G. S. Stockwell

The republic of Liberia

its geography, climate, soil and productions - with a history of its early settlement

G. S. Stockwell

The republic of Liberia
its geography, climate, soil and productions - with a history of its early settlement

ISBN/EAN: 9783742885326

Manufactured in Europe, USA, Canada, Australia, Japa

Cover: Foto ©ninafisch / pixelio.de

Manufactured and distributed by brebook publishing software (www.brebook.com)

G. S. Stockwell

The republic of Liberia

THE REPUBLIC OF LIBERIA:

ITS

Geography, Climate, Soil, and Productions,

WITH

A HISTORY OF ITS EARLY SETTLEMENT.

COMPILED BY G. S. STOCKWELL.

NEW YORK:
A. S. BARNES & CO., 111 AND 113 WILLIAM STREET.
1868.

PREFACE.

THE great interest awakened in this land in behalf of the African race, more especially since the abolition of slavery, has prompted the author in the preparation of the present volume. The interesting fact is here presented of a nation born in a day on the coast of Africa—a nation, indeed, having a form of government more in harmony with the teachings of divine revelation in its structure and application to the wants and well-being of the people than that of any human government. In this respect, it may be said to present a model, even in its youth, to the old nations of Europe and Asia, worthy of imitation. This is the more worthy of note when it is borne in mind that the continent of Africa is to-day the most degraded portion of our globe, and is less known to the civilized nations than any other.

But the little republic so recently planted upon the shores of that dark continent, and recognized by the great powers of Europe and America as a free and independent government, is already giving signs of growth and expansion, having passed the period of its infancy, and is now entering upon the great mission which Divine Providence has so manifestly assigned to her.

It becomes a question of vast importance to the African race what part the freed people in this country are to take in the great work of enlightening and elevating her children, thousands of whom have been enveloped in the darkness of heathenism, and are not able to rise till the blessings of civilization and the gospel shall be diffused among them. The following pages will give some idea of what has been done in Liberia and the adjacent country in abolishing the slave trade, and in the work of general education, along with missionary labors, the planting of Christian churches and Sabbath-schools, for the instruction of the young, both native and foreign, in a knowledge of the Scriptures; thus aiding in the intellectual and moral training of the rising generation, that they may come up to be good citizens and members of society.

It may be matter of surprise to some to learn that Liberia already has a college for her sons, having a president and professors, whose inaugural addresses, which may be found in the closing part of this volume, would do credit to any college in this land for rich and scholarly thought, and giving conclusive evidence to the world that there are men of African blood who are competent to fill the highest positions where cultivated intellect and brilliant talents are required.

The first chapters of the book are taken from a small work by J. W. Lugenbul, M.D., for many years resident in Liberia, and having, as United States agent, ample facilities for gaining correct information on the geography, climate, seasons, and productions of that portion of Africa, which will be of interest to the general reader.

The historical portions of the work are for the most part gathered from materials furnished by Wm. Coppinger, Esq., of Washington, to whom I am specially indebted, and may be regarded as furnishing a correct history of Liberia down to the present time. Much of this matter is in the form of letters, written by colored men in Liberia, and given in their own language, giving facts and incidents which go to make up the history of a people settling in a new country. The body of the work has been arranged in short chapters and paragraphs, to adapt it for use in schools among the freedmen in the North as well as for the general reader. Many of the colored people in the South will be able to gather much valuable information in regard to their friends who left them years ago and went to Liberia.

It is believed that more extended and reliable intelligence can be found in this work relative to the history of Liberia and that portion of Africa, than in any other work yet published. In a commercial point of view, the facts here presented in relation to the soil and productions of Liberia are of great importance; for with the development of its vast resources there will spring a commerce with foreign nations which will attract to her shores multitudes for the purposes of gain. And while this is going on, let the Christian teacher and missionary go also, to carry the blessings of education and the gospel of Christ, that the great work of elevating and saving the benighted millions of Africa may be hastened on to a glorious triumph.
G. S. S.

RICHMOND, *Nov.* 1, 1867.

CONTENTS.

CHAPTER		PAGE
I.	Geography	9
II.	Rivers	11
III.	Settlements	14
IV.	Settlements	16
V.	Settlements	18
VI.	Climate and Seasons	20
VII.	Climate and Seasons—*continued*	23
VIII.	Productions	28
IX.	Productions—*continued*	31
X.	Productions—*continued*	34
XI.	Productions—*continued*	36
XII.	Productions—*continued*	39
XIII.	Productions—*continued*	41
XIV.	Productions—*continued*	44
XV.	Productions—*continued*	48
XVI.	Animals	50
XVII.	Emigration to Liberia	55
XVIII.	Emigration to Liberia—*continued*	57
XIX.	Emigration to Liberia—*continued*	60
XX.	Emigration to Liberia—*continued*	64
XXI.	Emigration to Liberia—*continued*	68
XXII.	Emigration to Liberia—*continued*	71

CONTENTS.

CHAPTER		PAGE
XXIII.	Emigration to Liberia—*continued*	75
XXIV.	Emigration to Liberia—*continued*	79
XXV.	Prosperity of the Colony	82
XXVI.	Colonial War against the Slave Trade	84
XXVII.	More Trouble with Slave Traders	87
XXVIII.	The Colonial Navy—Literature—Peace	89
XXIX.	Arrival of Arms and Emigrants	92
XXX.	Schools—Commerce—New Territory	96
XXXI.	Domestic Condition of the Colony	99
XXXII.	Death of the Colonial Agent	101
XXXIII.	Commercial and Agricultural Prospects	105
XXXIV.	Death of the Vice-Agent—Election of Waring	108
XXXV.	Explorations—More Emigrants	111
XXXVI.	Large Accessions of Natives and Emigrants	114
XXXVII.	Monrovia—Schools—Temperance	118
XXXVIII.	Trade—The Courts—Religion	121
XXXIX.	War with the Dey and Gourah Chiefs	124
XL.	Health—Buying Wives—Grand Bassa	126
XLI.	1833—The Population of the Colony	130
XLII.	A New Agent—Missionaries	136
XLIII.	Judiciary—Trouble with the Natives	143
XLIV.	New Settlements—Imports—Finance	147
XLV.	Civilizing the Natives	150
XLVI.	Arrival of Governor Matthias	155
XLVII.	Progress of Missionary Labors	160
XLVIII.	A Large Planter—The Dey People	164
XLIX.	A Republic talked of—The Governor Murdered.	167
L.	A Lyceum—Paper Currency	171
LI.	Monrovia	175
LII.	New Virginia and Millsburg	177
LIII.	The Jaloff and Mandingo Races	180

CONTENTS.

CHAPTER		PAGE
LIV.	Liberia—Past, Present, and Future.	183
LV.	The St. Paul's River in 1866	187
LVI.	Extract from Message of Pres. Warner, 1865.	189
LVII.	Views of an Intelligent Emigrant	193
LVIII.	Address of the Hon. Abraham Hanson.	196
LIX.	Africa at the Present Day	201
LX.	Native Africans in Liberia	205
LXI.	The Superstitious Customs of the Natives.	211
LXII.	Emigration in 1851-52	217
LXIII.	The Chesapeake and Liberia Trading Company.	222
LXIV.	The Pessay Tribe	227
LXV.	Letter from G. W. Hall, Esq.	231
LXVI.	Letter from Monrovia	235
LXVII.	New Settlement.	239
LXVIII.	The Future of Africa.	240
LXIX.	Resources of Africa	243
LXX.	Voyage to Liberia	247
LXXI.	Hope for Africa	255
LXXII.	The New Nationality	258
LXXIII.	New Georgia.	263
LXXIV.	Foreign Relations in 1862.	266
LXXV.	The Colony in Danger.	272
LXXVI.	Inaugural Address of President Benson, 1860.	274
LXXVII.	Treaty between the United States and Liberia.	281
LXXVIII.	The Original Constitution of the Republic of Liberia.	286

LIBERIA.

CHAPTER I.
GEOGRAPHY.

1. THAT portion of the western coast of Africa which has received the appellation of Liberia, embraces a tract of country included between the parallels of 4° 20′ and 7° 20′ north latitude, extending from the Sherbro River on the north (near the southern boundary of the British Colony of Sierra Leone) to the Pedro River on the south, a distance along the coast of about six hundred miles. The political jurisdiction of the Republic of Liberia embraces about five hundred miles of this territory; that of the Colony of "Maryland in Liberia" embraces about one hundred miles, to the north and east of Cape Palmas.

2. All the territory which lies between these two points (except two or three small tracts) has been purchased from the original proprietors and rightful owners of the soil. The first tract was purchased in the early part of 1822, embracing a small extent of territory in the vicinity of Cape Mesurado. Other portions have, at different times, been purchased—the greater part within the last few years. The interior boundaries of the purchased tracts extend from about ten to forty miles from the coast. These boundaries may readily be extended as far as may be desirable, as the interior tribes are generally very willing, and some of them anxious, to sell their territories.

3. In no instance have the natives, from whom the land was purchased, been required to remove their residences, or to abandon their usual customs, except that of trading

in slaves, and the practice of such superstitious rites or ceremonies as tend to deprive any of their fellow-beings of life. And in all the written contracts which have been entered into between the agents of the Colonization Society, or the authorities of the Republic, and the native chiefs, the latter have invariably obligated themselves, in behalf of the people over whom they presided, to conform to the laws and regulations of the Liberian Government.

4. As in most other countries similarly situated, the land in the immediate vicinity of the ocean in Liberia is generally low; and in some places it is very marshy. There are some elevated spots, however, such as those on which the towns of Monrovia and Harper are located. The land generally becomes more elevated toward the interior, and in some places within fifty miles of the coast it is quite mountainous.

5. Far as the eye can reach from the highest points of land in the vicinity of the ocean, the whole country presents the appearance of a deep, unbroken forest, with hill-top rising above hill-top toward the vast interior; the country consisting, not, as is supposed by some persons, of arid plains and burning sands, but of hills and valleys, covered with the verdure of perpetual spring. The country is well watered; many beautiful streams may be seen winding their way amid blooming flowers and wild shrubbery; and many cooling springs of clear, sparkling water invite the weary traveler to linger and quench his thirst.

6. In all the settlements in Liberia good water can be procured without much difficulty; and though in the dry season, as in this country after a long dry spell in summer, some of the springs fail for a time, yet as good water can always be obtained by digging wells; and as many of the springs never fail, there need not be any fear about getting plenty of good water at any time in the year.

7. The soil of Liberia, like that of other countries, varies in appearance, quality, and productiveness. That of the uplands, though generally much inferior to that of the

lowlands, is better adapted to some articles. The upland soil usually consists of a reddish clay, more or less mixed with soft rocks and stones, containing considerable quantities of iron. That of the lowlands, in the immediate vicinity of the ocean, consists principally of sand. Besides this sandy soil, there are two other varieties of lowland soil—one of which is that on the banks of the rivers, within a few miles of the sea; this consists of a loose, deep, black mold, which is peculiarly adapted to the growth of those kinds of vegetables that thrive best during the dry season.

8. The other variety is that which is generally found extending back from the banks of the rivers, farther from the sea than the last-named; this consists of a light-colored clay, more or less tempered with sand, and it is well adapted to almost every kind of vegetables that will thrive in tropical climates.

CHAPTER II.

RIVERS.

1. There are no very large rivers in Liberia; and though some of them are from one fourth to three fourths of a mile wide, for fifty miles or more from their entrance into the ocean, yet none of them are navigable to a greater distance than twenty miles—the navigation being obstructed by rapids. The St. Paul's, the St. John's, and the Junk are the largest; and, indeed, they are the only rivers of any considerable length or width.

2. The other principal rivers are the Gallinas, the Cape Mount, the Mechlin, the New Cess, the Grand Cess, the Sanguin, the Sinou, and the Grand Sesters. Some of these present a bold appearance at their mouths, but they are

all comparatively short, and none of them are navigable for boats, or even for canoes, more than twenty or thirty miles, without obstruction by rocks or rapids.

3. The St. Paul's River is a beautiful stream of water. It is three fourths of a mile wide at the widest part (at Caldwell), and about three eighths of a mile wide at Millsburg, about fourteen miles from its mouth. The banks of this river rise from ten to twenty feet above the water, and except in places that have been cleared, they are covered with large forest trees, among which may be seen the graceful palm, rearing aloft its green-tufted head, and standing in all its pride and beauty, the ornament and the glory of its native land. The St. Paul's is perhaps the longest river in Liberia.

4. It is studded with many beautiful islands, abounding in camwood, palm, and many other valuable forest trees, and its banks furnish many beautiful sites for residences. Many native hamlets may be seen on the banks of this lovely river—the homes of the untutored children of the forest, the benighted sons and daughters of Africa.

5. The St. Paul's separates about three miles from its mouth; the principal stream rolls on toward the ocean, while the other fork flows in a southeasterly direction, almost parallel with the beach, and unites with the little Mesurado River near its mouth, and thus an island is formed, about eight miles long and from one to two in width, called Bushrod Island. This latter fork of the river is called Stockton Creek, in honor of Commodore Stockton, who kindly aided in effecting the first purchase of territory.

6. The St. John's River is also a beautiful stream. It is about sixty miles southeast of the St. Paul's, and it flows through that part of Liberia known as the Grand Bassa country. At the widest point it is nearly or quite a mile wide. Its length, however, is supposed to be less than that of the St. Paul's. The St. John's is also studded with numerous islands, the largest of which is Factory

Island, about three miles from its mouth. The banks of this river also rise considerably above the water, and the land bordering on it is also very productive.

7. The Junk River, which is about equidistant from the other two named rivers, is the third in size and importance. The main branch is supposed to be equal in length to the St. John's. The northern branch, which is only about forty miles long, is noted as a thoroughfare between Monrovia and Marshall. At the place of embarkation, a few miles below its source, it is not more than five yards wide, but it gradually expands to the width of more than half a mile. The appearance of the country along the banks of these rivers, and of the numerous little islands which they form, is highly picturesque.

8. The banks of the St. Paul's and the St. John's in many places present encouraging scenes of agricultural industry; showing the handiwork of a people whose social condition is vastly superior to that of their aboriginal neighbors, and who are thus placing before the indolent and improvident natives illustrations of the great superiority of the habits of civilized people to their own degrading customs; examples which must eventually exert a powerful influence on the minds and practice of the contiguous native tribes.

9. And thus, while the mind of the traveler is oppressed by the melancholy consideration of the moral and intellectual darkness of the scattered tribes of human beings, whose desolate-looking hamlets frequently meet his view, as he wends his way amid the dense forests of the uncultivated hills and dales of Africa, he is encouraged to believe that the time will come when this extensive " wilderness shall be made glad" by the labors of industrious agriculturists, and when this vast desert of intellectual and moral degradation " shall rejoice and blossom as the rose."

CHAPTER III.

SETTLEMENTS.

1. THE principal settlements in the Republic of Liberia are—Monrovia, New Georgia, Caldwell, Virginia, Kentucky, Millsburg, Marshall, Edina, Buchanan, Bexley, Greenville, Readsville, Lexington, and Louisiana. Besides these, there are a few other localities, which are sometimes called by one name and sometimes by another.

2. Monrovia is the largest and oldest of all the settlements, and it is the metropolis and the seat of government of the Republic. It is located near the mouth of the Mesurado River (a small stream about fifteen miles long), about four miles southeast of the entrance of the St. Paul's River into the ocean, on an elevated site immediately in the rear of Cape Mesurado, in latitude 6° 19′ north. The highest part of the hill on which the town stands, and which is near its center, is about eighty feet above the level of the ocean, and about three fourths of a mile from the summit of the cape, which is about two hundred and fifty feet above the sea.

3. Cape Mesurado is a bold promontory covered with massive forest trees and dense undergrowth, except in places that have been cleared. On the summit of the cape is a light-house and a fort, and along the sloping declivity toward the town there are several cleared lots on which small houses have been erected, in some places affording very pleasant places of residence. The greater part of the promontory, however, is very rocky. The course of the coast north of the cape forms a kind of bay, which generally affords safe anchorage for vessels; and the cove near the base of the cape affords as good a landing on the beach as can be found on almost any other part of the coast.

4. The town of Monrovia, although more compact than any of the other settlements in Liberia, occupies a considable extent of ground, being about three fourths of a mile in length. It is laid off with as much regularity as the location will allow, and the streets, of which there are about fifteen in number, have received regular names. The town is divided into lots of one fourth of an acre, and most of the dwelling-houses have a lot attached to each of them. Most of the lots, and several of the streets, are adorned with various tropical fruit-trees, and some of the gardens present a handsome appearance.

5. The houses are generally one story or a story and a half high; some are two full stories. Many of them are substantially built of stone or brick; and some of the best houses are built partly of both these materials. The State House is a large stone building which was erected in 1843. In the rear of this building is a substantial stone prison. There are three commodious stone houses for public worship in the town—Methodist, Baptist, and Presbyterian; nearly all of the professing Christians in the place being attached to one of the religious denominations.

6. At the base of the hill on which stand the principal dwelling-houses, there are several large stone buildings, which are occupied as stores and warehouses. The dwellings of many of the citizens of Monrovia are not only comfortably, but elegantly, and some of them richly furnished; and some of the residents of this little bustling metropolis live in a style of ease and affluence which does not comport with the contracted views of those persons who regard a residence in Africa as necessarily associated with the almost entire privation of the good things of this life. The population is about fifteen hundred, exclusive of native children and youths who reside in the families of the citizens.

7. New Georgia is a small township located on the eastern side of Stockton Creek, about five miles from Monrovia. It is occupied principally by native Africans who were

formerly slaves. Upward of two hundred of the liberated Africans who have been, or who now are residents of New Georgia, were sent to Liberia by the United States Government at different times. Many of these have married persons who were born in the United States, and have thereby become more strongly identified with the Liberians as citizens of the Republic. Some of them are partially educated, and a few years ago one of them occupied a seat in the Legislature. As most of the citizens of New Georgia have taken the oath of allegiance, they are permitted to enjoy equal immunities with other citizens.

8. Caldwell is situated on the southern side of the St. Paul's River. The whole settlement, which is divided for convenience into Upper and Lower Caldwell, is about six miles in length, extending along the bank of the river, the nearest part to Monrovia being about nine miles distant. The houses are from one hundred yards to a quarter of a mile, or more, apart; and, of course, this settlement has not much the appearance of a town. Some of the most enterprising farmers in Liberia reside at this place. The land about Caldwell is generally remarkably productive.

CHAPTER IV.

SETTLEMENTS.

1. VIRGINIA, or New Virginia, as it is sometimes called, is a new settlement, commenced in the early part of 1846. It is also on the St. Paul's River, opposite Caldwell. This is the site of the United States receptacle for liberated Africans, erected in 1847.

Kentucky is an agricultural settlement between Virginia and Millsburg, on the northern bank of the St. Paul's River, commenced a few years ago.

SETTLEMENTS. 17

2. Millsburg is the farthest settlement from the sea-coast of any in Liberia. It is situated on the northern bank of the St. Paul's River, about fourteen miles from its mouth, and about twenty miles from Monrovia. Like the other farming settlements, the houses generally are separated at a considerable distance from one another, so that the whole township extends about a mile and a half along the bank of the river. Millsburg is perhaps the most beautiful and one of the most healthy locations in Liberia. The land is remarkably good and of easy cultivation. A flourishing female academy is in operation at this place, under the care of Mrs. Wilkins, missionary of the Methodist Episcopal Church. And on the opposite side of the river is White Plains, a mission station of the same church.

3. Besides these settlements, there are numerous other points along the St. Paul's River which are occupied by farmers, so that the banks of this beautiful stream present in many places the appearance of agricultural industry and comfort.

4. Marshall is situated at the mouth of the Junk River, about thirty-five miles south of Monrovia. Most of the houses in this place are built along the sea-shore. This place is particularly noted for the manufacture of lime, which is obtained altogether from oyster and other shells. Most of the lime that is used in Liberia is made in the vicinity of Marshall. The river at this place abounds in oysters, and though they are not quite equal to those procured in some parts of the United States, yet they are quite palatable when properly served up.

5. Edina is located on the northern bank of the St. John's River, about half a mile from its mouth. It is handsomely situated, and in reference to the healthiness of the location it is perhaps equal to most others in Liberia. Some of the citizens of Edina are engaged in the cultivation of exportable articles of produce.

6. Buchanan is located at the junction of the Benso River (a small stream) with the St. John's, nearly opposite

Edina. Several of the citizens of this place also have given considerable attention to the cultivation of coffee, arrow-root, and ginger during the last few years. A steam saw-mill introduced in 1851 is in successful operation at this place.

A new settlement has recently been formed at the site of the one destroyed by Grando, a native chief, and his allies, in November, 1851, near Fish Town, a native village, about three miles below the mouth of the St. John's River.

7. Bexley is situated on the northern side of the St. John's River, about six miles from its mouth. This place, like the settlements on the St. Paul's River, occupies a considerable extent of territory. It is divided into Upper and Lower Bexley, both together extending about four miles along the river. Bexley is a fine farming settlement, the land is excellent, and the location is comparatively healthy. Several of the citizens of this place are pretty actively engaged in cultivating articles for exportation. This is certainly one of the most interesting settlements in Liberia. The mission of the Baptist Board of Foreign Missions is located at this place, also the headquarters of the Southern Baptist Mission.

CHAPTER V.

SETTLEMENTS.

1. GREENVILLE is situated at the mouth of the Sinou River, about one hundred and thirty miles by sea southeast of Monrovia. Like the settlement of Marshall, most of the houses are located along the sea-shore. Greenville presents a handsome appearance from the anchorage. It is one of the most healthy settlements in Liberia. The land in the immediate vicinity of Greenville, and indeed

of all the other settlements near the sea-shore, is much inferior to that on the banks of the rivers several miles from their entrance into the ocean. Consequently, those persons who expect to live by "the sweat of their brow," in the cultivation of the soil, will find it greatly to their advantage to locate beyond the sound of the breaking surf of the ocean. A steam saw-mill is in operation at this settlement—the first one introduced into Liberia.

2. Readsville, Lexington, and Louisiana are farming settlements on or near the Sinou River, from two to five miles above Greenville. In every settlement there is one place or more of public worship, in which religious services are regularly held. And in nearly every settlement there is one regular day and Sunday-school, or more. The principal deficiency in the system of education in Liberia consists in the inability to procure the services of a sufficient number of competent teachers. There are several very good schools at Monrovia and some of the other settlements, but the facilities for thorough intellectual training are not commensurate with the wants of the people in all the settlements.

3. As the census has not been taken for several years, I can not give the exact population of the different settlements, and the exact aggregate population of the Republic. The whole number of inhabitants of the Republic, exclusive of the natives, is probably at present about seven thousand. The native population is probably about two hundred thousand, many of whom have adopted habits of civilized life; and many of the youth of both sexes have enjoyed, or are enjoying, advantages of education.

The colony of "Maryland in Liberia," which has always maintained a distinctive character, and which has always been under a different government from the Republic of Liberia, was established in the early part of the year 1834. Ever since that period it has continued to progress in interest and importance, and at present it occupies a prominent position as an asylum for the proscribed descendants of Ham, to whom the siren song of "My native land" loses its mellowing cadence in the thrilling patriotic sound of "Sweet land of liberty."

5. This interesting colony is located about two hundred and fifty miles by sea southeast from Monrovia. Harper, the principal town or settlement, is situated near the point of the cape (Cape Palmas, a bold projecting promontory, which is one of the most prominent points or landmarks on the western coast of Africa); and from the anchorage it presents a handsome appearance. At the distance of about half a mile from Harper is the town of East Harper, in which are several beautiful sites for residences, commanding a fine view of the ocean and of the adjacent hills and vales. Between these two villages there are two large native towns, comprising several hundred houses, which present a marked contrast with the comfortable-looking dwellings of the colonists.

6. At the distance of about two and a half miles beyond East Harper is another settlement, called Tubmantown. Most of the land near the road between these two villages is occupied by the colonists, so that on both sides of this highway many neat little cottages may be seen, and many handsome gardens and small farms.

The whole population of Maryland in Liberia, exclusive of aborigines, is about one thousand.

CHAPTER VI.

CLIMATE AND SEASONS.

1. THE territory of Liberia being within a few degrees of the equator, of course the nature of the climate is essentially different from that of the United States, the vicissitudes of spring, summer, autumn, and winter not being

experienced in the equatorial regions of the earth, there being continued summer weather throughout the year, interrupted only by occasional slight variations in the thermometrical state of the atmosphere, caused by the greater strength of the ordinary breezes, and by clouds and rain; which latter prevail so much more during one half of the year than during the other half, as to give rise to the usually recognized division of the year into two seasons— the *wet* or *rainy season* and the *dry season*—or, in common parlance, "the rains" and "the dries;" the former of which answers nearly to summer and autumn, and the latter to winter and spring, in temperate latitudes.

2. This unqualified and somewhat arbitrary division of the year, however, has led many persons into error respecting the real state of the weather during these two seasons, some supposing that during the rainy season more or less rain falls every day; and on the other hand, during the dry season, an uninterrupted spell of hot and dry weather prevails for six successive months. This is so far from being the case, that, as a general rule, it may be stated, that some rain falls in every month in the year; and in every month there is some fine, clear, pleasant weather.

3. During my residence in Liberia I seldom observed a deviation from this general rule. Much more rain, however, falls during the six months beginning with May than during the remaining six months beginning with November. It is difficult, however, to determine at what time each of the two seasons actually commences and closes. As a general rule, I think the middle of May may be set down as the beginning of the rainy season, and the middle of November that of the dry season. In order, however, to give an accurate and comprehensive statement of the character of the climate and seasons of Liberia, it may be the best plan to note the vicissitudes of each month in the year as they are usually presented.

4. January is usually the driest and one of the warmest months in the year. Sometimes, during this month, no

rain at all falls, but generally there are occasional slight showers, particularly at night. Were it not for the sea-breeze, which prevails with almost uninterrupted regularity through the greater part of the day, on almost every day throughout the year, the weather would be exceedingly oppressive during the first three or four months of the year. As it is, the oppressiveness of the rays of the tropical sun is greatly mitigated by the cooling breezes from the ocean, which usually blow from about ten o'clock A.M. to about ten P.M., the land-breeze occupying the remainder of the night and morning, except for an hour or two about the middle of the night, and about an hour in the forenoon.

5. During these intervals the atmosphere is sometimes very oppressive. The regularity of the sea-breeze, especially in the month of January, is sometimes interrupted by the longer continuance of the land-breeze, which occasionally does not cease blowing until two or three o'clock P.M. This is what is called the *harmattan* wind, about which a great deal has been written, but which does not generally fully accord with the forced descriptions of hasty observers or copyists.

6. The principal peculiarity of the harmattan wind consists in its drying properties and its very sensible coolness, especially early in the morning. It seldom, perhaps never, continues the whole day, and usually not much longer than the ordinary land-breeze at other times in the year. When this wind blows pretty strongly, the leaves and covers of books sometimes curl, as if they had been placed near a fire; the seams of furniture and of wooden vessels sometimes open considerably, and the skin of persons sometimes feels peculiarly dry and unpleasant in consequence of the rapid evaporation of both the sensible and the insensible perspiration.

7. But these effects are usually by no means so great as they have been represented to be. What is generally called the harmattan season usually commences about the

middle of December, and continues until the latter part of February. During this time, especially in the month of January, the atmosphere has a smoky appearance, similar to what is termed Indian summer in the United States, but generally more hazy.

8. The average height of the mercury in the thermometer during the month of January is about 85°. It seldom varies more than ten degrees during the twenty-four hours of the day, and usually it does not vary more than four degrees between the hours of ten A.M. and ten P.M. In this month, however, I have seen the mercury stand at the lowest mark at which I ever observed it in Liberia—that is, at 68°. This was early in the morning, during the prevalence of a strong and very cool land-breeze. In this month I have also seen the mercury stand at the highest mark at which I ever observed it—that is, at 90°. The air is sometimes uncomfortably cool before eight o'clock A.M. during this month.

CHAPTER VII.

CLIMATE AND SEASONS.—*Continued.*

1. DURING the month of February, the weather is generally similar to that of January. There are, however, usually more frequent showers of rain, and sometimes, toward the close of this month, slight tornadoes are experienced. The harmattan haze generally disappears about the last of this month, and the atmosphere becomes clear. The range of the thermometer is about the same as in January.

2. March is perhaps the most trying month in the year to the constitutions of new-comers. The atmosphere is usually very oppressive during this month, the sun being

nearly vertical. The occasional showers of rain, and the slight tornadoes, which occur in this month, do not usually mitigate the oppressiveness of the atmosphere, as might be supposed. The variation in the state of the atmosphere, as indicated by the thermometer, seldom exceeds 6° during the whole of this month. The average height of the mercury is about 85°.

3. April is significantly called the "tornado month," the most numerous and most violent tornadoes usually occurring during this month. The ordinary state of the weather, in reference to the degree of heat, and its influence on the system, is not very different from that of the three preceding months.

4. The showers of rain are usually more frequent, however, and the visitations of those peculiar gusts, called *tornadoes*, are much more common in April than in any other month. These are sudden and sometimes violent gusts, which occur much more frequently at night than during the dry. Although they usually approach suddenly and rapidly, yet certain premonitory evidences of their approach are almost always presented, which are generally easily recognized by persons who have frequently observed them. They generally commence from the northeast or east-northeast, and rapidly shift around to nearly southeast, by which time the storm is at its height.

5. At the commencement of a tornado, dark clouds appear above the eastern horizon, which rapidly ascend until a dense, lurid-looking mass spreads over the whole hemisphere. As the heavy mass of clouds ascends and spreads, the roaring sound of the wind becomes stronger and louder, until suddenly it bursts forth in its fury, sometimes seeming as if it would sweep away every opposing object. Very seldom, however, is any material injury sustained from these violent gusts. The scene is sometimes awfully grand for fifteen or twenty minutes, during the formation and continuance of a heavy tornado.

6. Sometimes the whole hemisphere presents a scene of

the deepest gloom, the darkness of which is momentarily illuminated by vivid flashes of lightning in rapid succession, and sometimes tremendous peals of thunder burst upon the solemn stillness of the scene. The rain seldom falls until the violence of the gust begins to subside, when a torrent usually pours down for a short time, seldom more than half an hour; after which the wind shifts around toward the west, and generally in about an hour from the commencement of the tornado the sky becomes serene, and sometimes almost cloudless.

7. The weather during the month of May is usually more pleasant than in the two preceding months. The atmosphere is generally not quite so warm and oppressive. Sometimes copious and protracted showers of rain fall during the latter half of this month. Tornadoes also occasionally appear in the month of May. The average height of the mercury in the thermometer is usually two or three degrees less than during the four preceding months.

8. June is perhaps the most rainy month in the year. More or less rain usually falls nearly every day or night in this month. Although there are sometimes clear and pleasant days in June, yet there are seldom twenty-four successive hours of entire freedom from rain. The sun is, however, seldom entirely obscured for a week at a time, and he frequently shines out brightly and pleasantly in the interstices between the floating clouds several times during the day, occasionally for several hours at a time. During this month, as in all the other rainy months, more rain always falls at night than in the daytime; and, indeed, there are very few days in the year in which the use of an umbrella may not be dispensed with some time during the ordinary business hours.

9. In the month of June the atmosphere is always considerably cooler than in the preceding months, and I generally found it necessary to wear woolen outer as well as under garments, and to sleep beneath thick covering at night in order to be comfortably warm. The sensible per-

spiration is always much less during this month, and the five succeeding months, than during the other six months in the year. The mercury in the thermometer seldom rises above 80° in this month, the average height being about 75°.

10. During the months of July and August a great deal of rain also generally falls, but perhaps less in both these months than in the preceding one. There is always a short season of comparatively dry and very pleasant weather in one or both of these months. This season usually continues from three to five weeks, and generally commences about the 20th or 25th of July. Sometimes for several successive days the sun shines brilliantly and pleasantly all day, and no rain falls at night. The air, however, is always refreshingly cool and agreeable. This is perhaps the most pleasant time in the year. This is what is commonly called "the middle dries." It seems as if Providence has specially ordered this temporary cessation of the rains for the purpose of permitting the ripening and gathering of the crops of rice, which are generally harvested in August.

11. September and October are also generally very rainy months, especially the former. Sometimes more rain falls in September than in any other month in the year. Toward the close of October the rains begin to be less copious, and sometimes slight tornadoes appear, indicative of the cessation of the rainy season. The sea-breezes are usually very strong during these two months, and the atmosphere is generally uniformly cool and invigorating to the physical system.

12. During the month of November the weather is generally very pleasant, the temperature of the atmosphere being agreeable to the feelings—not so cool as during the five preceding months, and not so warm as during the five or six succeeding ones; the average height of the mercury in the thermometer being about 82°. Frequent showers of rain usually fall in this month, both in the day and at

night, but generally they are of short duration. Slight tornadoes also generally appear in this month. The sun may usually be seen a part of every day in the month, and frequently he is not obscured by clouds during the whole of the time in which he is above the horizon.

13. December is also generally a very pleasant month. Occasional slight showers of rain fall during this month, sometimes several sprinklings in one day, but seldom for more than a few minutes at a time. The mornings in this month are peculiarly delightful. The sun usually rises with brilliancy and beauty, and the hills and groves, teeming with the verdure of perpetual spring, are enriched by the mingled melody of a thousand cheerful songsters. Nothing that I have ever witnessed in the United States exceeds the loveliness of a December morning in Liberia.

14. On the whole, I regard the climate of Liberia as decidedly pleasant, notwithstanding the scorching rays of the tropical sun, and the "abundance of rain" which falls during the year, especially in the months of June, July, September, and October. So far as the pleasantness of the climate and weather is concerned, I would decidedly prefer a residence in Liberia to one in any part of the United States.

15. The extremes of the thermometrical state of the atmosphere may be set down at $65°$ and $90°$. I have never heard of the mercury in a good thermometer having sunk below the former, nor arisen above the latter point in the shade. The average height of the mercury during the rainy season may be set down at about $76°$, and during the dry season at $84°$. The mean temperature for the year is about $80°$.

16. In regard to the comparative healthiness of the two seasons, I may state that my observations fully convinced me that the rainy season is more conducive to health than the dry season, in both new-comers and old settlers. In reference, however, to the acclimating process, I think that no great advantage can be gained by arriving at any par-

ticular time of the year more than at any other time. Unnecessary exposure to the heat of the sun in the dry season, and to the rain in the wet season, should alike be avoided. Care and prudence should be exercised by new-comers at all times during the year.

CHAPTER VIII.
PRODUCTIONS.

1. NEARLY all the different kinds of grain, roots, and fruits, peculiar to intertropical climates, thrive well in Liberia; and many garden vegetables that belong more properly to temperate climates may be raised, in quality not much inferior to the same kind of articles produced in climates peculiarly adapted to their growth and maturation.

2. The only kind of grain, however, that has yet been cultivated to any considerable extent is rice, which is the great staple of intertropical Africa, and the principal article of food of the numerous aboriginal inhabitants. It is also used extensively by the Liberians; and it is undoubtedly the most wholesome article of food which can be used in that country. It is not cultivated very extensively by the Liberians, in consequence of their being able generally to purchase it more cheaply from the natives than the cultivation of it would cost. In consequence, however, of the increasing demand, it has of late years commanded a better price than formerly, which has induced some of the citizens to engage in raising it.

3. Until within the last few years, scarcely any persons attempted to raise it, but at present this valuable grain may be seen growing in the neighborhood of several of the settlements in Liberia. Although it grows much bet-

ter in low, wet land, yet it thrives very well in land more elevated, such as will produce most other articles usually cultivated. It is generally sowed in April and harvested in August. Sometimes two crops may be made in one year, but generally only one is made. It yields so abundantly, that, notwithstanding the extreme indolence of the natives, who do not work on their farms three months in the year, they usually raise much more than they require.

4. Indian corn, or maize, will grow very well on some lands in Liberia; and although it does not thrive so well as in some parts of the United States, yet I am quite satisfied that it might be cultivated much more extensively in Liberia than it ever yet has been. I have seen some fine, large ears of corn that were raised on the St. Paul's River. The small-grained corn, usually called Guinea-corn, no doubt will grow well in Liberia (Guinea, whence its name), but strange to say, I seldom saw it growing there. The natives in the vicinity of the settlements seldom, if ever, raise it.

5. A variety of esculent roots may be raised in Liberia; the most common of which are the sweet potato, cassada, yam, and tania. Sweet potatoes may be raised in great abundance with very little labor, on almost every kind of land, at any time during the year. I have seen them growing freely in the sandy soil within fifty yards of the ocean. The poorest persons may easily have a sufficiency of this nutritious vegetable. Those raised in some parts of Liberia are very fine. They generally thrive better in the rainy season, especially on the high lands; but in some places they thrive very well in the dry season, especially on the flat land bordering on the rivers; and in many places they may be gathered during every month in the year from the same piece of land.

6. The cassada (as it is usually called, but perhaps more properly *cassava*) is a shrub which grows from four to eight feet in height, having several white fleshy roots covered with a coarse, rough skin. The stem of the shrub is

round and jointed, having numerous branches, which are furnished at the upper part with alternate leaves, divided into three, five, or seven acute lobes. The root, which is the only part that is used, arrives at perfection in from nine to fifteen months. The roots vary in size from six to eighteen inches in length, and from three to eight in circumference. In taste, when not cooked, it very much resembles that of a fresh chestnut.

7. This vegetable may be raised abundantly on any kind of soil. It is the only vegetable, except rice, that is cultivated to any extent by the natives. It is usually prepared for use by being boiled, after the skin or rind has been removed, or by being roasted in ashes; and when properly cooked it is very palatable and nutritious. The tapioca of the shops is the fecula of the root of the cassada.

8. The yam is a slender, herbaceous vine, having large tuberous roots, sometimes nearly round, but generally elongated, like the cassada, but much larger. The roots of the yam are sometimes three feet long, and weigh twenty or thirty pounds. They usually arrive at perfection in four or five months, and yield very abundantly. The root of the yam is more farinaceous or mealy, when cooked, than that of the cassada—almost as much so as the Irish potato. They are more digestible than the cassada, and I think more palatable. The yam is one of the most wholesome and nutritious esculent roots of any country, and it may be produced in any desired quantity in Liberia.

9. Tania is a delicate, broad-leafed plant, about two feet in height, having a bulbous root, which, when prepared like Irish potatoes, resembles those excellent vegetables very nearly in taste; and it is a very wholesome and nutritious article of food. It may be raised easily and abundantly.

CHAPTER IX.

PRODUCTIONS.—*Continued.*

1. There are other esculent roots, peculiar to tropical climates, which have not yet been introduced, but which, no doubt, would thrive well in Liberia. I have alluded particularly to those only which have been introduced and which are cultivated there—those which I have seen and eaten myself. And in addition to those articles to which I have alluded, I may name a few other garden vegetables that I have seen growing in Liberia, the most common of which are—Lima or butter beans, snap beans, black-eyed peas, cabbages, tomatoes, cucumbers, watermelons, pumpkins, muskmelons, cantelopes, beets, radishes, and carrots.

2. Lima beans may be raised abundantly at any time during the year. In consequence of the absence of frost, the vines live and bear for several years; and as the beans are being continually reproduced, they may be gathered from the same vines during every month in the year, and for three, four, five, or more successive years. The vines yield in a few months after the planting of the bean, so that no family ought ever to be without this excellent vegetable. They are equal to those raised in any part of the United States.

3. Black-eyed peas may be raised in any necessary quantities. They come to maturity in about six weeks from the time of planting, and they may be raised at any time during the year. Cabbages do not thrive so well in Liberia as they generally do in the United States—that is, they do not produce so fine heads. They grow very rapidly, and sometimes the stalk attains the height of several feet. They do not generally go to seed. When, however, good seed can be procured from other countries, and proper attention is given to the cultivation of

the cabbage, fine, large, tender heads may sometimes be produced.

4. Tomatoes may be easily raised; and when the seed are procured from abroad, the fruit is large and well flavored—equal to the produce of most other countries. Cucumbers will perhaps thrive as well in Liberia as in any other country. Watermelons thrive as well in some parts of Liberia as in most parts of the United States, especially when good seed can be procured from abroad. Some as fine watermelons as I ever saw were raised in the vicinity of Monrovia. So far as I could learn, the best time to plant the seed is in March or April.

5. All the other articles that I have enumerated, and several other garden vegetables that seem to belong more properly to temperate climates, may be raised in Liberia without any difficulty, if the seed can be obtained from those countries to which these vegetables seem to be peculiarly adapted. Hence the necessity of importing seeds, if persons wish to have American vegetables on African tables. And here I would particularly recommend to persons who intend to emigrate to Liberia, to take with them a variety of garden seeds. And in order to protect them from being injured by the salt air of the ocean, I would advise that they should be sealed up in vials or bottles, or wrapped in paper and packed away in saw-dust.

6. A great variety of fruits is raised in Liberia, many of which are indigenous. The principal fruits are the orange, lime, lemon, pine-apple, guava, mango, plantain, banana, okra, papaw, cocoa-nut, tamarind, pomegranate, grandilla, African cherry, African peach, sour-sop, sweet-sop, sorrel, cacao, rose-apple, and chiota.

7. The orange tree thrives as well perhaps, and bears as fine fruit, in Liberia as in any other part of the world. The tree, when full-grown, is about the size of ordinary apple-trees in the United States, but much more handsome. One tree usually bears as many oranges as an apple-tree of the same size bears apples. Although ripe oranges may

be procured at any time of the year, yet there are two seasons at which they are more plentiful than at other times. One season is about the middle of the year, and the other about the close of the year. It is not uncommon to see blossoms, buds, young fruit, and full-grown fruit on the same tree at the same time; so that while some of the oranges are ripening, others are being produced. In the town of Monrovia many orange-trees may be seen adorning the sides of the streets, as well as in the yards and gardens of the citizens.

8. Limes and lemons are in superabundance in nearly every settlement in Liberia. Pine-apples grow wild in the woods in great abundance, and when allowed to ripen, before being pulled, they are very finely flavored. The apple grows out of the center of a small stalk, one or two feet high, and it is surrounded by prickly pointed leaves or branches. I have seen thousands of them in half an hour's walk. They are considerably improved by cultivation in good, rich land. They are not, however, a wholesome fruit, although very palatable, and many persons have made themselves sick by eating them too freely.

9. Guavas grow very abundantly on trees about the size of ordinary peach-trees. This fruit resembles the apricot in appearance, but not in taste. It is not very palatable when uncooked, though some persons are very fond of it. It, however, makes the best preserves and the best pies of any fruit with which I am acquainted. The guava jelly, which is almost universally regarded as a very delicious article, is made from this fruit. Though I believe the guava-tree is not indigenous to Liberia, yet it grows so luxuriantly as to be a source of much inconvenience in some places.

10. The mango (or mango-plum, as it is usually called in Liberia) also thrives well. It is the product of a handsome tree about the size of an ordinary apple-tree. The fruit is about the size of an ordinary apple, but oval, or egg-shaped. In taste, it approaches more nearly to the American peach than any other tropical fruit I ever ate.

CHAPTER X.

PRODUCTIONS.—*Continued.*

1. THE plantain is a beautiful, broad-leafed, tender, fibrous stalk that grows to the height of from eight to fourteen feet. The leaves, which are the continuation of the fibrous layers of the soft, herbaceous stalk, are generally about six feet long and from one to three feet broad. The fruit-stem proceeds from the heart of the stalk, and when full-grown it is about three feet long and beautifully curved, extending about two feet beyond the cluster of fruit, and terminating in a singular and beautiful purple bulb formed of numerous tender layers that can be easily separated. One stalk produces only one cluster or bunch of fruit, and when this is removed, by cutting the stem, the stalk dies; but cions spring up from the original root around the old stock, and in a few months these also bear fruit, and then die, giving place to other new stalks.

2. So that in two or three years from the time of the first planting, the number of stalks and bunches of fruit will be increased six-fold, or more. The venerable parent-stock, as if loth to leave her rising progeny unsheltered from the sweeping tornado, generally continues to spread her broad leaves over them until they shall have attained a sufficient size to stand firmly before the destroying blast of the storm-king, and then one by one the expansive leaves or branches wither and fall to the ground, leaving the aged, worn-out stalk to be prostrated by the passing breeze.

3. The fruit of the plantain is cylindrical and slightly curved, somewhat tapering toward the end. It is usually from six to nine inches long and one to two in diameter. At first it is of a pale green color, but when fully ripe it is yellow. It arrives at maturity in about eight months.

Most persons in Liberia cut the bunches before the fruit has ripened, but it is much better when it is allowed to ripen before being separated from the stalk. It is usually prepared for the table by being boiled, baked, or fried, and it is perhaps the most luscious and wholesome vegetable of tropical climates, and one of the most valuable fruits in the vegetable kingdom. It may be produced at any time in the year, and with a little judicious management, every family may have this excellent and nutritious article every day in the year.

4. The banana is so much like the plantain in every respect, except in the taste and a slight difference in the appearance of the fruit, that the description of one will answer for both. Indeed, it is difficult to distinguish one from the other when they are growing. The fruit of the banana is only about half the length of the plantain, and not so much curved. It is also much softer when ripe, and is more frequently eaten uncooked, although it may be prepared in the same manner as the plantain. The taste of the plantain very much resembles the taste of apples cooked in the same way, while that of the banana is *sui generis*—unlike any fruit of the United States. The plantain and banana trees or shrubs are among the most beautiful vegetable growths of tropical climates.

5. Okra is the fruit of a small tree ten or twelve feet high. It is a soft, pulpy, and very mucilaginous fruit, which when boiled forms a thick, semi-fluid, pleasant, and nutritious article of food—an excellent adjuvant to rice. It may be raised easily and abundantly in Liberia.

6. The papaw is a tall, slender, herbaceous tree of very rapid growth, sometimes attaining the height of thirty feet. The body of the tree is usually naked to within two or three feet of the top, and is marked with the cicatrices of the fallen leaves, which wither and fall as the tree continues to grow, giving place to others above them. Sometimes, however, there are several branches attached to the upper part of the body of the tree, each of which branches

produces a cluster of fruit. The leaves are very large, have long footstalks, and are divided into numerous lobes.

7. The fruit is nearly round, of a pale-green color, becoming yellowish as it ripens, and is about the size of the head of a young infant. One variety of the papaw, however, bears fruit of an elongated shape, somewhat like a a pear, but considerably larger than the other variety. The fruit of the papaw has a sweetish taste. It is very soft, and when fully ripe and stewed it resembles in both appearance and taste the best pumpkins of the United States; when stewed before it has ripened, and made into pie, it so much resembles the green-apple pie, in taste as well as appearance, that the most fastidious epicure might be deceived by it, if he did not stop to think that apples do not grow in Liberia.

8. The cocoa-nut is perhaps the most beautiful tree of tropical climates. It has long, curved leaves or branches, that hang gracefully from the upper part of the body, which rises sometimes to the height of thirty feet or more. The fruit grows in clusters near the base of the stalks of the leaves. The cocoa-nut tree is seldom raised in Liberia, except as an ornament. A few of these stately and beautiful trees may be seen in some of the settlements.

CHAPTER XI.

PRODUCTIONS.—*Continued.*

1. THE tamarind is a large, spreading tree, having very small, deep-green leaves. The fruit grows in elongated pods, similar to the butter-bean. Although the tamarind is indigenous, and thrives as well perhaps in Liberia as in any other part of the world, yet the people do not give any attention to the gathering of the fruit, except for their

own use; and, indeed, very few seem to care anything about it. I think, however, it might be made a profitable article of exportation.

2. The pomegranate is a dense, spiny shrub ten or twelve feet high. It produces beautiful, brilliant, large red flowers, and the fruit is about the size of a large apple, and covered with a thick coriaceous rind. It is filled with a multitude of small seeds, and the pulp is slightly acid and astringent. This fruit is seldom cultivated in Liberia, although I presume it will thrive as well as in most other parts of the world.

3. The African cherry (so called in Liberia) is a very peculiar fruit. It is about the size of the ordinary Morello cherry of the United States, but in taste it more resembles the cranberry. The tree is usually about fifteen feet high. The great peculiarity in the growth of this fruit consists in the manner in which the short stems are attached to the tree—not to the twigs of the branches, but to the body and larger limbs of the tree, the stems of the fruit being about one third of an inch long. This fruit makes very fine tarts—equal to the cranberry.

4. The African peach, of which there are several varieties, is a large, round, acid fruit—one variety being about twice the size of the largest peaches in the United States. These trees, some of which are very large, grow abundantly in the forests of Liberia. The fruit is used only for making preserves, which when properly made are surpassed only by the guava.

5. The sour-sop is a large, pulpy, acidulous fruit which grows on a tree about the size of an ordinary apple-tree. The fruit is nearly pear-shaped, and is about as large as an ordinary cantelope. It is covered with a thick, knotty rind. When perfectly ripe, it is a very pleasant fruit, especially when a little sugar is sprinkled over the pulp. It is also very good when fried in slices, in which state it somewhat resembles in taste fried sour-apples.

6. The sweet-sop is a fruit somewhat similar to the sour-

sop, but not so acidulous nor so pleasant to the taste. It is seldom used. The cacao, from which chocolate is produced, though not yet extensively cultivated, thrives well in Liberia, and doubtless might be made a very profitable article of cultivation. The rose-apple is a small, round fruit, which takes its name from its delightful fragrance. It is not very palatable, however, and is seldom eaten.

7. The granadilla is a large fruit that grows on a vine. It is about as large as a moderate-sized cantelope. No part of the fruit is eaten, except the seeds and the mucilaginous substance by which they are surrounded. These are loosely confined in the center of the fruit. The taste of this mucilage resembles the American strawberry more than any other fruit with which I am acquainted.

8. The sorrel is a large shrub having deep-red blossoms, which are often used for making tarts. It grows freely in Liberia, and it is a very handsome ornament to a yard or garden.

9. The chiota is the fruit of a vine. It is about as large as an ordinary pear. When properly prepared by stewing, it affords a wholesome, palatable, and nutritious article of food, and it may be easily raised in Liberia.

10. The celebrated bread-fruit of the island of Tahiti, which was introduced into the British West India Islands, by order of the Government, will grow well in Liberia. But as there are so many other articles of a somewhat similar kind that are preferable to it, it is seldom used.

11. I have seen several other indigenous fruits in Liberia, some of which are very palatable; some very fragrant, but not very acceptable to the palate; and others not possessing any good qualities to recommend them. And there are many other kinds of fruits peculiar to tropical climates which, no doubt, would thrive well in Liberia, but which have not yet been introduced. I have alluded to those only that I have seen growing there, and of which I have eaten.

CHAPTER XII.

PRODUCTIONS.—*Continued.*

1. In addition to the vegetable productions of Liberia to which I have alluded, there are some others that are worthy of particular notice, especially as they are the principal exportable articles, some of which may be rendered very profitable articles of commerce. These are, coffee, ginger, pepper, sugar, ground-nuts, indigo, cotton, and arrow-root.

2. In reference to coffee, I am quite satisfied that the soil and climate of Liberia are as well adapted to the cultivation of this article as the soil and climate of any other part of the world. I believe that as good coffee can be raised in Liberia as in any other coffee-growing country, and I have no doubt that, by proper attention, it may be raised as plentifully as in any other part of the world. These opinions are not hastily formed, but are founded on personal observations in some of the West India Islands, as well as in Liberia, and on frequent conversations with persons who have visited various other parts of the world in which coffee is cultivated.

3. I have frequently seen isolated trees, growing in different parts of Liberia, which have yielded from ten to twenty pounds of clean dry coffee at one picking; and however incredible it may appear, it is a fact, that one tree in Monrovia yielded four and a half bushels of coffee in the hull at one time, which, on being shelled and dried, weighed *thirty-one pounds.* This is the largest quantity of which I ever heard as being gathered from one tree, and it was the largest coffee-tree I ever saw, being upward of twenty feet high, and of proportionate dimensions.

4. I have given particular attention to observations and investigations respecting the cultivation of coffee in

Liberia, and I think I may safely set down the average quantity that may be raised, by proper cultivation, at four pounds to each tree—that is, each tree six years old and upward. The coffee-tree will begin to bear in three years from the time at which the seeds are planted. At the end of the fourth year, the average quantity may be set down at one pound to each tree; at the end of the fifth year, two and a half pounds; and at the end of the sixth year, four pounds.

5. About three hundred trees can be planted in one acre of ground, allowing the trees to be twelve feet apart. Therefore in four years from the time the seeds are planted in the nursery, 300 pounds of coffee may be gathered, which, at ten cents a pound (a very moderate rate for Liberia coffee, which has frequently been sold for twenty cents a pound in this country), would be worth $30.* At the end of the fifth year, 750 pounds may be gathered—worth $75; and at the end of the sixth year, 1,200 pounds—worth $120. So that in six years from the time of the planting of the seeds, agreeably with this calculation, 2,250 pounds of coffee may be produced on one acre of ground—worth $225. And accordingly, ten acres, properly cultivated, will yield during the first six years an income of $2,250, and at least $1,200 during each succeeding year.

6. This calculation I regard as pretty nearly correct; but even admitting that I have set down the quantities and the value at one fourth more than they should be, it will still appear that the cultivation of coffee may be rendered a source of wealth in Liberia, even supposing that nothing else could be raised for exportation, which is by no means the case. I am quite satisfied that at least $100 a year may be realized by proper management from the produce of one acre of ground cultivated in coffee after the sixth year from the time of planting the grains in the nursery.

7. And as it does not require much labor, one person

---

* These prices approximate the prices in 1858.

may easily cultivate three acres, with a little hired assistance in clearing the land, and may devote one half of his time, or more, to the cultivation of other articles for the use of himself and family, and for sale, and he need not work more than five or six hours a day. So that, by industry, prudence, and economy, any man may realize at least $300 a year for his labor over and above the necessary expenditures of himself and family; the other articles which he may raise being quite sufficient for the comfortable support of his household.

8. I am aware that the truthfulness of this statement has seldom been exhibited in the agricultural operations of the citizens of Liberia; but this fact does not necessarily confute the truth of the statement, nor does it sufficiently exhibit the impracticability of its being fully and easily carried out. And I might add, that it does not require the exercise of profound wisdom, even in a cursory observer, to discover the real cause why the feasibility of the result of the foregoing calculation is not more frequently exhibited.

CHAPTER XIII.

PRODUCTIONS.—*Continued.*

1. COFFEE is indigenous to Liberia. It may frequently be seen wild in the woods. It is, however, much improved by cultivation. The most approved method of raising it is to plant the grains in a nursery, and to transplant when the tree has attained the height of a foot and a half. Some trees arrive at their full growth in five or six years, while others continue to grow more than double that length of time. The grains grow in pairs, covered with a hull, from which they can be easily separated when dry.

2. The coffee blossom is a beautiful and highly fragrant little white flower, and the berry when fully ripe is of a

pale red color. The average height of full-grown trees is about eight feet. They continue to bear from ten to twenty years. I have seen some fine flourishing trees which were upward of twenty years old. As the coffee-tree is easily cultivated, and as the fruit is easily cured, the cultivation of this profitable and useful article should occupy a portion of the time of every family in Liberia.

3. Next to coffee, perhaps ginger may be made the most profitable article of culture for exportation. The superior quality of this article, and the peculiar adaptation of almost every kind of soil in Liberia to its abundant growth, justifies the opinion that it may be rendered a profitable article of commerce. It will certainly grow as well in Liberia as in any other part of the world, and in quality it is scarcely inferior to the best that is produced in any other country.

4. I have no certain data from which I can determine the average quantity of ginger that may be raised on a given quantity of land; but from what I have seen, I am quite satisfied that it may be raised in great abundance with very little labor. The average increase is at least twenty-fold when properly cultivated. From six to eight months is the time usually required for its growth and maturation.

5. Bird pepper, which is known in the United States as "African Cayenne pepper," is an indigenous article that may be found almost every where throughout Liberia. I have frequently seen great quantities of it growing wild in the woods; and if a little attention were given to the cultivation of it, thousands of pounds might be annually exported. It grows on bushes about four feet high. The pods are generally about half an inch long and one third of an inch in circumference. One species, however, is four or five times this size. The smaller kind is generally preferred. In quality, it is perhaps not equaled by that raised in any other country.

6. The cultivation of it requires scarcely any attention,

and the only preparation of it for the market consists in picking the pods and spreading them out to dry. The shrub grows very rapidly, and the fruit arrives at maturity in six or eight months from the time of planting. It yields more abundantly about the beginning of the year; but as the fruit continues to be reproduced throughout the year, it may be collected at any time.

7. The natives use it very freely. It is not uncommon to see them with a bunch of pepper in one hand and a roasted cassada in the other, taking with each bite of the latter one of the pods of the former, one of which pods would serve to pepper a full meal for a person not so accustomed to its use. Perhaps the reader of this may wonder why pepper is not more freely gathered and exported, as it grows so abundantly in the wild state, and as it may be so very easily cultivated. To this I can only respond, echo answers, Why?

8. Sugar-cane will, perhaps, thrive as well in Liberia as in any other country. I have seen stalks more than fifteen feet high and two or three inches in diameter. The average size of the stalks is considerably larger than those raised in the island of Barbadoes, and the juice is equally sweet and proportionably more abundant. This I have tested by personal observations. Sugar, however, probably will not soon become a profitable article of exportation, in consequence of the inability of the Liberians to compete with the West India planters.

9. Liberia, however, may be, and ought to be, independent of all the rest of the world for this luxury. Every farmer ought to raise not only enough of this article for the use of his own family, but some to dispose of to his mercantile, mechanical, and professional neighbors; and even if he can not conveniently manufacture the sugar, in any considerable quantity, he can certainly express enough of the juice in a few hours, with his own hands, in a mill of his own construction, to make several gallons of *sirup* (not molasses, but a much better article),

which answers very well for every practical or necessary purpose.

10. Ground-nuts, or pea-nuts, may be raised in great abundance in Liberia. And as these nuts generally find a ready market in the United States and in Europe, they certainly will richly repay the Liberian farmer for the little trouble and labor which their cultivation requires. I do not know what quantity may be raised on a given portion of land, but I do know that they yield very abundantly.

CHAPTER XIV.

PRODUCTIONS.—*Continued.*

1. Although the cultivation of indigo has not met with much attention in Liberia—comparatively few persons having given any attention at all to it—yet as the indigo plant grows so luxuriantly, and may be raised so easily, the manufacture of Indigo is certainly worthy of particular notice. The plant grows so abundantly in Liberia that it constitutes one of the most troublesome weeds in the gardens, and even in the streets of the settlements. And with a little skill and industry in preparing the indigo, it may be rendered one of the most profitable crops that can be produced in tropical climates.

2. The plant arrives at maturity in three or four months from the time of planting the seed, and as it springs up again in a few weeks after having been cut, one crop will yield five or six cuttings in the course of the year. Several varieties of the indigo plant may be found growing wild in Liberia, all of which yield very fine Indigo, some of which is perhaps equal to that produced in any other part of the world. The preparation of indigo requires a little more patience and industry than the Liberians gen-

erally are in the habit of bestowing on any one article of agriculture, which is the principal cause why it has not been more extensively manufactured.

3. Cotton has not yet been cultivated to a sufficient extent to enable me to determine from observation whether it may be made a very profitable article of agriculture. Several old cotton planters, who had grown gray in raising cotton in Georgia, Mississippi, and other Southern States before they went to Liberia, have repeatedly told me that the cotton-tree or shrub will grow as well and yield as abundantly in Liberia as in any part of the United States. The natives in the interior manufacture cotton goods pretty extensively from the indigenous growth, of which there are several varieties. The best grows on trees or shrubs eight or ten feet high—similar to those raised in the United States, but larger in the average size. And as the trees are not injured by frosts, of course they continue to bear for several years. I doubt not that Liberia might become one of the most important cotton-growing countries in the world.

4. Arrow-root probably thrives as well in Liberia as in any other part of the world. This is a tender plant, which usually grows to the height of two or three feet. The stems, of which several rise from the same root, are round, branched, jointed, and leafy. The leaves resemble the common sword-grass. They are alternate, and are from three to six inches in length. The root, which is the only part used, is beautifully cylindrical, straight, and tapering (hence the name of the plant), fleshy, scaly, and furnished with numerous long, white fibers, and is usually from three to eight inches in length.

5. This plant is one of the most luxuriant growths in Liberia. It is easily propagated, and it arrives at maturity in about five months. In preparing it for use, the roots are washed and then beat into a pulp, which is thrown into a tub of water, and agitated so as to separate the fibers from the amylaceous part; the latter of which re-

mains suspended in the water, while the former is removed. The milky fluid thus formed is strained and allowed to stand several hours, until the fecula, or starch, shall have settled at the bottom of the vessel. It is then washed with a fresh portion of water, strained again, and allowed to subside again; this process sometimes being performed three or four times, after which it is spread out and dried in the sun. About eight pounds of the pure powder or flour may be produced from a bushel of the roots.

6. As arrow-root may be produced so abundantly in Liberia, and as it is one of the most important exportable articles, as well as one of the most valuable articles of food, it deserves particular notice. The cultivation of the plant requires so little labor or attention, and the process of manufacturing the fecula from the roots is so very simple and so easily performed, that I am quite certain this article may be rendered a source of wealth by exportation. From having frequently seen it growing, and having seen the quantity which a very small piece of ground produced, I think the average quantity that may be raised on almost every kind of soil in Liberia may be safely and truly set down at one hundred bushels to the acre—that is, eight hundred pounds of pure manufactured arrow-root, or fecula.

7. An old gentleman at Monrovia, who has raised a considerable quantity of it, stated to me, that from the quantity he has made from a certain portion of land he was quite satisfied that one acre, properly cultivated, will yield two thousand pounds. And a farmer at Caldwell assured me that he made one hundred and thirty pounds from the produce of one sixteenth of an acre of ground. But, as it will be perceived, I have placed the average quantity at less than one half of the proportionate quantity that has actually been raised; and this, I think, is not beyond a fair estimate. Assuming, therefore, that one half an acre will produce four hundred pounds (a quantity which almost any family may easily raise and manufacture), and allowing the average net price to be only fifteen cents a pound,

it will appear that $60 may be realized from this small quantity of land, with comparatively little labor.

8. During the last few years arrow-root has been used pretty extensively in Liberia as a substitute for wheat-flour; and as I have frequently eaten it, in various forms of bread, I hesitate not to say that I believe it to be not only a good substitute for flour, but much more suitable and wholesome for persons residing in tropical climates. It makes very fine biscuits, either alone or when mixed with a small quantity of sweet potatoes. It also makes very good pie-crust; and I have seen light or leavened bread made of arrow-root which so much resembled wheat-flour bread, in both appearance and taste, as to deceive professed judges. Besides these, I have eaten the nicest kind of pound and other sweet cakes made of this article instead of flour, with the ordinary adjuvants.

9. The foregoing-named articles constitute the principal exportable articles of agriculture that may be raised in Liberia, and I have endeavored to give faithful and truthful statements in reference to each of them. And while I regret that greater attention has not yet been given to the cultivation of these articles, I cherish the hope that the period will arrive at which all of them will be cultivated extensively; if not by the present inhabitants, by others who may emigrate thither, having more energy, industry, and perseverance. I candidly believe that a man may acquire more wealth in Liberia by judicious management in the cultivation of the soil than he could acquire in any part of the United States with double the quantity of land, double the amount of labor, and in double the length of time; even allowing for all the disadvantages under which he may have to labor in Liberia, and all the facilities which he might have in the United States.

10. I am quite certain that, by pursuing a regular, systematic, and persevering course of agricultural industry and frugality, the citizens of Liberia may, with no other

means than those which every individual can readily procure, produce not only enough of those articles that are peculiar to tropical climates for their own use, but a large surplus for exportation. And any man in Liberia, who enjoys a tolerable degree of health, and who does not live comfortably and independently, may, without any violation of the principles of truth or justice, charge the deficiency to his own account.

CHAPTER XV.

PRODUCTIONS.—*Continued.*

1. ONE of the most important and valuable indigenous articles of the vegetable kingdom in intertropical Africa is the palm, which is one of the most remarkable and useful trees in the world. There are two or three varieties of the palm in Liberia, one of which, by its towering height and graceful appearance, attracts particular attention. The tree that yields the nuts from which oil is extracted seldom grows to the height of more than twenty-five feet. It resembles the cocoa-nut tree, having, like that, long leaves or branches attached to the upper part of the body of the tree, and which hang in graceful curves.

2. The fruit grows in clusters or bunches near the base of the stalks of the leaves. The nut is oval, about an inch long, and when ripe is of a deep red color. The oil is extracted from the pulp of the nut, which yields very abundantly. It is manufactured by the natives, and several hundred thousand gallons are annually exported from Liberia.

3. Palm-trees may be seen in every part of Liberia, adorning the hills and valleys, and furnishing not only great quantities of oil for exportation, as well as for

domestic uses, but yielding a variety of other useful substances: a peculiar beverage called "palm wine," procured by tapping the tree, and which in taste very much resembles wine-whey; also a substance that grows at the top of the tree called "palm-cabbage," and which when boiled has an agreeable taste; and from the fibers of the leaves the natives get materials for making baskets, hats, etc.

4. Palm-oil is extensively used by the Liberians as a substitute for sperm-oil and candles, and also in culinary operations as a substitute for lard and butter; and for all needful purposes to which those articles are applied, it answers very well. The average price of palm-oil in Liberia is about thirty-three cents a gallon.

5. Another valuable tree, which is indigenous and peculiar to intertropical Africa, is the camwood, which grows abundantly in the forests about a hundred miles from the coast. This is one of the most valuable dye-woods in the world, and hundreds of tons are annually exported from Liberia.

6. The palma-christi, the seeds of which yield castor-oil, is also indigenous to Liberia, and I have no doubt that the regular cultivation of this valuable shrub would richly repay the laborer for the little trouble that it would require.

7. The tree which yields the medicinal balsam called copaiva, may also be seen occasionally growing wild in the forests of Liberia, and I doubt not that the juice might be collected in sufficient quantities to become a valuable article of exportation.

8. Several varieties of the acacia (gum-arabic tree) grow in Liberia, and some of the gum is of superior quality. I have seen some specimens of olibanum (frankincense), which, as the natives informed me, were collected from large trees that grow abundantly in the forest. I have frequently seen the caoutchouc, or gum-elastic tree, growing in Liberia, some of which are forty feet or more in height.

9. The forests of Liberia also furnish many different

kinds of valuable timber, well suited for ship or boat building, cabinet-work, and all the various operations in carpentry; the principal of which are—wistmore, brimstone, rose-wood, mulberry, bastard mahogany, saffron, mangrove, African oak, hickory, poplar, persimmon, and sassawood. Some of these make very beautiful cabinet-work.

10. A considerable variety of medicinal plants, besides those to which I have alluded, may be found in Liberia; among which is the croton tiglium, a small tree or shrub with spreading branches, yielding a capsular fruit, from the seeds of which croton-oil is extracted.

CHAPTER XVI.
ANIMALS.

1. THE principal wild animals which infest the forests or rivers of Liberia are the elephant, leopard, hippopotamus, crocodile, porcupine, wild-hog, boa-constrictor, several varieties of the deer, and several of the ape.

2. Elephants are quite numerous about a hundred miles back in the interior, and the natives make a regular business of hunting and killing them for the ivory of which their tusks are composed. These animals were formerly frequently seen in the vicinity of some of the settlements, but they are now seldom seen within fifty miles of the sea-coast.

3. Leopards are occasionally seen prowling about the outskirts of some of the settlements, and they sometimes carry away small domesticated animals at night. But they are much less numerous and troublesome than formerly. They never attack a person except after having been wounded.

ANIMALS. 51

4. Hippopotami are occasionally seen on the banks of the rivers, some of them of immense size—weighing a thousand pounds or more. They are sometimes killed by the natives. They are harmless animals, and they always endeavor to escape, when interrupted, by plunging into the water.

5. Crocodiles (erroneously called alligators) are frequently seen basking in the sunshine on the banks of the rivers, or on the little rocky islands. They always make their escape into the water when approached by a person on shore, or in a boat or canoe.

6. Boa-constrictors are sometimes killed in the forests in Liberia. The largest I ever saw was fifteen feet long and fifteen inches in circumference. Much larger ones have been killed. I never heard of their attacking an individual. Serpents, however, are much less numerous in Liberia than is generally supposed, and poisonous snakes are perhaps less common than in many parts of the United States.

7. Deer are very numerous, and they afford excellent venison. Monkeys are found in great numbers in the forests. I have seen a dozen or more at one time, jumping from tree to tree with great dexterity. Several species of the ape tribe are occasionally caught by the natives, among which is the chimpanzee, so remarkable for its near approximation in appearance to the human race. Some of these "wild men of the woods" have been seen as large as an ordinary-sized man. The largest that I ever saw was about the size of a child two or three years old. The old ones are never caught, and are seldom killed. They are very powerful as well as very active.

8. Besides these, the guana, the ichneumon, the sloth, the beautiful and ever-changing chameleon, many varieties of lizards, and several species of ants may frequently be seen. One variety or species of ants is very remarkable, in consequence of the immense conical mounds of earth which they rear and in which they make their nests. These

mounds are sometimes ten or twelve feet high, and eight or ten feet in diameter at the base. These ants are about the size of the large black ant in the United States. The queen, however, is much larger—some of them two inches in length and nearly two inches in circumference. In the interior of the mound, about half-way from the bottom, is a large vaulted chamber, the floor of which is very hard and smooth. In the center of the floor is the nest, in the inmost recess of which lives the queen in luxurious ease, accompanied by the king, whose size does not vary much from the ordinary ant, but who is easily recognized by a striking difference in physical conformation. When the queen dies, or is captured, all the ants desert the hill, which is left to "crumble into dust again." Many of these deserted mounds may be seen in almost every part of Liberia.

9. Another species of ants (familiarly known by the name of Drivers) is still more remarkable. They are about the size of the black ant of America—that is, about one fourth to one half of an inch in length. They may frequently be seen marching along in the most systematic order and regularity of movement. They move in a solid compact column of great length, and they appear to be under the direction of able leaders and rigid disciplinarians. No common obstacle turns them out of their course, and whoever is so unfortunate as to come in their line of march will have to pay for his temerity, and will be reminded to be more careful in future. Hundreds seize fiercely on the intruding foot, and the unwary object of their vengeance is compelled to retreat from the scene of attack.

10. These tiny warriors are very troublesome, but they are exceedingly useful in expelling noxious vermin from every place into which they may enter in the course of their perambulations. Whenever a battalion of drivers enters a dwelling-house, the inmates are obliged, for the time, to yield undisputed possession, at least of that

part of the house which the little warriors may be searching.

11. They are not, however, always unwelcome visitors, for they never fail to expel rats, mice, and every species of vermin—making a clean sweep as they go. Whenever they come to a small water-course, the larger and stronger ones dextrously form themselves into an arch by clinging to each other, thus making a bridge over which the smaller ones pass dry-shod. Even in their ordinary march over level ground they seem to cling to each other in a solid phalanx, the stronger ones occupying the flanks, and arching themselves over the weaker ones, who occupy the center, and who are thus protected by the others.

12. All kinds of animals, both large and small, are afraid of drivers, nor have they any regard to size in the objects of their warfare. They are very useful in chasing away or killing snakes, lizards, scorpions, centipedes, etc., which, were it not for the drivers, would be exceedingly troublesome, and even dangerous. Whenever they visit a house, they search it all over and expel every living, moving thing that they find; after which they retire peaceably, and yield possession to the former occupants. They make their nests beneath the surface of the ground; and I presume they sally forth from their quarters only in search of food, at which times the line of march is sometimes a hundred yards or more in length.

13. The principal domesticated animals in Liberia are bullocks or beeves, cows, goats, swine, geese, turkeys, ducks, and chickens. Beeves are frequently brought into the settlements for sale by the natives, and they are sometimes raised by the citizens. They may be raised easily in any desirable quantity.

14. Cows are numerous, but they do not give much milk. Some of the cows which are brought from the interior, one or two hundred miles from the coast, are as large as ordinary cows in the United States, but they do not give half so much milk. If properly attended to,

however, I think they would afford milk much more plentifully.

15. Sheep and goats can be very easily raised in Liberia—as easily, perhaps, as in any other part of the world; and they both afford good wholesome animal food. The sheep are covered with hair instead of wool. The goats furnish very good milk. Swine do not thrive so well in Liberia as in some parts of the United States, but they can be raised in sufficient abundance for the wants of the people.

16. Geese and ducks may be raised without any more difficulty than in the United States, and within a few years past turkeys have become much more plentiful than they formerly were. Perhaps in no other part of the world can chickens be raised more easily and more plentifully than in Liberia. With very little trouble, every family may always have a sufficient supply of chickens.

17. Horses are plentiful in the interior, within three hundred miles of the coast, but they do not thrive well in the settlements; perhaps in consequence, principally, of the want of proper management. They are occasionally brought down by the natives, and some of them are very beautiful. They are small—seldom more than twelve hands high. I am quite satisfied that they never can be used to much advantage, as draft animals, in the present settlements of Liberia.

18. But for all necessary purposes the native oxen can be used as a substitute for horses. I have seen some of the small bullocks broken to the yoke, and working steadily and effectually. The Liberians, however, have not yet given much attention to the breaking and working of oxen—by no means as much as they ought to give. I trust that the time may not be distant when the plow and the cart will be much more extensively used than at present.

CHAPTER XVII.
EMIGRATION TO LIBERIA.

1. The first emigration of colored people from the United States to Africa was conducted by the celebrated Paul Cuffee, in 1815. This remarkable man was born at New Bedford, Massachusetts, in 1759, of an African father and an aboriginal mother. His early years were spent in poverty and obscurity; but possessing a vigorous mind, by industry and perseverance, guided by practical good sense, he rose to wealth and respectability. He was largely engaged in navigation, and in many voyages to foreign countries commanded his own vessel.

2. His desire to raise his colored brethren of this country to civil and religious liberty in the land of their forefathers, induced him to offer some of the free people of color a passage to the western coast of Africa. About forty embarked with him at Boston, and landed at Sierra Leone, where they were kindly received. Only eight of these were able to pay their passage, the whole expense of the remainder, amounting to nearly $4,000, was defrayed by the noble-minded Paul Cuffee. Had he possessed the means, he might in 1816 have taken 2,000 people from New England to Africa, but he died the following year.

3. The American Colonization Society was founded in the city of Washington, in December, 1816, by patriotic and benevolent gentlemen from various parts of the country, for the purpose of colonizing the free people of color of the United States.

4. In 1818, Messrs. Samuel J. Mills and Ebenezer Burgess were commissioned by this Society to proceed by the way of England to the English settlements and other ports of the western coast of Africa, to acquire information and ascertain whether a suitable territory could be obtained

for the establishment of a colony. They visited all the ports from Sierra Leone to Sherbro, a distance of about 120 miles.

5. At this last place they found a small but prosperous colony of colored people settled by John Kizzel. This man had been brought from Africa when very young, and sold as a slave in South Carolina; during the Revolutionary war he joined the British, and at its close was taken to Nova Scotia, from whence, about the close of the last century, he sailed with a number of other colored persons to Africa. Here he prospered in trade, built a church, and preached the Gospel to his countrymen. By Kizzel and his people the agents were kindly received and hospitably entertained. After having fulfilled their arduous duties, they embarked for the United States, but Mr. Mills died on the passage.

6. The missionary character and efforts of this man were thus referred to in a public discourse by the Rev. Leonard Bacon: "A young minister of the Gospel once said to an intimate friend, 'My brother, you and I are little men, but before we die, our influence must be felt on the other side of the world.'

7. "Not many years after, a ship returning from a distant quarter of the globe paused on her passage across the deep. There stood on her deck a man of God, who wept over the dead body of his friend. He prayed, and the sailors wept with him—and they consigned that body to the ocean. It was the body of the man who, in the ardor of youthful benevolence, had aspired to extend his influence throughout the world. He died in youth, but he had redeemed his pledge, and at this hour his influence is felt in Asia, in Africa, in the islands of the sea, and in every corner of his native country.

8. "This man was Samuel John Mills, and all who know his history will say that I have exaggerated neither the grandeur of his aspirations nor the results of his efforts. He traversed our land, like a ministering spirit, silently

and yet effectually, from the hill country of the Pilgrims to the valley of the Mississippi.

9. "He wandered on his errands of benevolence from city to city, pleading now with the patriot for a country growing up to an immensity of power, and now with the Christian for a world lying in wickedness. He explored in person the desolations of the West, and in person he stirred up to enterprise and to effort the churches of the East. He lived for India and Owhyhee [Hawaii], and died in the service of Africa."

10. Mr. Burgess gave so satisfactory a report of his mission, that the Society was encouraged to proceed in its enterprise. By an Act of Congress of the 3d of March, 1819, the President of the United States was authorized to restore to their own country any Africans captured from American or foreign vessels attempting to introduce them into the United States, in violation of law, and to provide by the establishment of a suitable agency on the African coast for their reception, subsistence, and comfort, until they could return to their relatives, or derive support from their own exertions. It was determined to make the station of the Government agency, on the coast of Africa, the site of the colonial settlement; and to incorporate in the settlement all the blacks delivered over by our ships of war to the American agent as soon as the requisite preparations should be completed for their accommodation.

CHAPTER XVIII.

EMIGRATION TO LIBERIA.—*Continued.*

1. In February, 1820, the Rev. Samuel Bacon went to Africa as principal agent of the United States. He embarked at New York in the ship Elizabeth, chartered by

Government, and was accompanied by John P. Bankson, assistant, Dr. Samuel A. Crozer, agent of the American Colonization Society, and eighty-eight emigrants, who, in consideration of their passage and other aid from Government, agreed to prepare suitable accommodations for the reception of the Africans who might be delivered over to the protection of the agent.

2. This expedition proceeded by way of Sierra Leone to the island of Sherbro; and the emigrants landed at Campelar, the place which had been chosen for the site of the proposed settlement, while the sloop of war Cyane, which sailed from New York in company with the Elizabeth, was ordered to cruise on the coast for the prevention of the slave trade.

3. Mr. Bacon, after encountering great fatigue and many vexatious delays in fruitless negotiations with the natives for the purchase of lands, found himself obliged to turn his whole attention to the care of the emigrants. Campelar proved to be very unhealthy, on account of the low marshy ground and bad water. These, with the total absence of accommodations, the want of proper regulations, and the continued fatigue and exposure incident to their situation, soon spread disease in a frightful form among the people. Almost the whole care of the sick, as well as of those in health, finally devolved on Mr. Bacon.

4. But, notwithstanding, he labored more, was more exposed to heat and wet, hunger and thirst, than any one, yet he continued in health until all the rest, except six or eight, had become sick. At length he was attacked by the fever, when there was no one to administer medicine or allay his sufferings by the kind and assiduous attentions which he had for weeks bestowed on others; and after an illness of about a fortnight he expired, a worthy martyr to the glorious cause of African regeneration.

5. A short time before his death he wrote in his journal, after describing his own labors and the sufferings of the people: "Is it asked, Do I yet say colonize Africa? I

reply, yes. He who has seen ninety naked Africans landed together in America, and remarked the effects of the change of climate through the first year, has seen them as sickly as these. Every sudden and unnatural transition produces illness. The surpassing fertility of the African soil, the mildness of the climate during a great part of the year, the numerous commercial advantages, the stores of fish and herds of animals to be found here, invite her scattered children home. As regards myself, I counted the cost of engaging in this service before I left America. I came to these shores *to die*, and anything better than death is better than I expect."

6. All the agents and more than twenty of the emigrants died; the remainder regained their health in a few weeks. Early in 1821 four new agents were sent out with supplies and a small number of emigrants. These, with the survivors of the Elizabeth, were established at Sierra Leone until a more eligible site than Sherbro could be selected. Messrs. Andrews and E. Bacon visited different points on the coast, but returned to Sierra Leone without having made permanent arrangements, where during the summer two of the new agents died, and one returned sick to the United States.

7. The total failure of their first effort to establish a colony in Africa, attended as it was with the sacrifice of so many valuable lives, and other discouraging circumstances, only tended to arouse the energies of the Society to more vigorous and determined action. In November another agent, Dr. Ayres, was instructed to visit Sierra Leone, and after ascertaining the condition of the surviving emigrants, to proceed down the coast in search of a suitable place for a settlement.

8. Captain Stockton, with the United States schooner Alligator, was also ordered to the coast of Africa, with instructions to assist Dr. Ayres in making proper arrangements for the emigrants. These gentlemen proceeded to Cape Montserado, about 250 miles from Sierra Leone, to

obtain, if possible, territory for the Colony. They urged negotiations for several days with the chiefs of the country, and by the address and firmness of Captain Stockton they finally succeeded in obtaining a valuable tract of land including Cape Montserado.

CHAPTER XIX.

EMIGRATION TO LIBERIA.—*Continued.*

1. AFTER the purchase of this territory was effected, Dr. Ayres employed two small schooners, belonging to the Colony, in removing the emigrants from Sierra Leone to their new settlement. In the mean time the Dey people, of whom the purchase had been made, began to show signs of hostility and of the insincerity of their engagements.

2. On the arrival of the first division of emigrants, consisting chiefly of single men, the natives forbade their landing. The smallest of the two islands at the mouth of the Montserado had been obtained by special purchase of John S. Mills, at that time the occupant and proprietor, on which the people and property were safely debarked, without any actual opposition.

3. Dr. Ayres attempted in vain to conciliate the natives (who seemed bent on expelling the colonists), and was so far deceived by their imposing offers of accommodation as to trust himself in their power, when they took him prisoner, and detained him several days for the purpose of compelling him to annul the bargain.

4. The island on which the people had landed was entirely destitute of fresh water and fire-wood, and afforded no shelter, except the decayed thatch of half a dozen diminutive huts; thus exposed in an insalubrious situation, sev-

eral were again attacked by intermittent fever, from which they had but a few months before recovered at Sierra Leone.

5. Happily a secret *ex parte* arrangement was at this critical period settled with King George (who resided on the cape, and claimed a sort of jurisdiction over the northern district of the peninsula of Montserado), in virtue of which the settlers were permitted to pass across the river and commence the laborious task of clearing away the heavy forest which covered the site of their intended town. They pursued their labor with animated exertions, had made considerable progress in the erection of twenty-two buildings, when a circumstance occurred which obscured their brightening prospects and kindled around them the flame of war.

6. A small vessel, prize to an English cruiser, bound to Sierra Leone, with about thirty liberated Africans, put into the roads for a supply of water, and had the misfortune to part her cable and come ashore within a short distance of Perseverance Island. The natives pretend to a prescriptive right, which interest never fails to enforce in its utmost extent, to seize and appropriate the wrecks and cargoes of vessels stranded, under whatever circumstances, on their coast. The English schooner having drifted upon the mainland about one mile from the extremity of the cape, and a small distance below George's town, was immediately claimed as his property.

7. His people rushed to the beach with their arms to sustain this claim, and attempting to board the wreck, were fired upon by the prize master and compelled to desist. In the mean time the aid of the settlers was sent for, which, from an opinion of the extreme danger of their English visitants, they immediately afforded. A boat was manned and dispatched to their relief; and a brass fieldpiece, stationed on the island, discharged upon the assailants, when they hastily retired to their town, with the loss of two of their number killed and several disabled. The

English officer, his crew, and the Africans were brought off in safety, but suffered the total loss of their vessel, with most of the stores and other property on board of her.

8. By some accident in discharging the cannon, fire was communicated to the store-house of the Colony, and most of the provisions, ammunition, and utensils were destroyed. The exasperated natives, but for their dread of the big guns, would have attacked the settlers and destroyed them at once; as it was, they threw down the frames of their houses and continued to fire occasional shots at individuals who exposed themselves. This confined the settlers to the island until they were obliged to go up the river after wood and water.

9. On their return, their boat, though strongly manned and armed, was fired upon by the natives who lay concealed; two of their men were mortally wounded and two slightly. Their situation was now most alarming—compelled to fight for every drop of water, their stores and ammunition destroyed, their number reduced by sickness, and surrounded by a highly incensed and savage foe bent on their destruction.

10. But deliverance arose from a quarter the least expected, and in a manner so remarkable as to impress all minds with a grateful sense of the interposition of Providence. Ba Cara, the chief of a settlement on the neighboring island, who was friendly to the colonists, now applied to King Boatswain in their behalf. This famous chief, who, though living in the interior, had often assumed a dictatorial authority in the affairs of the maritime tribes, promptly responded to this application from his ally, and appeared at the cape, not, as he said, to pronounce sentence, but to do justice; and he had actually brought along with him a force sufficient to carry his decisions into immediate effect.

11. He convened the head chiefs of the neighborhood, sent for the agents of the Colony, and after allowing both parties to set forth their claims and grievances, briefly told

the Deys that having sold their land and accepted part of the payment they must abide the consequences; that their refusal to receive the balance of the purchase money did not annul or affect the bargain. "Let the Americans," said he, in a voice that was seldom disobeyed, "have their lands immediately." Then turning to the agents, "I promise you protection. If these people give you further trouble, send for me; and I swear if they oblige me to come again to quiet them, I will do it to purpose, by taking their heads from their shoulders, as I did old King George's, on my last visit to the coast to settle disputes."

12. Whatever might be thought of this decision, no one presumed to oppose it, and the settlers resumed their labors without molestation. On the 28th of April, their whole company having arrived from Sierra Leone, the emigrants passed over from the island and took formal possession of Cape Montserado. The excitement of this occasion, the pious gratitude and encouraging hopes which it inspired, could not long divert their attention from the difficulties which still surrounded them.

13. The houses were yet destitute of roofs, for which the materials were to be sought in the almost impenetrable forests of the country. The rainy season had already commenced. The island, if much longer occupied by all the colonists, must prove the grave of many. Sickness was becoming prevalent, and both the agents were among the sufferers. The store of provisions was scanty, and all other stores nearly exhausted. The active hostility of the natives had been arrested, but there was reason to fear its return. In this gloomy state of affairs, Dr. Ayres determined to abandon the enterprise and remove the people and stores to Sierra Leone.

14. The Society's agent, Mr. Wiltberger, convinced that if the colonists removed, the land purchased could not be recovered, opposed this project, and at his instance the colonists rejected it; choosing rather to brave the perils of their situation than to seek present safety and ease by the

abandonment of that cause which they believed fraught with blessings to their race. A small number accompanied Dr. Ayres to Sierra Leone. The remainder set about the completion of their houses with industry and perseverance; and after having endured great trials and hardships, were enabled, in July, entirely to abandon the island and place themselves beneath their own humble dwellings on the cape.

15. Soon after, Mr. Wiltberger returned to the United States, leaving the settlement in charge of Elijah Johnson, an intelligent and honest emigrant. The natives having treacherously waited the departure of Boatswain to the interior, and that of the agents on their voyage to the United States, put themselves in an attitude of hostility, and prohibited the conveyance of supplies to the Colony from the surrounding country. At that season of the year the colonists could not obtain a supply of provisions from the soil; no vessels were expected on the coast, and the most economical use of the stores on hand could not make them last longer than a few weeks. In the midst of these trying circumstances and alarming prospects, relief came as unexpected as it was necessary.

CHAPTER XX.

EMIGRATION TO LIBERIA.—*Continued.*

1. In August a vessel arrived from Baltimore with stores for the settlement and fifty-one emigrants, part of whom were recaptured Africans sent out by the United States Government. The Rev. Jehudi Ashmun, whose name will be honored wherever the history of Liberia is known and exalted public services are valued, came out as superintendent of this expedition. To his surprise and regret he

found that both the agents had left the country, and though he had not contemplated remaining in the Colony, he felt constrained, in view of its helpless condition and the wants of the people, to assume the charge of affairs.

2. Owing to bad weather, and the want of suitable boats, some weeks were consumed in landing the emigrants and stores, and great difficulty was experienced in providing for the accommodation of so large a number of persons. In the mean time the agent had lost not a moment in ascertaining the external relations of the settlement and the temper of its neighbors. He visited some of the principal chiefs, whom he thought it safe to bind to a pacific policy by encouraging them to open a trade with the Colony—by forming with them new amicable alliances, and receiving the sons and subjects of as many as possible to instruct in the language and arts of civilization.

3. All his attempts at reconciliation were, however, in vain. It soon became evident that the natives, under the conviction that their new neighbors were hostile to the slave trade, were determined to extirpate them. One of the most remarkable circumstances in that series of providential events connected with the history of the Colony was, that a native chief, in the councils of those who were plotting the destruction of the settlement, should have secretly, and without any known motive, determined to serve the cause of the Americans by communicating to the agent the plans and purposes of his enemies. The person to whom the Colony was indebted for these signal services (for which he has never been sufficiently rewarded) was Bob Gray, a king of the Bassa tribe, since known as the subject of many interesting anecdotes related by the agents of the Colonization Society.*

---

* One day, when sitting with the Governor in his library, he fixed his eyes upon the books in a thoughtful mood and said, " I wish America man steal me when a little boy." " Why so ?" asked the Governor. " I learn to read book, know too much, and be a great man."

4. Aware of his danger, the agent set about preparing for defense. The little town was closely environed, except on the side of the river, with the heavy forest in the bosom of which it was situated, thus giving to a savage enemy an important advantage, of which it became absolutely necessary to deprive him, by enlarging to the utmost the cleared space about the buildings. This labor was immediately undertaken and carried on without any other intermission than that caused by sickness of the people, and the performance of other duties equally connected with the safety of the place. The town was inclosed with pickets, cannon mounted, the colonists mustered, and officers appointed; all this labor was performed under the greatest disadvantages—not only a want of teams, but of mechanics and tools.

5. Only twenty-seven native Americans and thirteen African youth were capable of bearing arms, and these wholly untrained to their use. There were but forty muskets, much out of repair, and no fixed ammunition. Of one brass and five iron guns, the former only was fit for service, and four of the latter required carriages. The rains were immoderate and nearly constant. In addition to other fatiguing labors was that of maintaining the nightly watch, which, from the number of sentinels necessary for the common safety, shortly became more exhausting than all the other burdens of the people. No less than twenty individuals were every night detailed for this duty after the 31st of August.

6. At the commencement of the third week after his arrival, the agent was attacked with fever, and three days after experienced the greater calamity of perceiving the health of his wife assailed with symptoms of a still more alarming character. The sickness from this period made a rapid progress among the last division of emigrants. On the 1st of September twelve were wholly disabled. The burdens thus thrown upon their brethren accelerated the work of the climate so rapidly, that on the 10th of this

month, of the whole expedition only two remained fit for any kind of service.

7. The agent was enabled, by a merciful dispensation of Divine Providence, to maintain a difficult struggle with his disorder for four weeks; in which period, after a night of delirium and suffering, it was not an unusual circumstance for him to be able to spend an entire morning in laying off and directing the execution of the public works.

8. The plan of defense adopted was to station five heavy guns at the different angles of a triangle which should circumscribe the whole settlement—each of the angles resting on a point of ground sufficiently commanding to enfilade two sides of the triangle, and sweep a considerable extent of ground beyond the lines. The guns at these stations were to be covered by musket-proof triangular stockades, of which any two should be sufficient to contain all the settlers in their wings. The brass piece and two swivels mounted on traveling carriages were stationed in the center, ready to support the post which might be exposed to the heaviest attack.

9. After completing these detached works, it was the intention of the agent, had the enemy allowed the time, to join all together by a paling to be carried quite round the settlement; and in the event of a yet longer respite, to carry on, as rapidly as possible, under the protection of the nearest fortified point, the construction of the martello tower, which, as soon as completed, would nearly supersede all the other works, and by presenting an impregnable barrier to the success of any native force, probably become the instrument of a general and permanent pacification. Connected with these measures of safety was the extension to the utmost of the cleared space about the settlement, still leaving the trees and brushwood, after being felled, to spread the ground with a tangled hedge, through which nothing should be able to make its way, except the shot from the batteries.

CHAPTER XXI.
EMIGRATION TO LIBERIA.—*Continued.*

1. This plan was fully communicated to the most intelligent of the people, which, in the event of the disability or death of the agent, they might, it was hoped, so far carry into effect as to insure the preservation of the settlement. Their defenses were still very far from complete when, on the 7th of November, intelligence was received at the cape that the enemy were ready for an assault on the settlement, which was ordered in four days, but the plan of the attack was not ascertained.

2. Mr. Ashmun was only able, with great effort, to inspect the works, give directions and encouragement to the people, and arrange them in order of action. They lay on their arms, with matches lighted, through the night. The most wakeful vigilance was continued during the following nights, and patrols kept up through the day. Early on the morning of the 11th the attack was made by above 800 men. In consequence of the sickness of the agent, and his inability to enforce his orders personally, one pass had been neglected to be properly defended.

3. By this the enemy approached, drove the picket-guard, delivered their fire and rushed forward with their spears; several men were killed by the first fire, and the remainder driven from their cannon without discharging it. Had the enemy, at this instant, pressed their advantage, it is hardly conceivable that they should have failed of entire success. Avidity for plunder was their defeat. Four houses in that outskirt of the settlement had fallen into their hands, and while they rushed impetuously upon the pillage, Ashmun rallied his broken forces, and discharging the brass field-piece (double-shotted with ball and grape), produced great havoc among the enemy, and brought their whole body to

a stand; a few musketeers passing around upon their flank increased their consternation, and in about twenty minutes after the colonists rallied, the enemy began to recoil.

4. The colonists regained their post, and instantly brought a long nine to rake the whole line of the enemy. A savage yell was raised, which filled the surrounding forest with a momentary horror. It gradually died away, and the whole host disappeared. At eight o'clock the well-known signal of their dispersion and return to their homes was sounded, and many small parties were seen at a distance directly afterward, moving off in different directions. One large canoe, employed in re-conveying a party across the mouth of the Montserado, venturing within the range of the long gun, was struck by a shot and several men killed.

5. In the engagement the colonists had three men and one woman killed, two men and two women severely wounded, and seven children captured. Although thus completely discomfited, the natives did not abandon their design of exterminating the Colony. They determined to renew the attack with additional forces, collecting auxiliaries from as many of the neighboring tribes as they could induce to unite with them. The colonists, on their side, were equally on the alert, and made incredible exertions to prepare for repelling the assailants. They reduced the extent of their works, and thus rendered them more defensible. But the number of effective men was less, being only thirty.

6. The attack was made on the 30th of November, and incomparably better concerted than the former one. It took place almost simultaneously on three sides of the fortifications. The assailants displayed a tact and skill that would have done credit to more experienced warriors. But they were received with that bravery and determination which the danger of total destruction, in case of defeat, was calculated to inspire, and were finally defeated with severe loss. The garrison had one man killed and

two badly wounded. The skill and talent and energy of Mr. Ashmun mainly secured the triumph. He received three bullets through his clothes, but was not wounded.

7. This action, which continued an hour and a half, and was renewed three times with the utmost desperation, was still more interesting in its details than the other. The wounded suffered much for want of surgical aid. There was not even a lancet or probe in the settlement; a penknife was substituted for the first, and a priming wire for the last. An alarm, the night after the battle, induced an officer of the guard to open a fire of musketry and cannon, which providentially brought relief to the settlement.

8. The English colonial schooner Prince Regent, bound for Cape Coast, with Major Laing, the celebrated African traveler, and midshipman Gordon on board, was then in the offing, a little past the cape. So unusual a circumstance as a midnight cannonading induced the vessel to lay by till morning, when the officers communicated with the shore, and learning the situation of the colonists, generously offered any assistance in their power. Major Laing sought the chiefs, found them tired of the war, and disposed for peace. They signed a truce, and agreed to submit all their differences with the Colony to the Governor of Sierra Leone.

9. Midshipman Gordon and eleven seamen remained at the settlement on the departure of the Prince Regent, having generously volunteered their services to assist the colonists in their extremity. The lamented Gordon and eight of the seamen fell victims to the climate in less than four weeks after the vessel sailed.

10. On the 8th of December, a large privateer schooner, under Columbian colors, came to anchor near the cape. The commander, Captain Wesley, and several officers, who were natives of the United States, rendered important aid to Mr. Ashmun. By assistance obtained from this vessel, the settlement, in a few weeks, was put in a bet-

ter state of defense; while the sufferings of the sick and wounded were alleviated by the kind attentions of a skillful surgeon.

CHAPTER XXII.
EMIGRATION TO LIBERIA.—*Continued*.

1. In 1823, Mr. Ashmun's health, which had been improving for several weeks, sunk again under excessive exertion, and he continued for some time in a state of hopeless debility. He was at length restored by an extraordinary prescription of a self-taught French doctor, who arrived in a transient vessel at the cape, so that by the middle of February he was able to resume his active duties. Previous to this time two of the captive children had been recovered, and a few weeks after the remaining five were gratuitously restored. So kindly and tenderly were they treated by the old women to whose care they had been committed, that they were unwilling to leave them, and their foster-mothers were equally reluctant to give them up.

2. At this period the colonists were in a sad condition; their provisions were mostly consumed; their trade nearly exhausted; their lands untilled; their houses without roofs, except of thatch; the rainy season was approaching; and the people, as a natural consequence of their late irregular life, had, in many instances, become indolent and improvident, and finally were experiencing all that derangement in their affairs which is produced by a protracted war. In these desponding circumstances they were cheered by the arrival, on the 31st of March, of the United States ship Cyane, R. T. Spencer, Esq., commander. This gentleman proceeded to make the most active exertions for the benefit of the Colony.

3. He supplied their wants; repaired the agent's house; commenced and nearly completed the martello tower, before the 21st of April, when the rapid spread of the fever among his crew compelled him to sail for the United States. Dr. Dix, surgeon of the Cyane, had already died. This lamented man had watched with interest the progress of the Colony from its earliest existence, and had visited and administered relief to the emigrants when at Sherbro. The tears of a grateful people watered his grave.

4. The next victim was Richard Seaton, first clerk of the Cyane, an accomplished and promising young man, who voluntarily remained to assist the agent. The third was the lamented Dashiell, left in command of the schooner Augusta, which had been fitted up by Captain Spencer at Sierra Leone for the defense of the Colony. Of the crew of the Cyane, no less than forty died soon after their arrival in the United States. It is painful to record the death of so many whose generous devotion to the interests of the Colony claims for them our spontaneous gratitude.

5. The successful exertions of the officers and crew of the Cyane are the more remarkable from the fact that they were enfeebled by a cruise of several months in the West Indies. Captain Spencer especially was laboring under great debility.

6. The Board of Managers, aware of the weak state of the settlement, had, early in the preceding winter, determined to dispatch a reinforcement of emigrants, with stores, under the direction of Dr. Ayres, whose improved health now permitted him to resume his duties, as principal agent and physician in the Colony. This gentleman embarked at Baltimore, on board the brig Oswego, with sixty-one colored passengers, on the 16th of April, and arrived at Cape Montserado on the 24th of May.

7. On the arrival of Dr. Ayres, as principal agent, both of the Government and the Society, Mr. Ashmun was relieved from the weight of care and labor which had nearly worn him out. Dr. Ayres entered with zeal and vigor

upon his official duties. The erection of houses, the surveying and distribution of land to the new settlers, and the general care of the government gave him unceasing employment. The system of government was improved, arrangements were made for the better disposition of supplies from the public stores; the site of the town was accurately surveyed and judiciously laid off; and the distribution was made of the lots and plantations.

8. Some of the early settlers, however, were dissatisfied with these arrangements. As the founders and defenders of the Colony they considered themselves entitled to peculiar privileges, and earnestly contended for their right to retain the ground upon which they had originally fixed their habitations. The health of Dr. Ayres soon began to fail under the combined effect of the climate and his incessant labors, and in a few months he was reduced to such a state that his recovery, in Africa, was considered hopeless; accordingly, in December, he took passage for the United States in the ship Fidelity of Baltimore, and the government was again thrown upon Mr. Ashmun.

9. He had been placed in a most painful and embarrassing position by the arrival of Dr. Ayres. He not only found himself superseded in the government, but had the additional mortification to learn that his drafts had been dishonored, and no provision made to remunerate him for past services, or provide for his present wants. No man possessed a nicer sense of honor than Ashmun. Finding his services undervalued, and even the confidence of the Society withheld, he was justly indignant; although his attachment to the cause remained steadfast. Seeing the principal agent leaving the Colony, the colonists in a state of insubordination, Ashmun, with true Christian magnanimity, forgetting his own wrongs, resolved to remain and save, if possible, from destruction a cause in which he had done and suffered so much.

10. The prudence of his measures and the firmness of his conduct prevented any immediate outbreak of violence;

but causes of dissatisfaction existed, and the spirit of insubordination had acquired too much strength to be easily eradicated. Their stock of provisions was low, the native rice very scarce and dear on account of the supplies required by the slave vessels, which, at this time, were on the coast in great numbers.

11. Worse than all, several of the principal colonists avowed their determination to leave uncultivated the land assigned them, and to give up all further labor or attempts at improvements until their grievances were redressed by the Board in the United States, to which they had appealed. It was at that time one of the regulations of the Society, that every adult male emigrant should, while receiving rations from the public store, contribute the labor of two days in a week to some work of public utility.

12. About twelve of the colonists not only cast off the restraints of the Colony, but exerted themselves to seduce others from obedience. On the 13th of December, Mr. Ashmun published the following notice: "There are in the Colony more than a dozen healthy persons who will receive no more provisions out of the public store until they earn them." This notice proved inefficient, except as it gave occasion for the expression of more seditious sentiments and a bolder violation of the laws.

13. On the 19th, Mr. Ashmun directed the rations of the offending individuals to be stopped. The next morning they assembled in a riotous manner at the agency house, and endeavored by angry denunciations to drive the governor from his purpose; finding him inflexible, they proceeded to the store-house, where the commissary was at that moment issuing rations for the week, and seizing each a portion of the provisions, hastened to their respective houses.

14. The same day, Mr. Ashmun addressed a circular to all the colonists, in which he made so powerful an appeal to their patriotism and to their consciences, and so decidedly expressed his own determination to maintain author-

ity, that the disaffected returned to their duty. The leader of the sedition confessed his error, and by the rectitude of his after-life nobly redeemed his character.

CHAPTER XXIII.
EMIGRATION TO LIBERIA.—*Continued.*

1. On the 13th of February, 1824, the ship Cyrus arrived with 105 emigrants, mostly from Petersburg, Virginia. The accession of this company was hailed by all as a joyful event, especially as it comprised an unusual amount of intelligence, industry, and morality. But the cordial greetings and kind interchanges of friendly offices, which made this a scene of happiness and hope, were soon succeeded by sadness and gloom. Within four weeks all the new emigrants were attacked by the fever. There was no regular physician in the Colony, the number of buildings bore no proportion to the number of emigrants, and by a strange neglect the provisions supplied for the expedition were wholly inadequate, while the dispensary contained little that was suitable for the sick.

2. Rev. Lot Cary, a colonist, who had before rendered important service to the Colony, undertook the care of the sick, and indebted solely for his medical skill to his good sense, observation, and what experience he had gained in the Colony, his success was remarkable. Only three died.

3. All these evils were light compared with those which the spirit of revolt and anarchy threatened to bring upon the Colony. Deficient in education and ill-informed on many of the important relations and duties of human society, dazzled and misled by false notions of freedom, disappointed in some of their expectations, and tried by affliction, a few individuals still continued utterly to disre-

gard the authority of the agent, and sought to persuade others to imitate their example.

4. On the 19th of March the rations were reduced one half, and it was found that, so diminished, the supplies would last not more than five weeks. This act of prudence was counted by the malcontents an act of oppression, and they reproached the agent in his presence.

5. On the morning of the 22d, Mr. Ashmun assembled the people and represented to them the advantages and necessity of subordination, the evils which had already resulted to them from disobedience, especially that their neglect to cultivate the rich soil which surrounded them had reduced them to their present want; reminded them of the expenditures, toils, and sacrifices made by the Society and its officers in their behalf, the distinguished privileges they enjoyed, and the bright prospects in reversion; urged upon them the obligation of their oaths, and declared his determination to enforce the laws by a rigid exercise of his authority, unless they immediately returned to their allegiance.

6. Most of the settlers tacitly assented to the truth and justice of this address, and Mr. Ashmun adopted every measure in his power to relieve and preserve the Colony, but the colonists afforded him no vigorous support. The spirit of disorganization was at work, deranging all the movements of government. The agent had some months before declared to the Board, that in his opinion "the evil was incurable by any of the remedies which fall within their existing provisions." He now prepared and forwarded dispatches containing his reflections on the state of the Colony, and the increasing elements of turbulence and danger threatening its speedy ruin.

7. Soon after this, he was obliged to leave the cape on account of his health, which, under his accumulated trials, had become entirely prostrated; appointing E. Johnson superintendent of affairs, he sailed for Cape De Verd Islands on the 1st of April

8. The remonstrances sent home by some of the colonists, and the communications of the agent, had convinced the Board that immediate and strong measures were required to prevent the subversion of the Colony and the total extinction of their hopes. They wrote a reply to the remonstrance, and an address to the colonists generally, in which they declared that the agents must be obeyed, or the Colony abandoned. They asserted their determination to punish offenders, while they assisted the obedient, and affectionately encouraged all the sober and virtuous to maintain the peace, and guard, as their very life, the authority of the laws.

9. These documents were scarcely dispatched, when letters were received from the Colony charging Mr. Ashmun with oppression, the neglect of obvious duties, the desertion of his post, and the seizure and abduction of the public property. These charges were confirmed by various verbal reports of officers of the United States Navy, and others who had touched at Montserado soon after his departure, and there listened to these calumnies.

10. The Board applied to the Government to send a vessel to the Colony with some individual duly commissioned, both by the Government and the Society, to examine the condition of the Colony, redress grievances, and correct abuses. The Rev. R. R. Gurley, Secretary of the Society, was appointed to this service, and embarked at Norfolk, late in June, 1824, in the United States schooner Porpoise, Captain Skinner.

11. Arriving at the Cape De Verds 24th of July, Mr. Gurley there found Mr. Ashmun, to whom he communicated the object of his visit to Africa, and the extent of the powers with which he was clothed. Ashmun, who desired the fullest investigation of his official conduct, returned by the Porpoise to the Colony, where she arrived on the 13th of August. On a full inquiry, Mr. Gurley was not only satisfied of the integrity and purity of Mr. Ashmun's character, but of his firmness and sound judgment,

as well as the admirable adaptedness of his talents to the extraordinary crises through which he had passed.

12. Both these gentlemen applied themselves with the utmost diligence to removing all causes of complaint. Widows, orphans, the infirm and helpless were provided for. A large share in the management of their political affairs was conceded to the colonists.

13. The decisions of the commissioners, with the plan of government to be recommended to the Board, were read and explained to the colonists, which, without a dissenting voice, they pronounced satisfactory; and being assembled in the first rude house of worship ever erected in the Colony, they solemnly pledged themselves before God to support the constitution agreed upon, and faithfully to sustain the great trust committed to their hands. Mutual confidence was completely restored between the people and the agent, and if the colonists in the extremity of their suffering had injured Mr. Ashmun, their error was atoned for by the most respectful subordination to his authority and the kindest regard for his personal comfort during his future stay in Africa.

14. This period may be considered as almost the commencement of their establishment. Contentment, industry, peace, and general comfort now succeeded to the sufferings, disappointments, alarms, and dissensions which had prevailed in the Colony during the previous four years of its struggling existence.

15. The commissioner left, on his return to the United States, the 22d of August. Mr. Ashmun explored the country, and finding a rich tract of land lying on the south side of the St. Paul's River, possessing great advantages for agricultural purposes, he opened a negotiation with the kings of the country for the purchase, and succeeded in obtaining twenty miles on the river, and from three to nine miles back. On this tract a town was laid out on a beautiful point six miles from Monrovia, which was at first called St. Paul's, but afterward changed to Caldwell.

CHAPTER XXIV.

EMIGRATION TO LIBERIA.—*Continued.*

1. On the 13th of March, 1825, the brig Hunter, from Norfolk, Va., with sixty-six emigrants arrived. These emigrants were principally farmers, and settled at Caldwell, preferring this situation, although an unbroken forest, and exposed to the depredations of the wild Africans, on account of the rich soil. The fever, which attacked nearly all within a month after their arrival in the Colony, was greatly protracted, and increased in violence from the want of proper medical treatment. The Board had failed to procure a physician. Lot Cary again interposed his good offices and acted as their friend and physician, and was very successful in saving his patients.

2. Recovered from the seasoning fever, these emigrants applied themselves with so much industry, that soon their farms extended a mile and a half on the rich flats of the river, and they were enjoying health and plenty.

3. At this period the slave trade was carried on extensively within sight of Monrovia. Fifteen vessels were engaged in it at the same time, almost under the guns of the settlement; and in July of this year a contract was existing for eight hundred slaves to be furnished, in the short space of four months, within eight miles of the cape. Four hundred of these were to be purchased for two American traders.

4. The agent had no power either to arrest or punish these pirates, but he determined to employ the whole influence of the Colony against this accursed traffic. He explored the whole line of coast from Cape Mount to Trade Town, and sought, by treaties with the chiefs, to effect the exclusion of the slave traders from the country, while within the legitimate jurisdiction of the Colony

he determined to enforce the laws against them with the utmost rigor.

5. In the month of August, a flagrant piracy was perpetrated by the crew of a Spanish schooner (the Clarida), employed in the slave trade, on an English brig lying at anchor off the town of Monrovia. Mr. Ashmun did not hesitate as to the course of duty. Ample testimony was taken to prove the piracy. The English brig was placed under his direction. A call upon the colonial militia was promptly responded to, and an expedition was immediately set on foot against the Spanish factory a few miles north of Monrovia.

6. The Spanish schooner was not to be found; the factory, with a small amount of property and a number of slaves, was captured without resistance, and the native chiefs bound themselves to assist in no way in collecting or transporting out of the country any of the slaves bargained for by the commander of the Clarida.

7. In proof of the good discipline of the colonists, and their sense of justice toward the natives, it may be stated that not a single instance of disorderly conduct occurred among the fifty-four men who composed this expedition. The natives, into whose country they had marched, expressed their amazement at the regard paid to their persons and property, and several of the chiefs sent deputations to thank the governor for his justice and humanity.

8. About this time a most daring robbery was committed by a Krooman on the public stores at Monrovia, and these offenses having become of frequent occurrence, it was deemed important to arrest the offender. A party of militia was ordered to accompany the sheriff to the Kroo town and to demand redress. Two or three of the party fell behind, one of whom fired at a Krooman and mortally wounded him. Ashmun had the man arrested and tried by a jury. It was proved on trial that the offender had misunderstood his orders; he was however sentenced to six months' imprisonment or a fine of one hundred bars, which

sum was paid over to the family of the deceased, and was perfectly satisfactory to the Kroo nation.

9. A short time after the destruction of the Spanish slave factory, Mr. Ashmun discovered that a plan had been formed, between the captain of the Clarida, some of the native chiefs, and a French slave dealer on the St. Paul's, for violating the engagement by which the slaves originally destined for the pirate were to be delivered over to the Colony. He was induced, in consequence, to break up two other slave factories, and to offer to the chiefs concerned in the transactions of the Clarida a bounty of ten dollars for each slave, which, in pursuance of their agreement, they should resign to the colonial agent. The consequence of this was, that *one hundred and sixteen slaves* were soon received into the Colony as freemen.

10. At the close of this year the agent presented to the Managers a complete view of the condition, relations, character, and prospects of the Colony. He stated that health had been for some months restored; that adults, resident for some time in Africa, preferred its climate to any other, and enjoyed as good health as in America, and that the settlers generally lived in a style of neatness and comfort. Two commodious chapels, each sufficient to contain several hundred worshipers, had been erected and consecrated to God.

11. A small schooner had been built, and put in the rice trade between Cape Montserado and the factories at the leeward, adapted to the passage of the bars of the rivers on that part of the coast. The militia of the settlement was well organized, equipped, and disciplined. In addition to the valuable tract of country purchased on the St. Paul's, the right of occupancy and use had been obtained to the lands at the Young Sesters, and at Grand Bassa, and factories established at both of those places. Five schools, exclusive of Sunday-schools, were in operation.

12. The people were obedient to the laws; their moral character had improved; the preponderance of example

4*

and of influence was on the side of virtue; and the Colony was, in *reality*, a Christian community. He observed that as "the great secret of the improving circumstances of the Colony is in the controlling influence of religion on the temper and happiness of the people, I should greatly wrong the cause of truth by suppressing a topic of such leading importance.

13. "The holy Author of our religion and salvation has made the hearts of a large portion of these people the temples of the Divine Spirit. The faith of the everlasting Gospel has become to them the animating spring of action, the daily rule of life, the source of immortal hope and of ineffable enjoyment. Occurrences of a favorable or desponding aspect are regarded as dispensations of the Almighty, and followed with corresponding feelings of gratitude or humiliation."

14. He testified to the good effects of the Colony on the neighboring tribes. They had been treated as men and brethren of a common family; they had been taught that one of the ends proposed in founding civilized settlements on their shore was to do them good; they had learned something of the great and interesting truths of the Christian religion, and sixty of their children had been adopted as children of the Colony. No man of the least consideration in the country would desist from his importunities till at least one of his sons was fixed in some settler's family.

CHAPTER XXV.
PROSPERITY OF THE COLONY.

1. On the 4th of January, 1826, the brig Vine, with thirty-four emigrants, a missionary (the Rev. Calvin Holton), and a printer, accompanied by the Rev. Horace Sessions, an agent of the Society, sailed from Boston, and arrived at Monrovia on the 7th of February. A printing-

press, with necessary appendages, a valuable supply of books, and other important articles were sent out in this vessel by the generous citizens of Boston, who assumed the entire expense of the printing establishment for the first year.

2. The Indian Chief, with 154 persons, left Norfolk on the 15th of February and arrived on the 22d of March; 139 of these emigrants were from North Carolina. In this vessel Dr. John W. Peaco went out as United States agent for the recaptured Africans. He was also employed by the Society to act as assistant agent and physician of the Colony.

3. The entire company which arrived in the Vine were soon attacked by the worst form of African fever, and about half their number, including Messrs. Sessions, Holton, and Force (the printer), fell victims to its power. A large majority of this company of emigrants were pious, steady, industrious, and intelligent; and the young men, who in the spirit of Christian benevolence had accompanied them, were worthy to become martyrs in such a cause.

4. Of the emigrants who came in the Indian Chief, only three out of the whole number (and two of these small children) died in the course of the season, while the remainder suffered very little during the period of acclimation, and were soon actively engaged in the laborious duties of a frontier life.

5. A tract of land lying along the Stockton Creek and St. Paul's River was surveyed, and as early as June no less than thirty-three plantations on the creek and seventy-seven at Caldwell were occupied. Cheered and animated by the thriving condition of the Colony, and the prosperous settlement of the newly arrived colonists, the agent wrote to the Board for more emigrants. "If they come from the South," said he, "they can not come very unseasonably in any part of the year. More funds, more activity, more emigrants, and I am satisfied."

CHAPTER XXVI.
COLONIAL WAR AGAINST THE SLAVE TRADE.

1. A SPANISH schooner, the Minerva, while waiting for the collection of her cargo of 300 slaves, at Trade Town, had committed piracy on American and other vessels, and obtained possession of several recaptured Africans belonging to the United States agency in Liberia. Mr. Ashmun, as agent of the United States, demanded of the Spanish factor and native authorities of that place the restoration of these Africans, and threatened, in case of refusal, " to destroy, as soon as Providence should grant him power, entirely and forever, that nest of iniquity." The demand was treated with contempt. Intelligence of the character of the Spanish schooner was communicated by Mr. Ashmun to the commander of the French brig of war, who soon captured her, though her establishment on shore, at which 276 slaves were ready to be shipped to America, remained unmolested.

2. Early in January, goods were landed at Trade Town from a French schooner, the Perle, sufficient for the purchase of 240 slaves, though in April she had obtained but 126. A brigantine, the Teresa, from Havana, armed with seven large carriage guns, and manned with forty-two men, with goods for the purchase of 300 slaves, arrived in March, landed about one third of the cargo, and had commenced her traffic.

3. Three slave factories were in full operation at Trade Town, guarded by two vessels, mounting between them eleven carriage guns, and having a complement of sixty men and twenty more on shore, all well armed; when, on the 9th of April, arrived at Monrovia the Colombian armed schooner Jacinto, Captain Chase, who, in accordance with the instructions of his Government, offered to

coöperate with Dr. Peaco (then principal agent of the United States for the recaptured Africans) and Mr. Ashmun, in any plan they might adopt for the punishment of these offenders.

4. The offer of Captain Chase was accepted; and on the 10th of April, Mr. Ashmun, accompanied by Captain Cochran, of the Indian Chief, who generously offered to become his aid, and thirty-two volunteers of the colonial militia, embarked in the Jacinto, and arrived off Trade Town on the 11th, where they had the happiness to find anchored the Colombian brig of war El Vincidor, Captain Cottrell, mounting twelve guns, which had the same afternoon captured, after a short action, the brigantine Teresa.

5. Captain Cottrell agreed to unite his forces with those of the Colony and Jacinto in an attack on the place. It was resolved to attempt a landing on the morning of the 12th, on the bar of the river in front of the town, where the passage is only eight yards wide, lined on both sides with rocks, and across which, at that time, the surf broke so furiously as to endanger even light boats, and leave scarce a hope of the safety of barges filled with armed men.

6. The Spaniards were seen drawn up on the beach within half musket range of the bar. The brig and schooner were ordered to open a fire on the town; but owing to their distance, their shot produced no effect except to disperse the unarmed natives who had assembled as spectators of the scene. The two boats in advance, commanded by Captains Chase and Cottrell, were exposed to a rabid fire from the enemy, and were filled by the surf before they reached the shore. Their crews, though few of them landed with dry arms, forced the Spaniards back into the town. The flag-boat, in which were Mr. Ashmun, Captain Cochran, and twenty-four men, was upset and dashed upon the rocks, several of the men (among whom was Mr. Ashmun) injured, and some of the arms, with all the ammunition, lost. Captain Barbour, a colonist, observ-

ing the dangers of those who preceded him, run his boat a little to the left of the river's mouth, and thus landed in safety.

7. Though met by a galling fire from a party of Spaniards and natives at the water's edge, Captain Barbour formed the colonists, under his command, with the utmost coolness, and attacked the enemy with such vigor that they soon broke and fled to the town. The colonists, joined by the Colombians, advanced rapidly upon the town, broke down the slight palisades, and before the frightened enemy had time to rally behind their defenses, fell upon them, and drove them in the forest in the greatest confusion.

8. As soon as he found himself in quiet possession of the town, Mr. Ashmun dispatched a messenger to King West (the principal native chief) demanding the delivery of all the slaves belonging to the factories. He was told that if there was deception or unnecessary delay in the matter, Trade Town should not exist two days longer. On the same day the Kroomen of King West brought in thirty-eight slaves, and on the next morning fifteen more; the latter, a wretched company, evidently the refuse of all that had been collected at the station.

9. The natives assembled and united their forces to those of the Spaniards, and continued, from the rear of their towns and under cover of the woods, to pour in at frequent intervals their shot upon their invaders. Captain Woodside, surgeon of the Jacinto, was severely wounded, and several of the colonial militia slightly. Every man under the command of the colonial agent lay on his arms during the night of the 12th; and until noon on the 13th every disposition was evinced by Mr. Ashmun to settle peacefully the questions which had excited hostilities. But in vain.

10. At twelve on that day the boats were prepared, just outside the breakers, to receive on board the rescued slaves; at two the canoes began to carry off the mariners, and at half-past three all were embarked, the officers leav-

ing the shore last, having set fire to the principal buildings of the town. The flames communicated with the utmost rapidity to every roof, and the town exhibited a single immense mass of flame before the canoes could get off from the beach. The moment they reached the boats, the explosion of 250 casks of powder at the same instant swept every vestige of what was once Trade Town from the ground on which it stood.

CHAPTER XXVII.
MORE TROUBLE WITH SLAVE TRADERS.

1. THE destruction of Trade Town contributed more to the suppression of the slave trade on the western coast of Africa, north of the Bight of Benin, than any one single event, except only the enactments of the English and American legislatures.* It convinced every slave trader along the coast that his commerce was insecure, and the natives over a great extent of country, that a powerful enemy to their crimes had gained establishment on their shore.

2. From May to October Mr. Ashmun was confined to his room in consequence of the injury received at Trade Town. Dr. Peaco was absent from Liberia several weeks during this period, to settle certain claims held at Sierra Leone against the United States agency in Liberia. But the Colony was not neglected. Mr. Ashmun was able to attend to the business of his agency, and directed several important measures for improving the condition and extending the influence and territory of the Colony.

---

* The American Government at this time rigorously enforced her laws against the slave trade by means of armed cruisers on the coast.

3. To encourage agriculture, he granted leases of the public grounds in the vicinity of Monrovia for three years rent free, on condition that the lessees should proceed immediately to clear, inclose, and improve them. He imposed a tax of two dollars a head on all landholders for the purpose of raising funds for the construction of a town school-house. Although this act occasioned expressions of the wildest and most absurd notions on the subject of taxation and republican liberty, he persevered in collecting the tax.

4. The government of Sierra Leone had put the line of coast from that place to the Gallinas under blockade for the suppression of the slave trade. This measure operated favorably for the American colonies, as the exclusion of the ordinary commerce induced the chiefs of Cape Mount to open a regular trade with the colonists, which made the supply of rice and other African provisions unusually cheap and abundant.

5. The brig John, Captain Clough, from Portland, and the schooner Bona, from Baltimore, were plundered on the 27th July, when lying at anchor off the town of Monrovia, by a piratical brig, mounting twelve guns, and manned chiefly by Spaniards, the former of $2,500 and the latter of $2,860.

6. Intelligence reached the Colony nearly at the same time, that eight vessels engaged in the slave trade had resolved to make Trade Town the station for their traffic, that they had commenced a battery on shore, and were determined to defend themselves against any force which might be brought against them. It is well known that the slave trade was, at this time, the pretext for fitting out piratical vessels from Havana. Scarcely an American trading vessel had for the last twelve months been on this coast as low as six degrees north without suffering either insult or plunder from these Spaniards.

7. In this state of things Mr. Ashmun directed that a strong battery should be immediately erected near the

termination of the cape, for the protection of ships at anchor in the roadstead, while he represented to the Hon. Secretary of the Navy the absolute necessity of the presence of a sloop of war for the defense of American commerce on the coast.

8. His influence and authority with the native chiefs, however, contributed more than any other means to prevent the destruction of the colonial factories and the threatened subversion of the Colony. The boats furnished by the Government were of great utility; they enabled him to maintain the establishment at the Sesters, although within five miles of Trade Town, and to keep up an intercourse, even at that inclement season, along the beach with Bassa factory.

CHAPTER XXVIII.

THE COLONIAL NAVY—LITERATURE—PEACE.

1. On the 18th of August, Dr. Peaco, whose health was much reduced by repeated attacks of fever, embarked in the brig John for the United States. This vessel was the first of a regular line of packets intended to run between the United States and Liberia; an arrangement which promised a great benefit to the colonies, as well as profit to the owners; but on account of exposure to slave traders and pirates, and the general want of security for American vessels on the coast, the line was discontinued.

2. Coincident with the departure of Dr. Peaco was the death of Mr. Hodges, a boat builder from Norfolk, which left Mr. Ashmun, for the seventh time, the only white man in the Colony. The first political contest in the Colony occurred this year. A few individuals belonging to the Independent Volunteer Company, composed of high-spir-

ited young men, all excellent soldiers, but bad politicians, took offense at certain restrictive regulations, and particularly at the summary method which, on the failure of all others, had been adopted to raise money for most necessary improvements in the town.

3. By zeal and activity they soon formed a party, went forward in a body to the polls, and while the more sober part of the community were little aware of any political danger, elected their own candidate for the vice-agency. The colonial agent refused to confirm the chosen candidate in office, and stated his reasons, which were entirely of a political nature.

4. In the afternoon, a circular was issued to this effect: "That the right of election conferred by the Board of Managers on the people of the Colony, as it never had been, so it never should be interfered with by the agent; consequently appointments to offices of trust in the Colony, once legally made by the concurrence of the popular choice, with his own approbation, should never be rescinded by any arbitrary act on his part, and that the actual incumbents must remain in their office till removed in the only way prescribed by the constitution—that is, by vote of a majority of the electors of the Colony."

5. A minority only having voted, the polls were kept open until the next day; the whole body of voters attended, and by a large majority elected men well qualified for the offices, and whose appointment was immediately confirmed by the colonial agent.

6. The frames of two small schooners had been brought out in the Indian Chief; one of them, the Catharine, was completed and launched in October. Trifling as this circumstance may seem, it was really an important event to the Colony; although but ten tons burden, the Catharine carried a brass six-pounder, pivot mounted, and being strongly manned and well armed with muskets, boarding pistols, and cutlasses, she was thus prepared for defense against the piratical slave traders, afforded a commodious

conveyance for the produce of the country, and enabled the agent to visit a long line of coast, to extend the relations of the Colony, and bind together their establishments.

7. At the close of the year 1826, the Colony was blessed with health, peace, and prosperity. Its commerce had greatly increased, new settlements had been founded, and much progress made during the year, in the construction of public buildings and works of defense. Fort Stockton had been rebuilt, and a battery nearly completed on the extremity of the cape. A large building capable of accommodating 150 emigrants had been finished.

8. The new agency-house, market-house, Lancasterian school-house, and town-house in Monrovia were far advanced, and the government-house at Caldwell nearly completed. A room had been set apart in the wing of the old agency-house for the colonial library, consisting of 1,200 volumes systematically arranged in glazed cases. Files of American newspapers were here also preserved, and it was intended to render this department both a reading-room and a museum for African curiosities.

9. The purchase of Factory Island had been definitely concluded, and a perpetual grant, rent-free, obtained of a fine tract of country lying between the two Junk rivers. Five of the most important stations on the line of coast from Cape Mount to Trade Town, 150 miles, now belonged to the Colony, either by purchase or by deeds of perpetual lease; and all Europeans were excluded from any possession within these limits.

10. The tract granted to the Society at the Young Sesters River in 1825, situated in the midst of a fruitful rice country, abounding in palm-oil, camwood, and ivory, included all the land on each side to the distance of half a league, extending from the river's mouth to its source.

11. In December, of this year, the agent wrote thus to the Board: "We still enjoy a state of profound tranquillity, as regards our relations with *all* the tribes of the country. The last season was most abundantly prolific in rice;

and never have our settlements been in so favorable a state to admit, I may add, to *require*, a very large addition of settlers as at the present moment.

12. "All this region of Africa opens its bosom for the reception of her returning children. I rejoice in the testimonials furnished of a growing and enlightened interest in the objects of your Board among the American people. It is one of those great and benevolent designs on which the merciful Father of all mankind loves to smile, which the American Colonization Society has undertaken. Its root is deep, and its growth, however gradual, I believe to be entirely sure. But the greatest difficulties—for difficulties the cause has always struggled with—I never supposed to lie on this side the ocean. To obviate prejudices, and unite the exertions, and rouse the enterprise of the whole American people, this is the great labor, and to such as most successfully engage in, and prosecute it, will be chiefly due the acknowledgments of posterity."

CHAPTER XXIX.

ARRIVAL OF ARMS AND EMIGRANTS.

1. The repeated acts of piracy in the vicinity of the Colony, and the necessities of the United States agency within its limits, induced the Secretary of the Navy to dispatch to the coast the United States schooner Shark, under command of Lieutenant Norris, with a supply of arms and ammunition for the Colony. This vessel arrived at Monrovia on the 12th of January, 1827. The commander acting in concert with the colonial agent, did much to suppress the slave trade along that coast, and to strengthen sentiments of good-will toward the settlement among the neighboring tribes.

2. Early in the year, a treaty of peace was concluded between the colonial agent and the principal chief of Trade Town, by which the two parties were bound, mutually, to maintain and encourage between them friendly intercourse and an equitable trade, and to regard as sacred and inviolable the persons and property of each other. Soon after, the colonial factory at Young Sesters was suspended, in consequence of depredations committed upon it by the surrounding people, and especially on account of a fierce war beginning to rage between the chiefs of that country and Trade Town.

3. Mr. Ashmun visited both of these places, and for three days was engaged in unavailing efforts to reconcile the contending parties. Both agreed to respect the colonial property, and both offered to give to the colonial agent the whole country of their enemy, provided he would assist them to subdue it. Freeman (the chief of the Young Sesters country) and his allies engaged to enroll themselves, with all their people and country, as vassals and fiefs of the Colony, on condition that they were assisted by the agent and his forces against their foe of Trade Town. "But from the first," said Mr. Ashmun, "all were given to understand that our whole force was sacred to the purpose of self-defense alone,. against the injustice and violence of the unprincipled; that while we were ready to benefit *all* our neighbors, we could injure *none ;* and that if we could not prevent or settle the wars of the country, we should never take part in them."

4. This war terminated for the advantage of the Sesters, at an earlier period than was expected; the colonial property confided to King Freeman had been scrupulously preserved amid all the disorder and alarm of hostilities, and the factory was re-established. The chief would, he said, relinquish one half of all his territories rather than see the colonial settlement, in the midst of his people, abandoned.

5. In March, Mr. Ashmun, expecting soon to leave the

Colony, wrote to the Board that preparations were made for the reception of at least 100 emigrants and 200 recaptured Africans, and added, "At this point, formed by the junction of the St. Paul's and Stockton, where I reside, I have now a most commodious house completely furnished, and kitchen and out-houses separate. There is also a public store-house, an extensive fortification, a block-house, jail, and, now erecting, a receptacle for emigrants, 100 feet in length, overlooking both rivers.

6. "At the cape, I have just completed a new and extensive warehouse, of which the second story is fitted up for a printing-office. Besides this building, the three settlements contain no less than six public stores and warehouses, altogether sufficient to store commodiously more public property than will soon find its way into the Colony. I have been enabled to collect an ample supply of rice, and hope to leave a sufficient supply of provisions and other necessaries for all the dependent of the agency, should other sources by accident be closed against them during my absence."

7. On the 11th of April, the brig Doris, Capt. Mathews, with twenty-three emigrants, most of them from North Carolina, arrived at the Colony, after a passage of forty-five days. These people suffered but slightly from the effects of the climate, and at an early day took up their residence at Caldwell. Two young children only died. The most protracted case of illness, in the whole number, did not last longer than five days.

8. Soon after the arrival of the Doris, Mr. Ashmun wrote the Board: "I am at length reluctantly compelled by a sense of duty to the Colony to relinquish my intention, so long indulged, and so fondly cherished, of visiting the United States the present season. The arrival of so large a company at so late a period of the dry season—the absence of my colleague—the multiplicity of delicate and arduous duties devolving on an agent in consequence of the recent extension of our settlements—the very expen-

CHAPTER XXX.

SCHOOLS—COMMERCE—NEW TERRITORY.

1. THE whole system of schools which had been suspended by the death of Mr. Holton, was reorganized and in efficient operation this year, under the superintendence of Rev. G. McGill, an experienced colored teacher, though its influence was limited by the want of proper books and well-qualified teachers. The schools were all taught by colored people, and supported partly from the colonial treasury, and partly by subscriptions from the colonists.

2. They were sufficiently numerous to embrace all the children, including those of the natives; all were obliged to attend. The number of children in the six schools was 227, of whom forty-five were natives. Most of these were the sons of the principal men of the country, and more than half could, at the close of the year, read the New Testament intelligibly, and understand the English language nearly as well as the settlers of the same age. Had means been supplied, the number of these native pupils could have been greatly increased.

3. A school was opened in the Vey nation, thirty-five miles interior from Cape Mount, and sixty or seventy from Montserado, by the Baptist missionaries of the Colony. It commenced with thirty-five scholars, and was patronized by the Prince and head men of the nation, who were desirous to have their children clothed and trained to the habits of civilized life. Rev. Mr. Cary's school, for native children, was supported in part by the Baptist Missionary Society of Richmond.

4. The system of government adopted in 1824 had continued without any material alteration, and received the cordial support of the enlightened and influential part of

the colonists. Unused to freedom, and ignorant of the principles of social order, it was to be expected that the uninformed would be deficient in public spirit and subordination. The annual elections resulted in the reappointment of most of the officers of the preceding year.

5. Nearly the whole expenses of the colonial government and of the United States' agency had this year been defrayed by the profits realized in the trade of the factories. Four schooners were built and sent out under the flag of Liberia. The Colony was sustained in its growth almost wholly by its own industry. It was, however, a subject of regret that the life of this industry was rather in its trade and commerce than its agriculture.

6. Situated, as were the colonists, on the central point of an extensive coast, with a vast field of commercial enterprise opening before them, they were tempted to seek the immediate gains of trade, rather than the remote, though surer and more important advantages of agriculture. The premiums proposed by the Board to the most successful farmers were to some extent beneficial. At Caldwell an agricultural society was formed, at the weekly meetings of which the members reported their progress on their plantations, and discussed questions on husbandry.

7. The recaptured Africans had proved orderly and industrious. Familiar with the ordinary modes of African agriculture, and suffering nothing from the climate, they were busily and tastefully improving their settlements. A company was formed in the Colony for the purpose of improving the navigation of the Montserado River, one thousand dollars of stock subscribed, and pledges given to raise, if necessary, four thousand more.

8. The military force was newly organized, and four volunteer companies formed, the description of which, as given at the time, was quite *en militaire*. "The oldest of these companies is Captain Barbour's light infantry, composed of select young men, completely armed and equipped, highly disciplined (relatively), and consisting of about

forty men. Uniform, light-blue, faced with white. The next is Captain Davis' company. Uniform, white, with blue bars, well armed and accoutered. The third is a company of light artillery, composed of select young men, completely uniformed and equipped. This corps having been lately organized, consists only of about thirty men, but as it is exceedingly popular, will increase rapidly. Captain Devany is the present commander. Uniform, deep blue, with red facings. The fourth is a newly organized artillery company, commanded by Captain Prout."

9. Three enterprising citizens of the Colony, during this year, explored the interior to a considerable extent. One of them penetrated to the distance of a hundred and forty miles, where he discovered a country inhabited by a numerous people far advanced in civilization. The St. Paul's River was explored upward of two hundred miles.

10. The chiefs of Cape Mount (with whom negotiations had been commenced the preceding year) had stipulated to construct a large and commodious factory for the colonial government; to guarantee the safety of all persons and property belonging to the factory; to exact no tribute from those who might resort to it; to encourage trade between it and the interior; and forever to exclude foreigners from similar privileges, and from any right of occupancy or possession in their country.

11. The right bank of Bushrod Island, extending the whole length of Stockton Creek, which unites Montserado and St. Paul's, had been ceded to the Society. This island contains twenty thousand acres of fertile, level land. An invaluable tract of land, of indefinite extent, on the north side of the river St. Johns, contiguous to Factory Island, had also been added to the possessions of the Society. All the chiefs between Cape Mount and Trade Town had bound themselves to exclude all others, except the people of Liberia, from a settlement in their country. And at no less than eight stations on this line of coast had the colonial government obtained the right of founding settlements.

CHAPTER XXXI.

DOMESTIC CONDITION OF THE COLONY.

1. The following is a general view given of the domestic condition of the Colony at this time. About half of the entire population were settled in comfortable dwellings on their own cultivated premises, and in independent circumstances. Most of these were engaged in the coasting and country trade; some were turning their attention to agriculture; several were carrying on mechanical trades, and employing from four to twelve journeymen and apprentices.

2. A second class, in their new, and in some instances unfinished houses, were engaged in clearing their lands, and making those improvements which were requisite to secure their title. Some of these, having large families to support, without any accumulated means, like the pioneers of all new settlements, were suffering hardships, embarrassments, and privations, which nothing but the cheering prospect of ultimate success could enable them to sustain.

3. A third consisted of those less than a year in Africa, mostly in the public receptacles or rented houses, imperfectly inured to the climate, partially dependent upon the Society, and beginning moderately to labor for the older settlers, or on their own premises. The remaining class included all the idle and improvident, who, although contributing to the labor of the Colony, were securing no permanent interests to themselves.

4. In the month of December the United States ship of war Ontario, Captain Nicolson, touched at the cape on her return from the Mediterranean. The commander granted the request of eight of his crew, free colored mechanics, to remain in the Colony, and left a valuable donation of seeds which he had taken special care to obtain in the Archipel-

ago, Asia Minor, and Tunis. On his arrival in America, Captain Nicolson bore testimony to the general contentment and industry of the colonists, the rapid progress made by them in public and private improvements, and their salutary and growing influence over the native tribes.

5. To this may be added the testimony of the colonists themselves, given in a communication which they addressed to the colored people of the United States in the summer of this year. They declared that in removing to Africa they had sought for civil and religious liberty, and that their expectations and hopes in this respect had been realized.

6. The great mortality which had occurred in the earliest years of the Colony they attributed principally to the dangers, irregularities, privations, discouragements, and want of medical experience which are almost necessarily attendant on the plantations of new settlements in a distant, uncleared, and barbarous country. After a few months' residence in Africa, they enjoyed health as uniformly, and in as perfect a degree, as in their native country.

7. They believed that a more fertile soil than that of Liberia, and a more productive country, so far as it is culvated, did not exist on the face of the earth. The virtuous and industrious were nearly sure to attain there, in a few years, to a style of comfortable living which they might in vain hope for in the United States. "Truly," said they, "we have a goodly heritage; and if there is anything lacking in the character or condition of the people of this Colony, it can never be charged to the account of the country; it must be the fruit of our own mismanagement, or slothfulness, or vices.

8. "But from these evils we confide in Him to whom we are indebted for all our blessings, to preserve us. It is the topic of our weekly and daily thanksgiving to Almighty God, both in public and in private, and he knows

with what sincerity, that we were ever conducted by his providence to this shore. Men may theorize and speculate about their plans in America, but there can be no speculation here.

9. "The cheerful abodes of civilization and happiness which are scattered over this verdant mountain; the flourishing settlements which are spreading around it; the sound of the Christian instruction, and scenes of Christian worship, which are heard and seen in this land of brooding pagan darkness; a thousand contented freemen united in founding a new Christian empire, happy themselves, and the instrument of happiness to others; every object, every individual, is an argument, is demonstration, of the wisdom and the goodness of the plan of colonization."

CHAPTER XXXII.

DEATH OF THE COLONIAL AGENT.

1. On the 15th of January, 1828, the brig Doris arrived at Liberia, after a long passage from Baltimore, with 107 emigrants, principally from Maryland—sixty-two of them liberated slaves; and on the 17th, the schooner Randolph, from South Carolina, with twenty-six Africans manumitted by a single individual. On the same day Mr. Ashmun returned from a fatiguing visit of inspection to the factories south of Monrovia, and found these vessels with several others waiting his arrival; he had hardly dispatched them before the settlement was menanced by a strongly armed piratical vessel.

2. Immediately after her departure he received a proposition from the interior for opening a new trade path, on condition of forming a settlement and factory at the head of navigation on the St. Paul's River. This required him,

without delay, to explore that situation and visit, for negotiation, all the kings on both sides of the river. Returning from this expedition, he was engaged for the next four days in a tedious judicial investigation. The duty of assigning to the newly arrived emigrants their lands was next discharged, followed immediately by a session of the court.

3. The agent had felt his strength failing under this pressure of business, but there seemed no alternative, and his exertions were unremitted until, on the 5th of February, he was seized with a violent fever, which deprived him of his reason until the 21st. Subsequently he was favored with daily intervals of reason, which he employed in giving instructions to those who managed affairs during his illness.

4. On the 19th of February, the brig Nautilus arrived from Hampton Roads, with 164 emigrants, mostly from the lower counties of North Carolina. The emigrants by this vessel and those by the Randolph suffered but slightly from the climate, but those by the Doris were sorely afflicted. They arrived in bad health, in consequence of a protracted voyage, and twenty-four of the emigrants from Maryland died. Mr. Ashmun having been advised by his physician that a return to the United States afforded the only hope of his recovery, prepared for his departure, and on the 25th of March, accompanied to the beach by the inhabitants of Monrovia in tears, left Africa never to return.

5. He proceeded to the West Indies, when, after some weeks, he took passage for New Haven, Conn., arrived on the 10th of August, and died on the 25th. He fell a victim to his labors and sufferings in the cause of African colonization. The establishment which he found on the brink of extinction, he left in prosperity and peace. The people whom he began to rule when they were few, unorganized, and disunited, he trained to habits of discipline and taught to enjoy the blessings of rational liberty. In

his life he illustrated the power of Christianity to guide, to comfort, and to elevate, and died with a calm, thoughtful, untrembling confidence which none but the Christian can experience.*

6. At his funeral the Rev. L. Bacon, preaching from the words "*To what purpose was this waste,*" said: "Such was he whose life has been spent and prematurely exhausted in his zeal for Africa. Do you ask, to what purpose has he died? I would that we could stand together on the promontory of Montserado and see what has been accomplished by those toils and exposures which have cost this man his life. Hard by, we might see the island where, a few years since, there was a market for the slave trade. To that place crowds of captives were brought every year, and there they were sold like beasts of burden. From that place they were consigned to the unspeakable cruelties of thronged and pestilential slave ships; and those whom death released not in their passage across the Atlantic, went into perpetual slavery.

7. "At that time this cape was literally consecrated to the devil; and here the miserable natives, in the gloom of the dark forest, offered worship to the evil spirit. All this only a few years ago. And what see you now? The forest that has crowned the lofty cape for centuries has been cleared away, and here are the dwellings of a civilized and intelligent people. Here are twelve hundred orderly, industrious, and prosperous freemen, who were once slaves, or in a state of degradation hardly preferable to bondage.

8. "Here are schools, and courts of justice, and lo! the spire which marks the temple dedicated to our God and Saviour—strange landmark to the mariner that traverses the sea of Africa. Here, for a hundred miles along the coast, no slave trader dares to spread his canvas; for the

---

* Gurley's Life of Ashmun is recommended as containing much valuable information relating to colonization, as well as for the elegant style and sentiments of the author. This work has afforded much assistance in preparing the early part of this history.

flag that waves over that fortress, and the guns that threaten from its battlements, tell him that this land is sacred to humanity and freedom. Is all this nothing? Is it nothing to have laid on a barbarous continent the foundation of a free and Christian empire? This is the work in which our friend has died.

9. "But this is not all. I look forward a few years, and I see these results swelling to an importance which may seem incredible to cold and narrow minds. I see those few and scattered settlements extending along the coast and spreading through the inland. I see thousands of the oppressed and wretched fleeing, from lands where at the best they can have nothing but the name and forms of freedom, to this new republic, and finding there a refuge from their degradation. I see the accursed slave trade, which for so many ages past has poured desolation along twelve hundred miles of the African coast, utterly suppressed, and remembered only as an illustration of what human wickedness can be.

10. "I see the ancient wilderness, like our own wide forests of the West, vanishing before the march of civilized and Christian man. I see towns and cities rising in peace and beauty, as they rise along our Atlantic shore, and on the borders of our rivers. I see fair villages, and quiet cottages, and rich plantations spreading out, where now in the unbroken wilderness the lion crouches for his prey. I see the pagan tribes catching the light of civilization, and learning from the lips of Christian teachers to exchange the bondage of their superstitions for the blessed freedom of the Gospel. I see churches, schools, and all the institutions of religion and science adorning Africa as they adorn the country of the Pilgrims. I hear from the mountains, and the valleys, and along the yet undiscovered streams of that vast continent, the voice of Christian worship and the songs of Christian praise. In all those scenes of beauty or of gladness, I see, and in all those accents of thanksgiving, I hear, to what purpose this

servant of God poured out his noble soul in his labors of love.

11. "Who asks us to what purpose is this waste? To what purpose! Thousands and thousands of the exiled sons of Africa, going back from lands of slavery, to enjoy true freedom in the rich and lovely land which God has given them, shall one day answer in their shouts of joy. To what purpose! Africa, delivered from her miseries, her chains thrown off, her spirit emancipated from the power of darkness, rising up in strength and beauty, like a new-born angel from the night of Chaos, and stretching out her hands to God in praise, shall one day answer, to what purpose this martyr of benevolence has lived and died.

12. "What parent would exchange the memory of such a departed son for the embrace of any living one? Who would not that his brother or his friend had lived such a life, and died so nobly for so noble ends, than that he were still living, and living for no such noble and exalted purpose? He is not dead to usefulness. His works still live. The light which he has kindled shall cheer nations yet unborn. His influence shall never die. Years and ages hence, when the African mother shall be able to sit with her children under the shade of their native palm, without trembling in fear of the man-stealer and murderer, she will speak his name with words of thankfulness to God."

CHAPTER XXXIII.

COMMERCIAL AND AGRICULTURAL PROSPECTS.

1. On the departure of Mr. Ashmun from Liberia, the government devolved on the Rev. Lot Cary, vice-agent of the Colony. The measures adopted by his predecessor

were successfully prosecuted by Mr. Cary, and in a manner which proved not only satisfactory to the Board, but to the colonists themselves. The tract of country recently stipulated for on the St. Paul's was to be secured only by immediate occupancy and cultivation. A company of the oldest and most enterprising colonists commenced an agricultural settlement here in February, called Millsburg. They progressed with their improvements so rapidly, that by July they had built a range of houses sufficient to accommodate thirty or forty people, besides a large log factory, and each of the settlers had a small farm under cultivation.

2. The tract of country, including this settlement, abounds in streams of fresh water, the land is easily cleared, and equal in fertility to the rich bottom lands of the United States. The condition and prospect of the Millsburg settlement at this time were thus represented in a joint letter to the Board from several individuals who had taken the lead in its establishment. "We have to inform you that we have in good cultivation twenty-four acres of rice, cassada, cotton, corn, and other vegetables, and our crops promise better than any which have been raised since we have been in Africa. We have seen enough to convince us that we are doing well for the time. We must, however, inform you that ten acres of land is not sufficient for a farm. Here are large tracts of land which no persons inhabit. We have traveled about fifteen miles northeast, and found no person whatever; nothing but old country farms, and good brooks of water, and good land for cultivation.

3. "As we have made more discoveries for the good of the Colony than any other set of men, we take the liberty to request that you would give us more land, as we intend to pursue cultivation, for without cultivation we can not prosper. Although times are hard with us just now, yet we must do the best we can; as we came out to plant a nation in the deserts of Africa, and as there are many

waiting in America for us to clear the forest, we wish our rights for our children secured, which we hope you will grant us. As there are mill seats here, we wish you would send to us saw-mill irons and running gear for the same, also ox chains, reaping hooks, grass scythes, and stone hammers, from nine to ten pounds weight, with seed and grains of all kinds. Our rice is now shooting, and in six weeks we hope to be eating it."

4. Another colonist wrote: "There are many fine mill seats in our new territory, and also on the other side of the river. It would be almost incredible if I were to state the many advantages which are here visible to men of research. Nothing appears to be wanting but means and men of industry, and in a short time the whole of the present Colony might be supported by its own inhabitants along the banks of the noble Dey (St. Paul's), and in the adjacent country."

5. Another from Monrovia wrote: "I wish you and the Honorable Board of Managers would make some inquiries whether it would be prudent and safe for me to trust a vessel across the Atlantic with our stripes and cross; and whether we would be subject to foreign duties on tonnage? as Mr. ——— and myself are about contracting for a schooner; and we wish to be very particular, and not to move until we shall hear from the Board, as the subject is important, particularly in regard to the duties. The commercial interest of the Colony is increasing."

6. On the 25th of June, the colonists were alarmed by the appearance of three suspicious vessels, which induced them to turn out all their forces, man Fort Norris battery, and put themselves on the alert for the night. The next morning the captain of one of the vessels came ashore, who wished a supply of wood and water. Being convinced that they were all slavers, Mr. Cary refused to supply them, and allowed them but one hour to leave the roadstead. They were punctual to the time. In September, Mr. Cary located those recaptured Africans, whose terms

of service to the colonists had expired, between Stockton Creek and Montserado River. Before the close of the year they had built themselves comfortable houses, inclosed their lots, and had their cassada, plantains, and potatoes growing most luxuriantly.

CHAPTER XXXIV.
DEATH OF THE VICE-AGENT—ELECTION OF WARING.

1. In the fall of this year, the Colony's factory at Digby, a few miles north of Monrovia, was robbed by the natives, probably at the instigation of a slave dealer, as one was allowed immediately to take possession of it. Demands for satisfaction having been refused, Mr. Cary felt himself bound to assert the rights and defend the property of the Colony, and immediately commenced preparations for seeking redress by military force. On the evening of the 8th of November, while he and several others were engaged in making cartridges, in the old agency-house, a candle appears to have been accidentally upset among the powder, which caused an explosion that resulted in the death of eight persons, including the lamented Mr. Cary.

2. This remarkable man was born a slave, near Richmond, Va., and was early hired out as a common laborer in that city. Here, under the power of religion, he reformed his previous profane and vicious habits, and united with the Baptist Church in 1807. A strong desire to read was excited in his mind, on hearing a sermon soon after his conversion, which related to our Lord's interview with Nicodemus, and he commenced learning his letters by trying to read the chapter in which this interview is recorded. Such was his diligence and perseverance that, although he never attended school, he learned both to read and write.

3. By his ability and fidelity in business, he obtained a sum sufficient to ransom himself and family, and became a preacher of the Gospel, in which capacity he was the means of doing great good to the colored people on the plantations around Richmond. He became deeply interested in African missions, and was among the earliest emigrants to Liberia. When the appalling circumstances of the first settlers led to a proposition from the Government agent that they should remove to Sierra Leone, the resolution of Mr. Cary to remain was not to be shaken, and his decision induced others to follow his example. To him was the Colony indebted, more than to any other man, except Ashmun, for its preservation during the memorable defense of 1822.

4. In order to relieve, if possible, the sufferings of the people, Mr. Cary turned his attention to the diseases of the climate, made himself a good practical physician, and devoted his time almost exclusively to the relief of the destitute, the sick, and the afflicted. His services, as physician of the Colony, were invaluable, and for a long time were rendered without hope of reward, while he made liberal sacrifices of his property to the poor and distressed. But amid his multiplied cares and efforts he never neglected to promote the objects of the African Missionary Society.

5. He sought access to the native tribes, instructed them in the doctrines and duties of the Christian religion, and established a school for the education of their children. To found a Christian colony which might prove a blessed asylum to his degraded brethren in America, and enlighten and regenerate Africa, was with him an object with which no temporal good could be compared. In one of his letters he says: "There never has been an hour or a minute, no, not even when the balls were flying around my head, when I could wish myself again in America."

6. The election for a successor to Mr. Cary in the vice-agency was warmly contested by the partisans of the two rival candidates, Mr. Waring and Mr. Devany. But on

the election of the former, all submitted willingly to the constituted authorities. On the 22d of December, Richard Randall arrived as the Society's agent for the Colony, accompanied by Dr. Mecklin as the colonial surgeon. They found the Colony prosperous, and were struck with the inviting appearance of the settlements and the country. As no further hostility had been manifested on the part of the natives, and the slave factory, which was the original cause of difficulty, had been broken up, the colonists were inclined to pursue an amicable course toward their offending neighbors.

7. The system of education, commenced the preceding year, had been pursued through this. The teachers were attentive and faithful, and every child in the Colony enjoyed the benefit of their instructions; but these instructions, owing to the limited ability of the teachers, were confined to the simplest branches of knowledge, and were insufficient to form that intellectual character which the condition of the Colony required. The attention to morals and religion, which had for years characterized the settlers, was still maintained, and was exerting a salutary influence over the natives. Sabbath-schools had been established throughout the colonies—two of which were for native children.

8. An enlightened ministry was, however, greatly needed, and the well-timed purpose of several missionary associations to make establishments in Liberia added much to the encouraging prospects of the Colony, though they failed in a great measure of being realized. Of five missionaries destined to this field from the Evangelical Missionary Society of Switzerland, one arrived in December of 1827, and the others during the following year. They all remained at Monrovia a few months for acclimation, and were about commencing their mission at Grand Bassa, when they were interrupted by sickness, which caused the death of one, and obliged another to quit the Colony.

CHAPTER XXXV.
EXPLORATIONS—MORE EMIGRANTS.

1. THE early part of 1829 was marked by no extraordinary events in the Colony. Health prevailed, the inhabitants were prosecuting their various improvements, the agent was zealously engaged in the duties of his office, preparing for the reception of a large party of emigrants which was soon expected, exploring the country, and examining into its various relations and resources. He made an excursion up the St. Paul's, ten or fifteen miles farther than it had yet been explored by any white man. As far as he proceeded he found this river unobstructed, its waters clear and limpid, its banks and the surrounding country rich and beautiful.

2. As the underbrush is here the most dense that can be imagined, the exploring party could only proceed through the paths made by the wild cattle, or have one cleared by sending forward two or three of the natives, who, with their short cutlasses, rapidly removed the underbrush, and thus formed a perfect alcove entirely protected from the action of the sun, which was only now and then visible through an opening in the trees.

3. Though much had been done by Mr. Ashmun to banish the slave trade from the territory under colonial jurisdiction, it was this year carried on very actively at the Gallinas, and to the leeward of Monrovia, in consequence of which some of the native tribes in the vicinity were involved in war with each other; and at one time approached so near the Colony in pursuit of their victims that the inhabitants were alarmed and prepared for defense. They were, however, soon relieved by the departure of the hostile party, with their complement of slaves to the interior. It is impossible to imagine, says the agent,

the misery that such a war occasions among the vanquished. It has not been unusual for the population of whole towns to die of starvation, their crops of rice and cassada having been destroyed by the enemy.

4. On the 17th of March the brig Harriet, from Norfolk, arrived at Monrovia, and landed 155 passengers in good health and spirits. This company of emigrants were from Virginia, Maryland, and North Carolina. Upward of forty were slaves, liberated on condition of going to Liberia. Some had long been free, and acquired considerable property, and nearly all had been recommended as industrious and exemplary. Comfortable shelters had been prepared for them, against the rains which soon commenced. In about ten days after their landing they began to have the fever of the country. The indisposition which they first experienced was slight, from which, having partially recovered, they regarded the danger as past; and by imprudent exposures to the weather, and a free indulgence of the tropical fruits, brought on a far more fatal disease.

5. At the same time both the colonial agent and physician were so reduced by fever as to be unable, for the most part, to give personal attendance to their patients, twenty-six of whom died in the course of the summer. It is to be lamented that instructions from the Board to the colonial agent, on the importance of having these emigrants, immediately on their landing, removed to Millsburg, were by some oversight not sent by the Harriet.

6. Dr. Randall recovered from his first slight attack of fever without having been long interrupted in his devoted attention to the wants of the Colony. Fatigue and exposure brought on a relapse, from which he again recovered; by similar imprudence he was again taken down. His fourth and last attack proved fatal. He died on the 20th of April, the victim of an enthusiasm which it is impossible not both to admire and regret. His loss was deeply felt in the Colony, and by the friends of colonization in the United States, as it was hoped that upon him

had fallen the mantle of Ashmun. On receiving the tidings of Dr. Randall's death, the Board appointed Dr. Mecklin as his successor.

7. Both Sabbath and day-schools continued throughout the Colony, but the want of qualified teachers was still felt. Joseph Shipherd, an experienced colored teacher from Richmond, Va., came out in the Harriet, and Mr. J. B. Russwurm, a young man of color, who received his education at Bowdoin College, Maine, and came out to the Colony for the express purpose of superintending and improving the system of education, arrived on the 12th of November.

8. The celebrated Moorish prince, Abduhl Rahhahman, went out in the ship Harriet, and while waiting at the Colony to receive intelligence from his friends and brother, who was then the reigning king of Teembo, died of a sudden illness on the 6th of July. It was his intention, had he lived to visit his native country, to obtain means to liberate his children who were slaves in the United States, and with them to return and settle in the Colony, where it was hoped his influence would be the means of opening a direct communication for trade with Teembo, and thus divert at least a portion of the trade of that place from Sierra Leone to Liberia.

9. Two of the citizens made a trading excursion this year to Bo Poro, the capital of King Boatswain's dominions, 150 miles interior. He professed himself a warm friend of the Colony (toward which he had always been well disposed), and made a distinct proposal through these colonists for the establishment of a factory at his town, offering to send down people to assist in transporting goods from the Colony, should the agent determine to build a factory. The commerce of the country was still active, and the crops of the farmers greater than in any preceding year. The emigrants by the Harriet had their lands assigned them, and commenced clearing and building.

CHAPTER XXXVI.
LARGE ACCESSIONS OF NATIVES AND EMIGRANTS.

1. FIVE additional Swiss missionaries came out in 1830. They left Europe in 1829, accompanied by one of the five who had previously visited Liberia, but was obliged to return with his invalid brother missionary to Switzerland. They came by the way of the United States, where they spent several months in visiting the churches. On the 27th of February, fifty-eight emigrants arrived in the brig Liberia, from Norfolk, and with them Dr. Anderson, the colonial physician and assistant agent, also two of the Swiss missionaries (the others having come out a month previous); all landed in good health, and were highly delighted with the country.

2. Among these emigrants was the Rev. George Erskine, a Presbyterian minister, with his wife, five children, and his mother, about eighty years of age, who was born in Africa. All this family were born slaves, and their freedom was bought by Mr. Erskine. He was an intelligent man and an interesting preacher. During the passage he preached every Sabbath. He said one day to the captain, "I am going to a new country to settle myself and family as agriculturists, to a country where the complexion will be no barrier to our filling the most exalted stations." Another interesting passenger was Mr. Cook; he was about seventy years of age, and had a family of thirty persons, all of whom evidenced the beneficial effects of the good old man's counsel. They were Methodists, from Lynchburg, Va.

3. On the 4th of March, ninety-one recaptured Africans arrived. They sailed from the United States in August, 1829. But owing to the ignorance and obstinacy of the captain (who, disregarding the experience of navigators,

determined on pursuing a direct course to Liberia, which deprived him of the benefit of the trade winds), after being out eighty-nine days, they were obliged to put into Barbadoes; and the vessel being condemned as unseaworthy, another was here chartered in which to prosecute their voyage.

4. The whole of this company were entirely exempt from the fever of the country, though they had been some time in the United States. They were therefore able immediately to take possession of the lands assigned them, and commence building their huts, which they had thatched in a different manner from those of the natives adjacent, and quite superior to them. The entire settlement of recaptured Africans, containing about 400 inhabitants, was at this time one of the neatest and most flourishing in the Colony. It seemed almost incredible that these could be the same individuals who when in bondage evinced so little intellect and forethought. They furnished a large supply of vegetables, melons, fowls, etc., for the market of Monrovia.

5. Soon after the arrival of the Liberia, Dr. Mecklin was compelled, by the state of his health, to leave the Colony, and the administration of government devolved on Dr. Anderson, who was then in good health, and continued to discharge the duties of his agency until April, when he died, after an illness of ten days. The death, also, of three of the Swiss missionaries, which occurred in quick succession, cast a gloom over the settlement. The colored passengers by the Liberia had the fever slightly at first, and it was hoped would pass through their seasoning with safety. But having no physician to attend them, and, in general, disregarding the advice of the older settlers not to expose themselves to the heat, and rain, and evening dews, several, in the course of the summer, died; among them was the Rev. Mr. Erskine.

6. Early in June, seventy emigrants arrived in the Montgomery. Thirty of these were liberated by one gentleman

in Georgia; and as the climate has little effect on people from that section of the country, the deaths of two small children were the only ones that occurred among this hardy company during their acclimation. Among the other emigrants by the Montgomery, who were chiefly from Virginia, the sickness was more severe, and in a greater number of instances proved fatal.

7. More of an agricultural spirit seemed at this time to prevail in the Colony. The emigrants who came out the preceding year by the Harriet were chiefly men who knew the value of industry, and their application to business was manifest in the flourishing condition of their farms. Caldwell, the place of their residence, is a beautiful town, situated at the junction of the St. Paul's and Stockton Creek, consisting of one street about a mile and a half long, kept very clean, and planted on each side with rows of plantain and bananas. Between this and the water there is an open space, contributing to the beauty and health of the place.

8. Those who applied themselves diligently and perseveringly to farming from the first, were generally in a prosperous condition. But the mania for trading was too apt to seize new-comers, many of whom engaging in it, not only without adequate means, but wholly destitute of experience, would be cheated by the natives, lose their property, and become dissatisfied with the place. Those who expected to live comfortably, and get rich without labor, constituted nearly the whole class of murmurers.

9. The schools of the Colony were in a deplorable condition for the want of funds and competent teachers. Mr. Shipherd soon became so engrossed by his duties as colonial surveyor, that he gave up his school altogether, which left only two pay schools in operation, and these embracing but a small number of pupils. Mr. Kisling, one of the Swiss missionaries, had collected a school for orphans and natives, which the state of his health permitted him to attend to but very irregularly. One of the emigrants by the Liberia opened a school at Caldwell. There was none

at Millsburg, and none in the settlements of recaptured Africans at New Georgia.

- 10. The citizens, in general, felt no due sense of the importance of preparing their children, by education, for usefulness, influence, and self-government. Their sudden elevation of circumstances and privileges, and their rapid acquisition of property, had, to some extent, produced a spirit of emulation, display, and extravagance unfavorable to the moral and religious interests of the Colony. They had yet to learn, from experience, that economy and sober expectations best promote not only public welfare, but private happiness.

11. Friendly relations continued to exist between the colonists and the natives. Early this year, one tribe put themselves under the protection and adopted the laws of the Colony, the king, Long Peter, cheerfully giving up his title, and receiving the appointment of head man from the agent. His people were full of joy when they learned that the agent had determined to adopt them as subjects of the Colony. They were aware of the advantages of such an arrangement, which at once freed them from all the oppressive customs and laws of the surrounding native tribes, and secured them from being sold into slavery, as they were before liable to be at any moment, on account of some frivolous dispute or palaver, got up for the purpose by the head men whenever they wanted a supply of money.

12. Several of the petty kings made application to put themselves and their people under the government of the Colony, that they might not be molested by King Boatswain, who was at this time largely engaged in the slave trade; but the colonial agent hesitated to engage his protection to the more distant tribes. He, however, received Far Gay and his people, who were in the vicinity of the Colony.

13. On the 3d of December the Caroline arrived, bringing 107 colored persons, Dr. Mecklin, Dr. Humphries, as-

sistant agent and physician, and Mr. and Mrs. Skinner, missionaries, sent out by the American Board of Foreign Missions. Among the forty-five liberated slaves were the children and grandchildren of Abduhl Rahhahman. Several children of this company died of the measles on the passage, and several adults of fever after their arrival, amounting in all to twenty, including Mrs. Skinner and child. Dr. Mecklin resumed the duties of colonial agent, which, during his absence, had been ably performed by the vice-agent, A. D. Williams.

14. Twenty-five substantial stone and frame buildings had been erected in Monrovia; the spirit of enterprise was increasing among the people, who seemed determined to develop the resources of the country. The first newspaper in Liberia was commenced this year by Mr. Busswurm, and called the *Liberia Herald*.

CHAPTER XXXVII.
MONROVIA—SCHOOLS—TEMPERANCE.

1. THE brig Valador, with Dr. Todsen and eighty-three emigrants, arrived at Monrovia in January, 1831. Most of these were from the lower parts of Virginia and North Carolina. They arrived in good health, and were immediately transferred to Caldwell, and placed under the care of Dr. Todsen, who providentially continued well until nearly all his patients were recovering from the fever. It was no doubt in part owing to his skill and unremitting attention that, of this whole company, only three children, and not a single adult died, during the acclimation, while the mortality that attended those by the Caroline was partly attributed to their want of a physician, both Dr. Mecklin and Dr. Humphries being sick at the time when

their services were most needed. The latter died in February, of consumption, with which he had long been afflicted in the United States. The Rev. Mr. Skinner took passage for the United States, in hopes of thus recovering his health, but died on the voyage. The death of this devoted missionary and his wife was a great loss.

2. The colonial agent, in obedience to the instructions of the Board, made a sale of some public lots in Monrovia the beginning of the year, by which a considerable fund was raised for the purpose of education. A law was passed about the same time, by the agent and council, taxing all the real estate in the Colony, at the rate of five cents on a hundred dollars, which tax was to be exclusively devoted to the support of public schools. The duties on spirituous liquors were also to be thus appropriated. School-houses were erected at Monrovia, Caldwell, and Millsburg, competent teachers appointed under the supervision of trustees, and a new zeal in the cause of education was awakened throughout the Colony. The system adopted was designed to afford the means of instruction to every child.

3. A most encouraging letter, addressed to the colonists from the Female Colonization Society of Richmond and Manchester, on the importance of education, was published in the February number of the *Liberia Herald*. The editorial article in this paper, which closed its first year, contained the following paragraph: " The changes which have taken place in the Colony during the publication of the *Herald* are worthy of notice. Everything has improved—our agriculture, our commerce have each shared in the blessing. Monrovia has almost assumed a new garb, and should things continue to prosper as they have, our town will certainly present the most desirable residence, to a stranger, of any on the coast of Africa.

4. "In Monrovia alone, the number of comfortable stone and wooden dwellings erected during the year has been upward of fifty-five; and if we take into consideration that Caldwell, Millsburg, and the recaptured towns have

shared equally in this prosperity, we have abundant reasons to be thankful for the showers of mercy which have been extended to our infant Colony. Our commerce is daily extending, and we believe the day is not far distant when our port will be the emporium of the western coast of Africa.

5. "But the object which we consider of most vital importance to the future prosperity of the Colony is education. The subject has long lain dormant, but the late resolutions of the Board of Managers, and the fixed determination of our executive to carry them into effect, give us every reason to hope that a complete free-school system is about being put into operation."

6. It had been thought that the sale of ardent spirits was almost necessary to the commerce of the Colony, as the natives would prefer selling their brethren to the slave traders, who always supplied them with this pernicious article, rather than to trade with the colonists, if it could not be obtained from them. And besides, the facilities of introducing it clandestinely were such, that the Board of Managers, though they were grieved to have it so extensively introduced into the Colony, thought that to correct the evil by moral influence would be wiser and more effective than by legal restraints.

7. They therefore sent an address to the colonists, expressing their disapprobation of the use and sale of ardent spirits; recommending them to form temperance societies, and in every way to use their influence to produce a correct public sentiment on this subject, with the design of lessening the demand for this article, and of finally banishing it from the commerce of the Colony. This address, together with various pamphlets and tracts on the subject of temperance, was not unavailing. Many of the colonists determined to abandon entirely the use of ardent spirits, and to discourage its introduction into the Colony.

CHAPTER XXXVIII.
TRADE—THE COURTS—RELIGION.

1. THE excessive disposition to engage in commerce still continued. The substitution of an anchorage for a tonnage duty induced many vessels that formerly passed on to the leeward coast, to anchor now in the harbor of Monrovia, and do business to a considerable amount.

2. The *Liberia Herald* announced the arrival of eighteen and the departure of fourteen vessels in a single month. Several of these, however, were small schooners owned at the Colony. The *Herald* of December says: " The beach is lined with Liberians of all ages, from twelve to fifty years, eager in the pursuit of traffic and in the acquisition of camwood; and it is astonishing what little time is necessary to qualify even the youngest to drive as hard a bargain as any roving merchant from the land of steady habits, with his assortment of tin-ware, nutmegs, books, or dry goods. Here the simile ends, for it is to be wished that our Liberians would follow their prototype in the mother country throughout, and be as careful in keeping as acquiring.

3. " The Liberian is certainly a great man, and what is more, by the natives he is considered a white man, though many degrees from that stand; for to be thought acquainted with the white man's fashions, and to be treated as one, are considered as marks of great distinction among the Bassa and other nations." Forty-six vessels, twenty-one of which were American, visited the Colony in the course of the year. The amount of exports was $88,911.

4. The slave trade, though it had received some check in the immediate vicinity of the Colony, was still prosecuted on nearly every part of the African coast. In June, the colonial schooner Montserado was captured by a Span-

ish pirate off Little Cape Mount, and her crew consisting of eight persons either conveyed on board the Spanish vessel or put to death. During a visit of the colonial agent to one of the native towns in the vicinity this summer, eight or ten of the chiefs, after consulting with each other, united in the request that they might be received and treated as subjects of the Colony, and that settlements might be made on their territory. They expressed a confidence that in such case they would no longer be exposed to the incursions and cruelties of more powerful tribes.

5. The just and humane policy of the colonial government toward the natives induced the latter frequently to refer the settlement of their disputes to the colonists, instead of abiding by their own laws and usages. It was not unusual for them to attend the court of montbly sessions, either as plaintiffs or defendants; and its decisions were cheerfully acquiesced in even by the party against whom they were given. In the autumn of this year, the brig Criterion, after a passage of eighty-eight days from Norfolk, arrived at the cape with forty-four passengers, who were immediately landed and placed in the receptacle at Caldwell. This was represented to be a better company, more respected for their habits of industry and propriety of conduct than the generality of those who had emigrated for some time.

6. On the 9th of December, the schooner Orion arrived from Baltimore with thirty emigrants, all welL The same day a small tract of land at Grand Cape Mount was formally ceded to the American Colonization Society; healthy, fertile, and very advantageously situated for trade, the possession of this tract was considered a valuable acquisition. The chiefs of the country granted an unquestionable title to this land, on the sole condition that settlers should be placed upon it, and that schools should be established for the benefit of the native children. The young men declared their purpose of submitting to the laws of the Colony, and their willingness to make further grants of

land to any extent desired, whenever the terms of the present negotiation should have been complied with.

7. The liberality of the Pennsylvania Colonization Society enabled the managers of the American Colonization Society this year to build a schooner for the use of the Colony of about sixty tons. She was completed and sailed from Philadelphia, under the command of Captain Abels, with a colored crew, carrying a valuable supply of trade goods. She was called the Margaret Mercer. Two families of colored people embarked in her, one the Rev. W. Johnson's, of Connecticut, the other liberated by the Rev. Dr. Mathews, of Shepardstown, Va. They arrived on the 15th of December.

8. To the Christian who esteems worldly prosperity of little moment in comparison with that blessing of the Lord which bringeth salvation, the following letter from a colonist will not be uninteresting: "A great press of worldly business, and a great revival which the Lord was pleased to bless us with last year, and greater part of this, have occcupied all my time. Since Captain Sherman was with us, there have been nearly 100 added to our church. The work began in June, 1830, in Monrovia, and lasted till the early part of 1831. It then extended to Caldwell and Cary Town [New Georgia], a settlement of recaptured Africans.

9. "Among the latter it has continued ever since, so they make up the largest number that has been added to the church; and they seem fully to adorn the Christian character. They have built themselves a small house of worship, at which they meet regularly on the Lord's day, and twice in the week for prayer. We have appointed one of the most intelligent among them to take the oversight of them, and to exhort them, when none of the preachers are there from Monrovia. Monrovia may truly be said to be a Christian community; there is scarcely a family in it that some one or the whole do not 'profess religion."

CHAPTER XXXIX.
WAR WITH THE DEY AND GOURAH CHIEFS.

1. On the 14th of January, 1832, 343 emigrants arrived in the James Perkins. This vessel was fitted out at short notice, at the earnest request of those who embarked in her, and the unexpected arrival of her large company, in addition to the other recent arrivals occasioned some embarrassment in providing shelters for them all. Temporary arrangements were, however, made for their accommodation, until a receptacle which had been commenced should be finished, and some building frames which were brought out in this ship erected. It was an encouraging circumstance that many of this company were farmers, for the time had now come when those who could must till the soil for a subsistence or starve. More were already engaged in trade than could gain a livelihood by this means.

2. In February, the schooner Crawford, from New Orleans, brought out twenty-two emigrants under the care of Dr. Shane, of Cincinnati. The following was extracted from a letter written by this gentleman from the Colony: " I here see many who left the United States in straitened circumstances, living with all the comforts of life around them, enjoying a respectable and useful station in society, and wondering that their brethren in the United States, who have it in their power, do not flee to this asylum of happiness and liberty. I am certain no friend to humanity can come here and see the state of things without being impressed with the immense benefits the Society is conferring on the long-neglected sons of Africa. Nothing but a want of knowledge of Liberia prevents thousands of honest, industrious free blacks from coming to this land, where liberty and religion with all their blessings are enjoyed." All that is wanting here is industry to make

the emigrants not only easy in their circumstances, but wealthy.

3. In March, the colonists were called to take the field against a combination of the Dey and Gourah chiefs. Several slaves about to be sold had escaped from King Brumley and sought protection among the recaptured Africans of the Colony. A demand being made for them by Brumley's son, the agent refused to treat with him, but requested the king to visit the Colony, and declared himself ready to do justice in the case. Soon after the return of the young man, King Brumley died, and his sons immediately resolved on war. They secured the aid of several of the Dey and Gourah chiefs (the latter of which secretly furnished men for the contest), and commenced aggressions by seizing and imprisoning several of the colonists.

4. A messenger sent to them by the colonial agent was treated with contempt, and the settlements of Caldwell and Millsburg threatened with destruction. About 100 recaptured Africans were sent against the hostile forces, but on approaching the town of a native chief, which had been fortified as a place of retreat for the aggressors, they were repulsed and compelled to retreat with the loss of one man. Prompt and energetic measures were now required; accordingly the agent, at the head of 270 men, armed with muskets and a field-piece, proceeded toward the fortified town just mentioned, and arriving about midnight, commenced an attack upon the barricade.

5. For twenty minutes the firing on both sides was incessant, and in less than half an hour the colonists were in possession of the town, with the loss of one man killed (Lieutenant Thompson) and two wounded. Kai Pa, the instigator of the war, received a wound when about to apply the match to a three-pounder, which doubtless prevented the destruction of many lives. Of the natives, fifteen were killed and many wounded. The courage and ability exhibited by the colonial agent, as well as by the officers and men under his command on this occasion, left

an impression on the minds of the natives, favorable to the future peace and security of the Colony.

6. In a few days, six Dey chiefs appeared at Monrovia and signed a treaty of peace, by which it was agreed that traders from the interior should be allowed a free passage through their territories, and that all matters of difference which might arise between citizens of Liberia and the Dey people, with the evidences thereon, should be referred to the decision of the colonial agent. A few weeks after this affair with the Dey people, the agent received a message from King Boatswain, expressing his regret that he had not been made acquainted with their hostility, as he would have rendered it unnecessary for the colonists to march against them.

7. This spring the agent visited Grand Bassa, and obtained a deed of a tract of land on the south side of the St. John's River, containing from 150 to 200 square miles, together with four large islands in the river a little above Factory Island. The chiefs from whom the purchase was made agreed to build three large houses in the native style, for the accommodation of the first settlers.

CHAPTER XL.

HEALTH—BUYING WIVES—GRAND BASSA.

1. On the 30th of July, the ship Jupiter anchored in the harbor of Monrovia, with 172 emigrants; a part of them suffered from sickness on the passage, and several were infirm when they landed. This was considered one of the most promising expeditions which had been sent out for some time. Several were men of intelligence and education, superior to the generality of their class. They were mostly from Virginia, the two Carolinas, and Georgia.

2. In contrast to the character of this company was that of the emigrants by the America, 182 in number, who arrived on the 15th of September. The following is the account given of them by the colonial agent, in his letter announcing to the Board their arrival: "With respect to the character of the people composing this expedition, I regret to be compelled to state that they are, with the exception of those from Washington, the family of the Pages from Virginia, and a few others, the lowest and most abandoned of their class.

3. "From such materials it is in vain to expect that an industrious, intelligent, and enterprising community can possibly be formed; the thing is utterly impracticable, and they can not but retard instead of advance the prosperity of the Colony. I am induced to be thus unreserved in my remarks, as it is from the sufferings of people of this stamp, occasioned by their own indolence and stupidity, that the slanderous reports circulated in the United States have originated. Our respectable colonists themselves are becoming alarmed at the great number of ignorant and abandoned characters that have arrived within the last twelve months, and almost daily representations are made by those who have applied themselves to the cultivation of the soil, of the depredations committed on their crops by the above-described class of people, who can not be induced to labor for their own support."

4. The health of the Colony had never been better than this year, with the exception of intermittent fever in the summer at Caldwell, attributed to local causes. The diseases of the climate yielded so generally to the skill and attention of the physicians, and the deaths from acclimating fever among the emigrants, by the several late expeditions, had been so very few, that it seemed as if the climate was no longer to be dreaded.

5. A manifest improvement in the schools was reported this year, and a more general desire of the colonists for the promotion of education. Besides the six day-schools for·

children, there was an evening school for adults. The female schools at Monrovia and Caldwell were well conducted, and attended by nearly a hundred girls. The teachers, Mrs. Johnson and Mrs. Cesar, were paid by a society of ladies in Philadelphia. At Millsburg there was no good school, and none of any kind among the recaptured Africans, except Sunday-schools, which were well attended and taught by their own people, many of whom could read.

6. Each tribe had a house of worship, and a town or palaver house built by voluntary subscription and joint labor. A street separated the neat and well-built villages of the Eboes and Congoes; their farms adjacent to the village were under excellent cultivation, and they were stated to be the most industrious and thriving of any people in the Colony, but they had very imperfect notions of republican government. They had several times attempted to choose a chief without success, the minority refusing submission to the person chosen. This year they solicited the colonial agent to superintend their election; it was held in his presence, and after he had explained to them the object of an election, and the necessity of submitting to the will of the majority, they appeared perfectly satisfied.

7. These recaptured Africans not unfrequently procured wives from the adjacent tribes by paying a small sum to the parents of the girls. The women thus obtained were married and dressed according to the customs of the Colony, and in a short time adopted the habits of the settlers, so as scarcely to be distinguished from those who had been several years in the United States.

8. The settlement of Grand Bassa was commenced on the 18th of December, by thirty-eight emigrants, under the most encouraging circumstances. The chiefs and people of the country received them in the most cordial manner, assisted them in building houses, and constructing a barricade upon which their guns were mounted, though there was no prospect of their being required for defense. Bob

Gray, one of the chiefs from whom the territory was purchased, had planted a large quantity of cassada and sweet potatoes on their land for the use of the settlers. Mr. Williams, the vice-agent, who accompanied these emigrants, performed divine service several times during his stay, and found among the natives (most of whom could speak English) a numerous and attentive congregation. They were anxious to have a school established among them.

9. The following extracts of letters written from Monrovia will show how the colonists estimated their own advantages—one wrote to her former mistress in Virginia: "Our house has one front room, a shed-room, and one above stairs. When Mr. Hatter returns, he intends to build a stone house. Our lot is in a very pretty part of the town, and I have a great many very pretty trees growing in it. I send you, by Mr. Hatter, some tortoise-shell and a little ivory tooth; and some shells to Miss —— and ——. Give my love to them, and tell them I wish they had such a sweet beach to take their morning and evening walks on as we have here. My dear mistress, you do not know how thankful I am to you for buying my husband." The same wrote to her sister: "I never was better satisfied in my life, if I only had my dear relations and friends with me. We enjoy the same liberty here that our masters and mistresses do in America. I am so well pleased with my situation, I would not change it for all America.

10. "You need not be afraid to come; every person has to see trouble and inconvenience at first, in a new country. I have seen about as much trouble as anybody, and I know I am satisfied. I get a great deal of work to do. I keep a girl, ten years old, for her victuals and clothes. I have taught her to read and sew, and she assists me in cooking and cleaning. I have coffee in my lot, a good many other trees, and the guava, which makes nice sweetmeats. If I only had you and your family, mother and her family, and if my dear husband was returned, I should be as happy as the day is long."

11. Another wrote to his mistress: "It gives me great satisfaction that everything I do is for myself and my children. I would not give the enjoyment I have had since I have been in Africa for all I have seen in America. I have set out all kinds of trees that are in Africa. As soon as my coffee-trees bear, I will send you some. We have preaching every Sunday, and prayer-meeting every night through the week. Many of the recaptured Africans come to be baptized, and we expect more shortly; they appear to be more diligent than the Americans."

CHAPTER XLI.

1833—THE POPULATION OF THE COLONY.

1. In 1833, 649 emigrants were landed at Monrovia, from six different vessels, five of which left the United States the latter part of 1832. The arrival of so great a number of emigrants in so short a time had not been anticipated by the agent, nor were the means provided by the Board sufficient to furnish the provisions and accommodations necessary for the health and comfort of these new-comers. The consequence was suffering, discontent, and complaint.

2. In July, the brig Ajax arrived from New Orleans, with a large company of emigrants from Kentucky and Tennessee, nearly all of whom were manumitted that they might proceed as freemen to Liberia. The entire company were of the most respectable character, and only eleven, out of the 150 that left the United States, were over forty years of age. They were accompanied by an agent from Tennessee, and Mr. Savage, from Ohio, who had devoted himself to the moral and intellectual improvement of Africa. The cholera was just beginning its ravages in New Orleans at the time the Ajax sailed from that port,

and twenty-nine of the emigrants fell victims to that disease during the early part of the passage.

3. A large company of emigrants from South Carolina were enterprising, intelligent, and industrious. Many of them possessed capital. Such as were farmers drew their plantation lots in a body, for their mutual convenience and benefit. Agriculture did not, in general, receive the attention which its importance demanded—the mania for trade still prevailing. The settlement at Grand Bassa increased this year from 33 to 170, and the pioneers, already settled on their inclosed town lots, were making commendable progress in agricultural improvements. Their town, named Edina,* was laid out on a tongue of land on the north side of the St. John's, and presented a fine view from the ocean. A short distance from Edina was the native town of Bob Gray, who considered himself highly honored by having Americans so near him.

4. Between the two settlements was the ancient Devil Bush of the Grand Bassa people, which they reserved in their sale of lands to the colonists, though it was no longer used for the performance of their superstitious rites. "It is evident," said the editor of the *Herald*, "to the most casual observer, that the natives in the vicinity of our settlements are gradually becoming more enlightened, and consequently less observant of their superstitious notions and idolatry.

5. "It is pleasing to reflect that the spot near which the nameless bloody rites of Moloch have been perpetrated for centuries, is soon to be the site of a mission-house, which is erecting by the direction of the Rev. Mr. Cox, missionary from the United States." This was the first Methodist missionary to Liberia. He arrived in March, having on

---

* Through the able and generous efforts of Elliott Cresson, large contributions were obtained in England and Scotland in aid of the American Colonization Society. It was in honor of the liberality of the citizens of Edinburgh that the name Edina was given to the settlement.

his voyage touched at Cape de Verds, Bathurst, on the Gambia, and Sierra Leone, and conferred with many intelligent and religious men at the English settlements.

6. He regularly organized the Methodist Episcopal Church at Monrovia, purchased the mission-house which was built by Mr. Ashmun, and selected several important points for missionary stations. But his health, which had long been feeble, failed before he had done much toward the accomplishment of his enlarged plans of benevolence, and on the 20th of July his career of usefulness was closed by death. His own words better express his zeal and devotedness than a volume written in his praise. "*Let thousands fall before Africa be abandoned.*"

7. The following paragraph in the *Liberia Herald* shows that the colonists themselves were doing something for the missionary cause: "According to the resolutions of the managers of the Board of Domestic and Foreign Missions in the town of Monrovia, and Colony of Liberia, held on the 17th of May, 1833, at the Monrovia Baptist Church, Adam W. Anderson, by proposal to said Board, was unanimously appointed a missionary by all present, to locate himself, for the space of one year, at Grand Cape Mount (West Africa), among the Vey people, to teach the children of natives, as far as possible, the English language, and to preach, when opportunity would offer itself, to the adult part of the tribe. He will leave Cape Montserado in a few days, in prosecution of so arduous and important a duty. O! may much good be done through his instrumentality, among that idolatrous and perverse people, that the Saviour of mankind might receive abundant honor, even among the heathen, to His great name."

8. In regard to the moral and religious condition of the Colony generally, but little change had taken place. There were nine houses of worship in the various settlements, and the Sabbath and public worship were well observed. This was a year of unusual sickness and mortality. Out of the 649 emigrants that had arrived, 134 died. Those of no

particular class, nor from no particular section of the United States, were exempt from the fatal effects of the fever, though the emigrants from the North suffered most. The Colony had been deprived of the services of Drs. Todson and Hall; both having returned to the United States on account of ill-health, the duties of physician, for the whole Colony, devolved on the agent, Dr. Mecklin, who himself was enfeebled by the fever, caused by exposure.

9. The emigrants were located in settlements widely separated from each other. When attacked with fever, one physician could not, even if in good health, give them proper attention. The emigrants from the South, believing they were in no danger, imprudently exposed themselves to the various exciting causes of the fever, and when attacked, relied for remedies on some of their own company, rather than on the advice of those more experienced.

10. Among the deaths that occurred this year, none was more lamented than that of Francis Devany (of consumption). He was originally a slave, belonging to Langdon Cheves, Esq., of Charleston, S. C., and emigrated to Liberia at an early period of its settlement. He engaged in commerce, and accumulated a handsome fortune. He held for some time the office of high sheriff of the Colony, and in the various relations of life sustained and deserved the character of an honest man.

11. In their annual report, the Board of Managers of the American Colonization Society, while they deplored the suffering and loss of life experienced in the Colony, expressed undiminished confidence in the final success of their enterprise, and referred to still more disastrous events in the early history of American colonization. The comparative view given by them was as follows: "The number which had been sent to the Colony before the arrival of the expeditions above mentioned, as so severely afflicted, was 1,872 persons, and the actual population of the Colony (not including the recaptured Africans) in 1832, 1,097. The

whole number of emigrants, including the expeditions of last year, and the recaptured Africans (a part of whom only were removed from this country), has been 3,123, while the present population of the Colony is stated to be 2,816. About fifty of the colonists are believed to have been absent in the country at the time this census was taken.

12. " Now, it should not be forgotten that the early emigrants were exposed to almost every variety of hardship and suffering, that several fell in a contest with the natives, that from twenty to fifty at least have returned, that some have perished by disasters upon the rivers and at sea, that all have had to contend with difficulties, inseparable from their enterprise, in an untried climate and on a distant and uncultivated shore, and finally, that neither the information nor the pecuniary means of the Society have at all times been such as to enable it adequately to fulfill the dictates of its own benevolence.

13. " While the facts just stated must excite painful emotions in the breast of every member of this Society, while all will feel that human life is not to be wantonly exposed or lightly regarded, neither (the Managers may be permitted to say), on account of ordinary or temporary calamities, should a great cause, undertaken from the purest motives, and for purposes of large and lasting good to mankind, be abandoned. The history of colonization in America proves how impotent were events, in themselves most afflictive and disheartening, to arrest the progress of settlements founded by men who grew wise in adversity and gathered resolution and strength from defeat.

14. " The genius of our nation, sprung from the colonies of Plymouth and Jamestown, rebukes the despondency which would augur destruction to Liberia because dark clouds have hung over it and many valuable lives perished in its foundation. Nearly one half the first Plymouth emigrants died in the course of four months. The first three attempts to plant a colony in Virginia totally

failed. In six months, 90 of the 100 settlers who landed at Jamestown died. Subsequently, in the same brief period, the inhabitants of this Colony were reduced from 500 to 60; and long after, when £150,000 had been expended on that Colony, and 9,000 people had been sent thither, its population amounted to but 1,800 souls."

15. The report of Capt. Voorhees, of the United States ship John Adams, to the Secretary of the Navy, dated 14th of December, 1833, gave some interesting facts in relation to the condition of the Colony. "The importance of this settlement here is daily developing itself in various ways, and is always felt as a refuge of security and hospitality, both to the oppressed natives and the shipwrecked mariner. Lately a French oil ship was cast away to the south of Grand Bassa, where the crew, about twenty in number, were kindly received by the settlers at that place, and from which they safely traveled, uninterrupted, along the sea-shore to Monrovia. Here the generous hospitality of the people of Liberia (though with humble means, and at their own expense) prompted them to fit out a conveyance for the seamen, by the Government schooner, in which they were carried to their own settlement of Gorée. And on our arrival here, I found a French man-of-war barque, the commander of which had been dispatched by the governor of Gorée, to express the thanks of his country to the people of Liberia for the charitable services which they had rendered their countrymen.

16. "Monrovia appears to be in a thriving condition, and bears an air of comfort and neatness in the dwellings quite surprising. Several stone warehouses and stone wharves line the banks of the river; others are building, which, with schooners loading and unloading or repairing, afford an aspect and an air of business common to a respectable white population. All seem to be employed, good order and morality prevailing throughout. But cultivators of the soil are mostly needed here. A few mechanics might do well, such as ship-carpenters, blacksmiths, sail-

makers, boat-builders, masons, and house-carpenters. The settlement must move onward, and with all its disadvantages it appears a miracle that it should be in such a state of advancement.

17. "An intelligent man, about sixty years of age, with whom I conversed, stated that he had been here about eighteen months, and was getting on cleverly for himself and family, and that on no account would he return to the United States. 'It was true he had not yet the luxuries nor the accommodations which he had been accustomed to in America, but the want of these was not to be brought into competition with his rights and privileges as a man in Liberia; for here only, in the consciousness of having no superior, did he feel himself a MAN, or had he ever before known what it was to be truly happy.'"

18. The colonial agent, Dr. Mecklin, who had done much to enlarge the territory and extend the influence of the Colony, returned to the United States, and resigned his office as colonial agent. His health had been impaired by the arduous labors of his station and the influence of the climate. A removal from a tropical region seemed to offer the only hope of his recovery.

CHAPTER XLII.

A NEW AGENT—MISSIONARIES.

1. The first day of this year, 1834, welcomed the arrival of a new colonial agent, the Rev. J. B. Pinney, which is thus announced in the *Liberia Herald* for January: "On the 31st ult. the ship Jupiter arrived in our harbor, having on board, as passengers, Rev. J. B. Pinney, recently appointed colonial agent by the Board of Managers of the American Colonization Society, Dr. G. P. Todsen, colonial

physician, Rev. Messrs. Spaulding and Wright, with their ladies, and Miss Ferington, missionaries of the Methodist Episcopal Church; Rev. Mr. Laird and lady, Rev. Messrs. Cloud and Temple, missionaries of the Presbyterian Church; and Messrs. Williams and Roberts of this Colony. The Jupiter also brings out about fifty emigrants.

2. "On New Year's day, at ten o'clock A.M., the new agency boat, recently procured from the United States ship John Adams, was dispatched to the ship Jupiter for the colonial agent, Rev. J. B. Pinney. About noon, he landed at Waring's wharf, where he was received by the civil and military officers, and the different uniform companies of the Colony; he was then escorted to the agency-house, where he was welcomed by the acting agent, G. R. McGill, Esq. Minute guns were fired from the time the boat left the ship till she arrived at the wharf." Mr. Pinney had visited Liberia the preceding year as a missionary, and after examining several places on the coast and in the interior, and making arrangements for the prosecution of his work, he returned to the United States to improve his impaired health, report his prospects, and obtain associates in his enterprise.

3. At the earnest solicitation of the Board, he accepted a temporary agency; on his arrival he immediately applied himself to the discharge of his duties, which were arduous indeed. The agency-house and other public buildings needed repairs to render them fit for occupancy. The public store was without trade goods, the provisions were nearly exhausted, the paupers, or those who were a charge on the Colony, were numerous and badly provided for, and the public schooner used in obtaining provisions coastwise, could not be used without expensive repairs.

4. Late changes in the mode of appointing officers, and in the local regulations among the recaptured Africans, who were of different tribes, had produced dissatisfaction, and they were in a state of great disorder. The financial affairs of the Colony were in great derangement. The

mode of compensating officers employed by the Society had induced speculation, and orders of the former agent, to the amount of several thousand dollars, were held by colonists clamorous for their pay.

5. The want of correct surveys, maps, and land-marks was a source of great trouble, among both farmers and owners of town lots; the field notes of the original surveys having been lost, it was impossible to settle the bounds of lots; and as the lots and farms had increased in value, the difficulty was the more felt. Mr. Pinney corrected many abuses, satisfied the public creditors, and relieved the sufferings of the poor, but in accomplishing this he only consolidated the colonial debt by drafts on the treasury of the Society. This debt had been accumulating for the last two years, the funds of the Society being insufficient to meet the expenses of sending out and providing for the unusual number of emigrants which had arrived during that time.

6. To make the expenses on the public buildings, and provide for the various and necessary repairs of the Colony, he was under the necessity of negotiating drafts on the treasury of the Society for $11,000 over and above all means furnished him by the Board of Managers. He succeeded in restoring order among the recaptured Africans, by allowing the Congoes and Eboes each to elect their own civil officers. Although these people had made great advances in civilization, their notions of caste were, to some extent, still retained. The farms and lots were resurveyed and permanent land-marks established. In addition to the emigrants by the Jupiter, another company of about fifty arrived this winter in the Argus. These were the last that came out this year under the patronage of the American Colonization Society.

7. An expedition sent out in the brig Ann, by the Maryland Colonization Society, to form an independent settlement, after visiting Monrovia and Grand Bassa, and taking with them twenty or thirty acclimated citizens, proceeded

to Cape Palmas, where they arrived on the 11th of February. This Society had taken every precaution to insure the success of their colony. They furnished a large stock of trade goods, tools, and agricultural implements; the emigrants were well selected, and the Society was fortunate in securing the services of an excellent agent, Dr. Hall, whom they instructed to exclude ardent spirits in trading with the natives. He succeeded in procuring an eligible tract of land on the Cavally River, well adapted to agriculture, to which employment the industry of the colonists was to be exclusively directed.

8. The native kings, from whom the purchase was made, expressed much satisfaction at the proposal of the Americans to settle among them, and a great desire for the establishment of schools. Messrs. Wilson and Wynkoop, who accompanied the expedition, after taking a survey of the coast from Monrovia to Cape Palmas, with reference to a missionary establishment, returned to the United States.

9. In the summer, the Jupiter returned to Monrovia with stores, agricultural implements, and trade goods to amount of $7,000. Among her passengers were Rev. Ezekiel Skinner, missionary and physician, Dr. McDowall, a physician from Scotland, and Charles H. Webb, one of the colored medical students educated by the Board, and who was to complete the study of his profession in the Colony. Mr. Searle and Mr. Finley, both young men of liberal education, came out as teachers, under the patronage of the Ladies' Association of New York city.

10. Mr. Pinney's health was so bad during this summer as to render him incapable of attending to his public duties, and several works and improvements which he had commenced were consequently retarded or suspended. Dr. Skinner was employed to aid in the transaction of public business, while, at the same time, he successfully pursued the practice of his profession as a physician, and attended to his missionary duties.

11. Mr. Seys, of the Methodist Episcopal Church, ap-

pointed to the charge of their Liberia mission, arrived in October. A more judicious selection could scarcely have been made. A native of the West Indies, he had nothing to fear from the climate; was acquainted with the agriculture of tropical latitudes, experienced in business, industrious and persevering, conciliating in his manners, and a zealous Christian. He visited the various settlements, and in a few weeks after his arrival had established a school at New Georgia, in which twenty-eight children and fifty-eight adults were taught, and one at Edina with forty-three scholars.

12. The colonial council had passed an ordinance for the suspension of the public schools, until some plan should be devised for conducting them more successfully. There was a great want of suitable teachers, school-books, and stationery; and besides, the council wished to appropriate the public funds to the erection of a new court-house and jail. The girls' schools, at Monrovia and Caldwell, were flourishing. An interesting notice was given of them in the following extract of a letter, written by an old and respectable colonist: "I am happy to inform you that the schools supported by the ladies of Philadelphia continue to exert the most beneficial influence on our rising generation, and many will live to bless the name of Beulah Sansom. We had an exhibition of Mrs. Thompson's school, in the Methodist meeting-house, and I can not express the great interest felt on the occasion.

13. "Our warehouses were shut up, so that all might attend. It was very largely attended, although each had to pay twelve and a half cents. Mr. Eden's school, at New Georgia, among the recaptured Africans, is doing well. Our new and excellent Governor Pinney is quite indefatigable in his labors to push forward the interests of the Colony, and strongly reminds us of the sainted Ashmun. He has determined upon taking measures to re-establish a public farm near Caldwell, on the plan of Mr. Ashmun, where all idle persons and vagrants may be placed. Many

persons are going to farming, and I am within bounds when I say that three times the quantity of ground will be put under cultivation this season over any preceding year."

14. The cause of African missions suffered severely this year by the death of the Rev. Mr. Laird and wife, and the Rev. Mr. Cloud, of the Presbyterian Church, and the Rev. Mr. Wright and wife, of the Methodist Episcopal Church, individuals who, by their talents, zeal, and piety, were qualified for extensive usefulness in the work to which their lives were cheerfully devoted. There had been a number of deaths among the emigrants who came out in the Argus, but few instances of mortality had since occurred; among these were the death of Rev. C. M. Waring, who emigrated from Virginia in 1823, pastor of the first Baptist Church, member of the colonial council, and who had twice filled the office of vice-agent; and the Rev. G. V. Cesar, from Connecticut, a minister of the Episcopal Church, and surveyor of the Colony. Chas. H. Webb, who promised to be very serviceable to the Colony in the practice of medicine, fell a victim to the local fever, or to his own imprudence while it was upon him.

15. A very valuable tract of land at Bassa Cove was purchased for the Young Men's Colonization Society of Pennsylvania, whereon to establish a colony. This was deemed as favorable a location for a settlement as any on the coast of Western Africa. The land was rich, lying on the St. John's River, which affords boat navigation far into the interior; the anchorage in the roadstead is good; the sites for towns on the sea-coast eligible. The first expedition to this place was by the ship Ninus, which carried out 126 emigrants, 110 of whom were manumitted slaves, freed by the will of Dr. Hawes, of Virginia. They were settled under the agency of Dr. McDowall, and it is worthy of remark that the planting of this colony broke up an extensive slave factory. This settlement was made on strict temperance and peace principles, furnished with neither arms nor liquors.

16. The native tribes on the sea-coast who had leagued together ten years before to destroy the colonists, and met with such signal defeat, had ever since courted their favor, and to save themselves from the attacks of the more powerful nations in the interior, had applied for the protection of the colonies, which was extended to ten kings and head men with their people; all of whom were subject to the jurisdiction of the Colony, and enjoyed the protection of their laws.

17. Dr. Skinner's opinion of the influence of colonization in ameliorating the condition of the native Africans is forcibly expressed in the following extract: " I become daily more convinced that the colonization cause is the cause of God. Slavery in a form far more horrid than in the United States, exists in an unknown extent, spread over this vast continent. A general effort to civilize and Christianize the natives is the only means of putting it down. Slave factories are established all along the coast, *Liberia only excepted*, from which thousands every year are carried into perpetual bondage. There is no other conceivable means to abolish it but by the establishment of colonies on the coast. I would aid the cause of Christianity and colonization here, if Jew or infidel, and so would every man that knew the facts, and had the least regard for the temporal welfare of millions that are in this land.

18. "Had I a thousand lives I would devote them all in such an enterprise as is now going forward here. All the money necessary would be furnished, did the Christian public know the facts, and what was needed. That there are difficulties in our way is true, and that there has been some bad management here is also true; but shall these things discourage us, and lead us to give up the only conceivable means of meliorating the condition of millions of our fellowmen? Shall we forsake the last plank, the only ground of hope, for causes such as these? What would have been the fate of Christianity had such been the dastardly spirit of its first propagators?"

CHAPTER XLIII.
JUDICIARY—TROUBLE WITH THE NATIVES.

1. At the annual meeting of the colonial council in January, 1835, an ordinance was passed giving township powers to the various settlements. This was considered a favorable measure for the cause of temperance, as it enabled the several corporations to prohibit the introduction of ardent spirits by fines. It also gave them power to levy taxes for the support of schools, and the building of roads, bridges, etc. An important improvement was made in the judiciary by creating a Court of Appeals, which measure, however, was not carried without considerable and warm debate.

2. The temperance cause had become the subject of much interest in the Colony. Two meetings were held in January for the purpose of promoting it, a society was formed, and other measures used to enlist popular feeling in its favor. The society, which at first consisted of forty-three persons, was soon increased to 503, upon the pledge of total abstinence. A temperance society was also formed at Edina this year. Captain Outerbridge, of the brig Rover, who spent some time at Monrovia, wrote, "I saw but one man the worse for liquor while I was at Monrovia, that is among the Americans, but before I arrived I expected to see them lying about the streets drunk as we do in the States."

3. On the 18th of January, the brig Bourne, of Baltimore, touched at Monrovia on her way to Cape Palmas, with fifty-four emigrants. In April, the brig Rover, from New Orleans, arrived at Monrovia with seventy-one emigrants. These were not inferior in good character and intelligence to any company of emigrants that had ever come to the Colony. At a public meeting held at New Or-

leans before their departure, they all formed themselves into a temperance society on the principle of total abstinence; some of them possessed considerable property.

4. The August number of the *Liberia Herald* (edited at this time by Hillery Teage) announces the following arrivals: " On the 9th instant, the brig Louisiana, Capt. Williams, arrived from Norfolk, Va., with forty-six emigrants, thirty-eight of whom are recaptured Africans, principally, we believe, from the Nunez and Pongas. They are a strolling people. A number of their countrymen, and among them some acquaintances, have found their way to this settlement. They were hailed by their redeemed brethren with the most extravagant expressions of joy.

5. " On the 12th instant, the Susan Elizabeth, Capt. Lawlin, arrived from New York. Passengers, Dr. E. Skinner, colonial agent, and daughter. Rev. Mr. Seys and family, of the Methodist Episcopal Mission. Rev. Messrs. Crocher, and Myln and lady, of the Baptist mission. We hail with joy the arrival of the passengers by this vessel. We are led to hope that this portion of the moral vineyard is about to be regarded with special interest. Surely if any portion of the earth has a claim upon another, Africa has a claim upon the United States. On the 14th instant, the schooner Harmony, Capt. Paschal, from Baltimore, with twenty-seven emigrants for Cape Palmas, arrived. This expedition has been long expected at Cape Palmas, and will, no doubt, prove an acceptable reinforcement to Dr. Hall.

6. " On the 19th instant, the ship Indiana, Capt. Wood, arrived from Savannah, with sixty-five emigrants, among whom was Dr. Davis and family. These repeated arrivals, following so closely in the track of each other, seem to have given some degree of uneasiness to the natives. They do not understand it, and imagining that Americans move by the same principles that they do, that is to say, animal motives, they conclude that ' Rice be done for big 'Merica,' and hope they will plant more next year, or ' black man will no have place for set down.' "

7. Owing to the unfortunate result of the noble and benevolent experiment at Bassa Cove, the emigrants were landed at this place, to wait, as we suppose, orders from home. The Bassa Cove settlement had not been provided with the means of defense. The great anxiety expressed by the native kings to have a colony planted at that place, and their solemn pledges to protect it, induced the Pennsylvania Society to rely on their good faith; and when the colonists complained that a hostile disposition was manifested by the natives, the agent, Mr. Hankinson, took no measures of precaution, and even refused the proffered assistance of the people of Edina, who tendered their services to defend the Colony. On the same night the natives, under King Jo Harris and his brother, King Peter Harris, attacked the Colony, murdered twenty of the defenseless inhabitants, and burnt the town.

8. The agent, Mr. Hankinson, and lady, were saved by the friendly aid of a Kroo, who concealed them and secured their escape. This murderous act was induced by a slave trader, who, on coming to anchor in the harbor, discovered that a colony of Americans had been planted on the river, and refused to land his goods, alleging that the colonists would interrupt his trade. King Jo Harris finding that the trade in slaves was likely to be thus cut off, resolved on the destruction of the settlement. Had the colonists been armed, the attack would not probably have been made. One gun owned by a colonist, and often used by his next neighbor (which fact had been noticed by some of the natives), saved both houses unmolested, and the families uninjured. The colonists who escaped were carried to Monrovia and their wants provided for.

9. The agent at Monrovia took immediate measures to chastise the people who had committed this outrage. After demanding redress, which was refused, an armed force was marched against the aggressors, who were routed and their towns destroyed. The offending kings gladly accepted a peace, agreeing to abandon the slave trade for-

ever, and to permit the interior natives to pass through their country to trade with the Colony, and also to build a number of houses to replace those destroyed, and pay for or return the property carried away. As soon as peace was concluded, the agent of the American Colonization Society, Dr. Skinner, proceeded to lay out a town on a site which he described as healthy and beautiful. A part of the town plot was cleared, and buildings commenced for the reception of the dispersed citizens.

10. The native kings in the neighborhood of Cape Mount were engaged in a bloody war, carried on with more than ordinary ferocity; and King Boatswain was at war with several of the more interior nations, who had leagued together to resist this tyrant and prince of slave dealers. Commissioners were sent out by the colonial agent to negotiate a peace. They were well received, but unsuccessful in their mission.

11. A school was established on the Junk River for the instruction of the natives, by Mr. and Mrs. Titler (colored people), under the patronage of the Western Board of Foreign Missions, with very encouraging prospects of success. The head men provided the missionaries with a house, and promised a supply of rice and other necessary provisions for the pupils. The natives placed their girls as well as boys under the missionaries to learn "white man fash." The several schools in the Colony, supported by benevolent people in the United States, were prosperous. But had the colonists been able duly to appreciate the importance of public schools, it was impossible to obtain a sufficient number of suitable teachers from among themselves.

12. For a considerable time dissatisfaction had been expressed by some of the colonists with the administration of the Government, and as the executive power was vested in the colonial agent, who was often changed, and much of the time when in discharge of his official duties was enfeebled by sickness, no doubt some ground for dissatis-

faction existed. It was equally probable that men, having so recently commenced the study and practice of republicanism, should mistake salutary restraints for oppression, and regard as tyrants those who enforced obedience to necessary laws. Nor was it an easy task to furnish laws suited to the peculiar circumstances of the colonists; and when defects were ascertained, much time necessarily elapsed before the evil could be remedied. It was, however, creditable to the colonists that their real or supposed grievances gave rise to no violent measures for redress.

13. This year the fifth Baptist Church in the Colony was formed at Caldwell, and the first annual meeting of the Liberia Baptist Association held at Monrovia, in October, which was a joyful and profitable season. Quarterly and protracted meetings were held this fall in the Methodist churches, which were greatly blessed; and there were revivals of religion in nearly all the settlements.

CHAPTER XLIV.

NEW SETTLEMENTS—IMPORTS—FINANCE.

1. In 1836 most of the settlers had returned to Bassa Cove. They were greatly assisted in establishing themselves by Dr. Skinner. Soon after his return from that settlement he had the pleasure of welcoming Thomas Buchanan, agent of the New York and Pennsylvania Societies, who arrived at Monrovia on the 1st of January, with abundant supplies for the relief of their infant Colony. After collecting the remaining emigrants from Monrovia and the surrounding settlements, he proceeded, on the 8th instant, to Bassa Cove.

2. A much more eligible site for a town was now selected at the mouth of the St. John's, about three miles distant

from that on which the first company had located. By the activity and perseverance of the agent, the settlement was soon put in a condition to defy attacks from the natives. The settlers were placed in comfortable houses, and busily engaged in clearing and cultivating their farms; public buildings were erected, the necessary officers appointed to administer the laws, a church built, the town plot cleared, and the native kings who had destroyed the settlement compelled to fulfill the stipulations of their treaty, by which they were bound to pay for property destroyed or carried away.

3. A profitable trade was opened with the natives in the interior, and a valuable accession of territory acquired, lying around the bight of the Cove, adjoining the former purchase, and extending along the sea-coast ten or twelve miles. The acquisition of this territory gave the Colony jurisdiction over the only place accessible to the slavers in that vicinity, and was considered very important as the site of a sea-port town.

4. The tract of land near the mouth of the Junk River, which had been bought by Mr. Pinney, and the title afterward disputed by some of the Junk people, was this year secured to the Society by farther negotiations, on terms satisfactory to the former claimants. A town of more than a mile square was laid off in 392 lots during the spring, and a number of the colonists and recaptured Africans commenced the settlement of Marshall. This place was beautifully situated, on rising ground, between the Junk and Red Junk rivers, and fanned by fresh breezes from the ocean.

5. In April, the brig Luna, from Norfolk, arrived at Monrovia, bringing eighty-two emigrants, a majority of whom were young men, and several preachers of the Gospel. One of them, the Rev. B. R. Wilson, a missionary of the Methodist Church, had spent several months in the Colony, and returned to the United States for his family. This company of emigrants was destined for the new set-

tlement at Marshall, but circumstances detained them at Monrovia until they had taken the fever of the country, which, in several cases, proved fatal.

6. In July, forty-two emigrants arrived in the schooner Swift, from New Orleans. The character of this company was equally good as that of the preceding arrival. Most of them were industrious, and accustomed to work on plantations. They settled immediately at Millsburg. In August, the brig Luna, from New York, brought eighty-four emigrants to Bassa Cove. They arrived in good health and spirits, and being principally industrious and intelligent farmers, were a valuable acquisition to the settlement. Dr. Skinner purchased a small tract of land for the American Colonization Society, in the neighborhood of Edina, on the margin of the bay which forms the outlet of St. John's River.

7. At the request of the Mississippi Society, he also purchased a tract of land from the natives, on the River Sinoe, about half way between Bassa Cove and Cape Palmas, as the site of a settlement to be established by that Society, and appointed D. Johnson, an intelligent Monrovian, to prepare for the accommodation of emigrants. The conflicting claims for lots and farms, which grew out of hasty and imperfect surveys, frequent changes of agents, and carelessness in keeping records, had become a fruitful source of difficulty. Notwithstanding all that had been done by his predecessor, Dr. Skinner had much labor in resurveying lands, and making equitable settlements between contending parties. Persevering in his labors after his exposure had brought on repeated attacks of fever, he was at length so reduced as to be obliged to leave the Colony and return to the United States.

8. On his departure, the administration of government devolved on A. D. Williams, the Lieutenant-Governor. This title and that of Governor had, by order of the Board, superseded those of agent and vice-agent. The revenue arising from imports this year was $3,500, applicable to

colonial improvements and payment of the salaries of certain officers. It had been expended in a way not satisfactory to the legislative council; the money had disappeared, but the vouchers of the disbursing officers did not cover the amount which came into their hands. The editor of the *Herald*, after noticing the squabbles in the United States relative to the "sub-treasury," remarked that "their treasury was all *sub*."

9. But although speculation and fraud might have sometimes been committed by the receiving or disbursing officers, these practices were not without precedent in governments farther advanced in political science; and however imperfect the system of finance adopted by the colonial legislature, the general adaptedness of their laws to the condition and wants of the people would not suffer by comparison with the colonial legislation of the United States. Their laws for the collection of debts, enforcing the fulfillment of contracts, securing persons and property, prove that the colonists are not incapable of self-government.

10. The first murder that ever occurred in the Colony was committed this year. A recaptured African, of the Congo tribe, named Joe Waldburgh, was murdered by an Ebo, named John Demony, at the instigation of Waldburgh's wife. The crime was marked by the most aggravating circumstances. The parties were tried, Governor Skinner presiding, and condemned to be hung. The execution took place on the 22d of July.

CHAPTER XLV.

CIVILIZING THE NATIVES.

1. THE wars among the natives, which continued with little interruption, subjected the colonists to great inconvenience. Natives, under the protection of the Colony,

were sometimes seized and sold to the slave dealers, by whom every effort was made to set the natives against the colonists. Scarcity of provisions among the natives led some of them to make depredations upon the plantations of Millsburg and Caldwell. Rice was scarce and dear in the Colony, which occasioned much suffering, especially among the poorer classes. In November, some of the paupers were placed on the public farm, where they could be employed to advantage, with the prospect of soon being fed from the cassada and other vegetables, several acres of which had been planted for their use.

2. The Maryland Colony at Cape Palmas continued to prosper. From the commencement of this settlement, in 1833, the Society had sent out seven expeditions, containing in all about 300 emigrants. The village of Harper contained about twenty-five private houses, and several public buildings; a public farm of ten acres had been cleared, and about thirty acres put under cultivation by the colonists. Their influence on the natives was salutary; schools were established in the settlement, and the people were pronounced, by their late intelligent Governor, Dr. Hall, moral, industrious, religious, and happy. This gentleman had resigned his office, and J. B. Russwurm, former editor of the *Liberia Herald*, was appointed to that station.

3. The mission in this settlement, established by Mr. and Mrs. Wilson, was most successfully conducted. In addition to the missionaries already engaged in their work, the brig Niobe, from Baltimore, which arrived in December with thirty-two emigrants, brought out Thomas Savage, M.D., missionary of the Protestant Episcopal Church, Rev. D. White and lady, missionaries of the American Board of Commissioners for Foreign Missions, Mr. James, a colored printer, sent out by the same Board as an assistant missionary, and Mr. David James, a colored missionary of the Methodist Episcopal Church.

4. The blessings flowing from Christian ordinances and Christian communion continued to be enjoyed in all the

settlements. The heathen around and in the midst of them were not neglected by the ministers of Christ, and the zeal of the missionaries was unabated. The Rev. Mr. Seys, who had recently returned from a visit to the United States, and brought with him one white and one colored Methodist preacher, wrote under date of December 21st: "I preached in Krootown, this afternoon, to a congregation of Kroomen. I spoke without an interpreter, in broken English, compounded of the most common terms of our language, and many that are peculiar to the African, and were familiar to me from my infancy. They listened to us with deep attention, and when we went to prayer, in conclusion, they came around us, and not content to kneel simply, they bowed down their faces to the earth. Let me urge it upon the Church to have pity upon this intelligent and teachable tribe. O send us a missionary for Kroo Settra! They beg, they entreat us to send them a teacher—a man of God. We shall make an additional effort to plant the standard of the Redeemer among the Condoes."

5. The following will show the kind of influence which the colonists have over the natives: Dr. Hall, Governor of the Maryland Colony, finding the subjects of his neighbor, King Freeman, to be very great thieves, and being much annoyed by their continual pilfering, determined to make the king pay for the articles stolen by his people. The king complied for some time. The demands, however, became so frequent, that he at length objected. The Doctor told him that as he was king, he could make such laws as he pleased, and that if he did not make laws to surrender the thieves to him for punishment, he would hold him responsible. The king made many inquiries of the Doctor in relation to his laws, where he got them, the manner of executing them, etc. On being informed that they were made by the Society's Board at Baltimore, King Freeman resolved to send his head man, Simleh Balla, to Baltimore to get him a book of laws.

6. Simleh visited Baltimore, was introduced to the

Board, and delivered the following speech (as nearly as it could be written): "I be Balla, head man for King Freeman of Cape Palmas. Him send me this country. I come for peak his word. Pose him sava book, I no come; he make book and send him; but cause he no sava make book, I come for look country and peak him words. Long time past, slave man come we country. He do we bad too much, he make slave, he tief plenty man for sell. By and by all slave man knock off. This time we no sell slave, no man come for tief him. All man glad this palaver done sit. Beside that we have plenty trouble. All man have to go for ship for get him ting, iron, cloth, tobacco, guns, powder, and plenty, plenty little ting. Some time canoe capsize, man lose all him money. Some time he die, plenty water kill him; him can't come up.

7. "This hurt we too much, and make we heart sorry. By and by one white man come we country. He bring plenty black American man. Him buy we country, we give him land for sit down. Him say he come for do country good. Him build house—put all him money shore—make farm—make road—make all country fine. This time all good ting live shore—no more go ship. Ebery man can buy that ting him want. No money lose—no man lose. This make all men heart glad—made king's heart glad. King tell me, 'Balla, go that country; see how this ting be. Tell them people all we heart say. Thank him for that good ting them do for we country. Beg him for send more man, for make house, make farm—for bring money, and for make all ittle childs sava read book, all same America men. I done.'"

8. The Board kindly furnished a simple penal code in language that the natives could understand. On reading it to Simleh, the clause limiting every man to one wife alarmed him, and he expressed his disapprobation in the the following language: "'No good for my countryman.' 'Why not, Simleh?' 'Me tell you. I got four wives. Spose I send three away, and keep Bana—she pretty—she

7*

young—no man give 'em rice—no man take care of 'em—they die—pickaninny die too—no good law that?' There was so much reason in his objection, that an immediate reply was not made to him, and after a short pause he went on—' Me tell you. Spose that law no good law for me—well—that law good for my son—he pickaninny now —got no wife—by-um-by he want wife—I say, King Freeman say you only have one wife—so all men. When I got my four wives, I no saba that law. When my son get wife, he saba law—he do what law say. Yes, that good law for time come.'" Simleh's idea of an *ex post facto* law was correct, and he was instructed to explain this article of the code to King Freeman as prospective only in its operation.

9. After the return of Simleh to King Freeman, the laws being adopted and found to be popular and productive of the happiest results, the king applied to the Rev. Mr. Wilson to write him a letter of thanks to the Board at Baltimore, as follows:

"*King Freeman to the Gentlemen of the Colonization Board of Baltimore*—Naheveo, (greeting):

"Mr. Wilson be hand for me and Simleh Balla be mout for me for make dis book, but de word come from me own heart. He be true I send Balla for look you—he eye be all same me eye, and dat word he peak be all same he come out me own mout. You do Balla good when he lib to your hand, dat be all same you do good for King Freeman. I tank you for dat, Balla tell me you hab fine country, I believe what he say, cause he no fit for tell lie. I tank you berry much, gentlemen, for dem dash you send me. I like um plenty an go keep um all de time. But I tank you berry much for dem law you send me—he be good law, and all my people go do him. Pos' I hab dem law first time I no go do fool fash all time—dis time I go make all me people do dat ting what you law tell me. I tauk you plenty, gentlemen, for dem good law. I tell all man go hear Misser Wilson talk God palaver, and yiserday so much man go till plenty hab for to stand outside de house.

10. " Soon Balla go for 'Merica first time me go long way bush and tell all man say he must make fine road and bring plenty trade for Cape Palmas. Me heart tink say he guin do him soon. Me hear you say you hab plenty slave in you country. Me have one word for peak dem. You must come me country den you be *freeman* for true. Dis country be big and plenty room lib here. Pos' you come, I peak true, me heart be glad plenty for look you. Pos' any gentleman want come me want him for come too —me heart glad for see dem too much. Me word be done now—I tank you berry much for you dash and you law. I go lub you till me dead. Me send you one country chair for you look at. Me go put pickaninny country word for you see. A good child loves his father, he loves his mother.   KING FREEMAN, *alias* PA NIMMAH."

CHAPTER XLVI.
ARRIVAL OF GOVERNOR MATTHIAS.

1. THE Rondout, from Wilmington, N. C., arrived at Monrovia on the 4th of February, 1837, with thirty emigrants. Dr. D. F. Bacon, who had been appointed colonial physician, came out in this vessel, and immediately entered upon his professional duties. The following is extracted from his communication to the Board, dated February 15th: " I found the Colony in a peaceful, prosperous, and healthy condition. The public prosperity and general comfort have been greatly promoted under the faithful and active government of Mr. Williams, whose business-like management has effected a reform in affairs that has

given me a satisfaction which I know the Board and all the friends of the Colony will share on perceiving the results as reported by him officially. In my own department I have found much that required active attention; for although there is not a single case of the common fever in the Colony (unless at Edina, from which I have not yet heard), there are in all this section, besides a few light cases of croup, about fifteen or twenty cases of chronic disorders resulting from debility, mostly in old, broken-down constitutions, which have been long suffering for want of the aid of a regular physician; the Colony having been left entirely to the medical assistants ever since the departure of Dr. Skinner in September.

2. "The people, in general, I believe to be remarkably quiet, inoffensive, and peaceable, more so than in any part of the United States where I have lived. Ever since I have established myself on shore, all have combined to treat me with the greatest attention and kindness; and since beginning my business here as physician, I have met with nothing but the most polite and civil usage. My medical assistants in this quarter, Messrs. Prout, Brown, and Chase, have been very polite and attentive, and have promptly pledged themselves to become active and serviceable to the Colony under my directions. Dr. McDowall left your service long since, and resides wholly at Bassa Cove."

3. The Governor, in his official communication of the same date, wrote: "I am happy in being able to say that at present the Colony is peaceful and tranquil. A growing attention still continues to be paid to agriculture; indeed, the whole community seems to be awaking to the subject. No former period of the Colony can boast of as great an extent of land under tillage as at present. In order to afford some encouragement to the settlers at Junk, as well as to prevent their eating the bread of idleness at the expense of the Society, I have established a farm there, on which they will work a part of the time in return for the articles with which the store there may provide them.

4. "The emigrants by the Swift have proved themselves an industrious, thrifty people. They have already raised two crops of culinary vegetables and other produce. The farm established on Bushrod Island is doing remarkably well, and will, I think, realize my former hope respecting it. All the paupers that require constant assistance are now on the farm, and those able to labor have their work regularly assigned to them. You will be astonished, no doubt, when I inform you that the former fearful number of mendicants has dwindled, since the commencement of this system, to twenty, including those who are only occasionally beneficiaries.

5. "The emigrants by the Rondout are located at Millsburg, and already have their town lots assigned them; they will have their farms in a few days." In May an agricultural society was formed. One of the conditions of membership was a subscription of $500 to a joint stock fund to be paid in quarterly payments. The object of this society was the cultivation of the sugar-cane, and the manufacture of sugar. Stock was taken by the most wealthy and enterprising inhabitants, and the investment promised to be advantageous both to the stockholders and the Colony.

6. In June there were twenty acres of the public farm under successful cultivation, six acres of which were in sugar-cane. The crops on the public farm at Junk were also promising. With a view to encourage agriculture and the raising of stock, twenty acres, instead of five, were allotted to those who had not before drawn farms, on condition that deeds should not be given until five acres were under good cultivation. There were 450 acres of land under excellent cultivation in the Colony, exclusive of the settlements of Edina and Bassa Cove; at both of which places they were applying themselves successfully to agriculture. At Bassa Cove there were ten acres of rice in one field.

7. Owing to the wars, which for the last two years had

raged with little intermission along the coast, the natives were nearly in a state of starvation, and the Caldwell and New Georgia people had for some months supplied them with cassada, which was almost the only article of provision that could be obtained. Rice was very scarce. The Mississippi Society fitted out a company of emigrants for their new settlement on the Sinoe, which sailed in the Oriental from New Orleans in April, under the care of J. F. C. Finley. They arrived unexpectedly at Monrovia, where they were obliged to remain some time before proceeding to their place of destination.

8. In the summer the brig Baltimore brought fifty-five emigrants to the Maryland Colony. A majority of these were emancipated by the will of Richard Tubman, Esq., of Georgia, on condition of their emigrating to Liberia, and $10,000 bequeathed to the Colonization Society for the expenses of their emigration and settlement. They were of good character and experienced cotton planters. Many of them were acquainted with some trade. The Charlotte Harper arrived on the 4th of August, at Bassa Cove, with supplies for the Colony to the amount of $10,000. The passengers in this vessel were the Rev. John J. Matthias, who had been appointed Governor of the Colony, and his wife, Dr. Wesley Johnson, assistant physician to the Colony, David Thomas, millwright, Misses Annesley, Beers, and Wilkins, teachers, and Dr. S. M. E. Goheen, physician to the Methodist Mission at Monrovia, and four colored emigrants.

9. The thriving settlement of Edina, separated by the St. John's River from that of Bassa Cove, was this year, by an arrangement entered into between the American Colonization Society and the Pennsylvania and New York Society, transferred to the latter Society, the people of Edina consenting thereto. This was a favorable arrangement for both settlements, as it united their strength and identified their interest, while it lessened the expense of their government. Mrs. Matthias and Miss Annesley both

died in a few months after their arrival in Africa, and within two or three days of each other. These pious missionaries were intimately attached to each other in America. Together they consecrated themselves to the cause of Africa, and together were called from the field which they had barely been permitted to enter and survey.

10. Governor Matthias wrote from Bassa Cove, December 18, 1837: "There is not a finer climate for the colored man in the world, nor a soil more fertile. It is now summer. The thermometer for a month past has ranged from 79° to 84°, and the season will continue until May, during which period the thermometer will not rise above 86°. Although the *Watchman* has been pleased to ridicule our organization as a republic, nevertheless we are a State with all its machinery. The editor would be induced to change his views were he to see our well-dressed and disciplined troops and their management of arms. I should venture nothing in comparing them with the militia anywhere at home.

11. "Our courts of justice, of sessions, and the supreme court, the clerks and sheriffs, with the prosecuting attorney, with great readiness perform their respective duties. To see members of council gravely deliberating on matters of interest to the commonwealth and good government, together with merchants transacting their business with as much skill and propriety almost as at Middletown, is truly astonishing, considering the short period since our organization. Our chief clerk, for example, one of the children taken by the enemy in Ashmun's war, and restored after a detention of some months, besides writing a beautiful hand, can, in a twinkling, cast up any account, and make his calculations, without pen or pencil, in the sale of articles, with as much accuracy as any of your merchants. I am preparing, if well, to go up the St. John's, to hold a palaver with six or eight head men and kings for the purchase of their country. A great change has taken place among them; they seem desirous of being allied to

us, for the protection of themselves against each other's aggression.

12. "December 25. We have now as fine a court-house as there is in Liberia. Benson has finished quite an elegant house, and others are laboring not only to stay here, but to live. The government-house is nearly finished. We have laid out the yard into walks and grass plots; on the margin of the walks we have planted the cotton-tree and papaw. I have just returned from partaking of an agricultural dinner, not given by us of the government, but by the farmers. We had mutton, fish, and fowl, and a superfluity of vegetables. The table was set under some palm-trees in Atlantic Street; there were, I should judge, about fifty persons present. You need be under no apprehensions but that farming will go on. We mean to plant the coffee-tree throughout our farm.

13. "We have bought, as you have been apprised, of Yellow Will, a large tract of beautiful upland. There are four native towns on it. King Yellow Will is, therefore, considered as allied to us by the neighboring head men and kings, who appear to be jealous of the honor, and determined to share it. They have sent me word that they would sell their lands."

CHAPTER XLVII.

PROGRESS OF MISSIONARY LABORS.

1. THE native kings, in carrying on their wars in the vicinity of the settlements, always regard the territory of the Colony as neutral ground, to which the vanquished flee without fear of pursuit. Even slave traders have surrendered those who have been stolen from the territory of the Colony, on the demand of the colonial authorities—

hence the desire of the natives to sell their country to the colonists. They give up the jurisdiction of the country sold, and the right to buy and sell slaves, or engage in any way in the slave trade, or make war upon their neighbors. In return, the right to occupy their towns and farms, and have them enlarged at pleasure, the same as if they were colonists, is secured to them; they are no long exposed to be sold as slaves, or to be punished for witchcraft and other imaginary crimes. Thus, in Liberia, colonization, instead of destroying, gives protection to the natives, increases their comforts, abolishes the barbarous rites of devil-worship, by which multitudes have been yearly sacrificed, and is found to be a sure and effectual means of civilizing those brought under its influence.

2. The ninth expedition to Maryland in Liberia sailed from Baltimore, on the 28th of November, with eighty-six emigrants, in the Niobe. In the same vessel the Protestant Episcopal Church sent out three missionaries, the Rev. Mr. Payne and wife, and the Rev. Mr. Minor, to join Mr. Savage, who was at the head of their establishment at Cape Palmas. The emigrants by the Niobe were all from Maryland, and nearly all of them persons of good character, who had been accustomed to labor, and left America under the conviction that their happiness and prosperity in Africa were only to be secured by persevering industry, and not expecting exemption from the toils incident to early settlers in a new country.

3. It had been the wise policy of the Maryland Society's Board to send out industrious men, and by keeping general native trade in the hands of the Society, to make agriculture the main, and, indeed, except in the case of mechanics, the sole occupation of the colonists. The system of barter, which had been the chief means of inducing and cherishing the spirit of trade, so detrimental to the Monrovia settlement, and which was necessarily resorted to in the Maryland Colony, threatened to defeat the wishes of the Board in regard to native trade, by obliging each colonist

to keep on hand an assortment of goods to exchange for the articles wanted from the natives for the use of his family.

4. It was at first proposed to send small silver coin to the Colony, but the Board became satisfied, by the information they received, that it would be impossible to keep a sufficient quantity of silver there to answer any useful purpose, as it would soon be brought off by trading vessels stopping at the cape. They prepared and forwarded certificates for five, ten, twenty-five, fifty, and one hundred cents, receivable in payment for goods at the public store. To make these intelligible to the natives, there were represented on them objects to which they attached the value represented by the certificates; for instance, on the five cent certificate a head of tobacco; on the ten cent, a chicken; on the twenty-five cent, a duck; on the fifty cent, two ducks; and on the dollar certificate, a goat.

5. The report of the Liberia Mission of the Methodist Episcopal Church represented this as a year of unparalleled prosperity. "The fervent and united prayers," said the report, "with which we commenced 1837, have not been in vain. The thousands of pious hearts among the Christians of America, which have been supplicating a throne of Divine Grace for Africa, have not been pleading for naught." Seasons of revival had been extensively experienced in the Colony, and more than twenty of the natives had been converted. Some of these were living in the families of the colonists, and had been trained to the knowledge of the Christian's God, while others were "right out of the bush."

6. At Millsburg, the Methodist Church had increased, this year, from eleven to sixty-three. The White Plain manual labor school, near this settlement, had shared in the blessings of converting grace. One of the native boys at this school received a visit from his father, and on being inquired for at a certain hour of the day to go to work with the other boys, was missing. The missionary found

him in one of the upper rooms of the school-house, pleading with his father to "look for the American's God," and get his soul converted to Christ.

7. The number of church members within the bounds of this mission, embracing all the settlements except Marshall, was 578. The number of children in the schools, under its care, 221 attending day schools, and 303 the Sabbath-schools. One of the colored teachers at Monrovia (Mrs. Moore, formerly Eunice Sharp) wrote to a lady in New York: "I have a goodly number of pupils, from twenty years old to three, but not advanced in learning as they are in years. I have some very interesting little girls; I have watched them from the alphabet to more interesting things; I have seen them trying to point out the different countries on the map; I have heard them tell me the nature of a noun, conjugate a verb, and tell how many times one number is contained in another; but all this was not half so entertaining to me as when I saw them crowding to the altar of God. Give God the glory, O my soul! that mine eyes have seen the salvation of God upon my own people.

8. "I have heard the wild natives of Africa testify that God hath power on earth to forgive sin. Rejoice, then, ye daughters of benevolence! The Judge of all the earth is answering your prayers in behalf of poor benighted Africa. Yes, though they have laid long upon the altar, he has smelled a sweet savor, and it appears to me that the day is beginning to dawn, and the day star is rising on this dark division of the earth. The way is opening for the poor native, who is now worshiping devils, to become acquainted with the worship of the true and living God." The Rev. S. Chase, who came to Liberia in 1836 with a heart most zealously devoted to the cause of missions, and who promised to be extensively useful in spreading the Gospel among the natives, was obliged, in consequence of protracted ill-health, to return to the United States in the summer of this year.

CHAPTER XLVIII.

A LARGE PLANTER—THE DEY PEOPLE.

1. ARRIVED on the 12th of February, 1838, ship Emperor, with ninety-six emigrants from Virginia, of which sixty were emancipated by John Smith, Sr., Esq., of Sussex County. These people have all been bred to farming, and we hope they will prove an important accession to the agricultural interests of the Colony. The physicians of the Colony being united and unequivocal in their verdict in favor of the superior healthfulness of the inland settlements over that of Monrovia, these emigrants have all been placed at Caldwell and Millsburg, an event which will put this opinion to the test. Our opinion is that either place is healthful.

2. There is no earthly occasion that colored people should die in establishing themselves in Africa. Let them only avoid the actual and obvious causes of disease (which is neither more difficult nor more necessary to be done here than in all other countries), and they may live their three-score years and ten, and if they should have on their arrival good cheer and plenty, they may even attain their four-score years. There came passengers in this ship, Rev. Mr. and Mrs. Clark, to join the Baptist Mission at Edina, Rev. Mr. and Mrs. Barton and mother, of the Mission of the Methodist Episcopal Church, and Dr. Skinner and daughter. This latter gentleman has the medical charge of the Colony.

3. It was a great disappointment to the Governor not to receive a sugar-mill, which he expected by this vessel, as he had then six acres of promising thrifty cane, and was anxious to prove the practicability of cultivating and manufacturing the article, and thereby give an impulse to the

business; but the cane was lost for want of the means of grinding. In the early part of this year the Bassa Cove settlement received an accession of seventy-two emigrants, who came in the barque Marine, from Wilmington, N. C.

4. One of these emigrants was Mr. Lewis Sheriden, a distinguished colored man from North Carolina. On visiting Governor Matthias, and examining the laws for the government of the Colony, he expressed much dissatisfaction, and refused to take the oath required of those who became citizens, alleging that he had left the United States on account of oppression, and that he should not subject himself to arbitrary government in Africa, and such he deemed that of the Colony. However, after spending a few weeks in examining the country, and failing in an effort to induce the colonists to petition the Board for an amendment of the constitution, he resolved on locating at Bexley, six miles from Bassa Cove. As he was a man of wealth, and had been extensively and successfully engaged in business in Carolina, the rules observed in the allotment of lands to emigrants were dispensed with in his case. He took a long lease of 600 acres, and soon had in his employ a hundred men. Many of them were natives, who proved to be excellent laborers.

5. The inland and elevated situation of Bexley, and its rich soil, well adapted to the growth of sugar-cane and the coffee-tree, with such a man as Sheriden to excite to industry those around him, by his own example, may soon make it one of the most important agricultural settlements in Liberia. Some of the Dey people, residing on the Little Bassa, had forcibly taken colonial property from those to whom its transportation to Edina had been intrusted. On satisfaction being demanded for this outrage, the Deys readily agreed to pay for the property taken, also to pay a debt due by them, to the colonial agent, and to secure the payment in four months, pledged a portion of their lands, embracing the mouth of the Little Bassa.

6. The time of payment having expired, a commissioner

was appointed to remind the Deys of their promise, but only a renewal of it was obtained. The colonization agent, acting in accordance with the spirit of his instructions to treat the natives with all consistent lenity, pursued persuasive measures to induce this tribe to comply with their engagements, for eighteen months without success, when he sent two commissioners, accompanied by seventy-five armed men, with instructions to bring the business to a close by an amicable arrangement, if possible; but if no satisfaction could be obtained, they were to take possession of the land pledged.

7. The Deys, conscious of their own duplicity, and fearful of being chastised for the robbery they had committed, retired from the coast; and after spending eight days in fruitless efforts to bring them to a palaver, the colonists took possession of the territory pledged. This course was deemed necessary, for had the Deys escaped unpunished, their robberies would have become of frequent occurrence; forbearance is always interpreted by the natives to be weakness.

8. A man by the name of Logan, in disregard of the remonstrances of his friends, settled on the territory of the natives, north of the St. Paul's, and opened a farm. In a fracas with some Mandingoes in which he was concerned, one of them was killed. Logan was accused of the deed, arrested, and formally tried in the Colony, and acquitted of the murder. Having returned to his farm, the party to which the murdered man belonged, went, a few days after, to Logan's house, under pretext of trading; not suspecting their designs he admitted them.

9. As soon as they had entered, they seized and confined him, and after robbing the house of its contents, set it on fire, which, with the owner was consumed. Of three other persons in the house, an American, a Gourah, and a Bassa, the latter escaped, and the other two were taken captive. The Governor demanded of the Deys the surrender of the murderers, and satisfaction for the property destroyed.

This demand was made in conformity with a treaty existing between the parties.

10. The Deys pleaded ignorance of the murder and robbery, stating their weakness to be such that they were forced to submit to see their own property taken and carried away at pleasure by the Mandingoes and Gourahs; and although they admitted their obligations to protect Americans and their property, they alleged a want of ability to do so, and agreed to a proposal to relinquish a part of their territory, which would enable the Colony to extend their jurisdiction and settlements in a direction that would give protection to the Dey people. Twenty-five square miles on the St. Paul's was transferred to the Colony. The Board of Managers doubted the justice of these proceedings, and directed a full report to be made of all the circumstances in the case before assenting to the possession.

CHAPTER XLIX.
A REPUBLIC TALKED OF—THE GOVERNOR MURDERED.

1. Some of the evils anticipated by many of the friends of the American Colonization Society in the establishment of separate settlements in Liberia, independent of each other, and under distinct governments, began to be realized. In reference to this subject, the Lieutenant-Governor, in a communication dated May 8th, 1838, wrote as follows: "I regret to say our neighbors of Bassa Cove and Edina seem to entertain the most hostile feeling toward the old Colony, and everything connected with it. They have manifested such a disposition as will, if continued, lead to serious difficulties between the settlements.

2. "The policy which the colonizationists are now pursuing is assuredly a bad one, and will inevitably defeat the

object they aim to accomplish. Nothing can be conceived more destructive to the general good than separate and conflicting interests among the different colonies. And this consequence will certainly follow the establishment of separate and distinct sovereignties contiguous to each other. If societies must file off and have separate establishments, their very existence depends upon their union by some general and well-settled relations. They might be so far separate as to have peculiar local and internal regulations, but they should be controlled by general laws, and general supervision, and be so connected as to move on to one object in harmonious operation." The editor of the *Liberia Herald* expressed his views on the same subject in the following article from the July number for 1836:

3. "The formation of colonies along the coast is beyond doubt the surest way of breaking up the slave trade, as far as their influence may extend. But while we view with much satisfaction the success of the colonization scheme and the formation of new settlements, we would observe that we deem it highly necessary that the several, and all the colonies now in existence, and those that may hereafter be formed, should be under the guidance of general laws; such a connection would promote union, without which they could never prosper. Each settlement, independently, should have its own laws and regulations for its internal government, like the several States of the Union in America, and, like them, should be bound and cemented together by one general government and by one common interest.

4. "Such a union, of so much vital importance to the future prosperity and peace of the whole, would elevate the character of the colonies in a degree to which they could not otherwise attain. By it, moreover, their strength would be increased, as well as their permanency, according to a common but true saying, '*united we stand.*' Instead of a few isolated settlements, often at variance with each other from selfish motives and conflicting interests, they

would then present to the view of the beholder a number of small settlements, or states if you please, forming a rising republic in Africa of one people and of one language, after the model of the great Union of America."

5. On the 9th of July a company of emigrants arrived at the Mississippi Colony,* by the brig Mail, from New Orleans. These emigrants were well provided with clothes, tools, and farming utensils; working animals were purchased for them at the Cape de Verd Islands, and with great cheerfulness they commenced improving their farms, which were already laid out. An agent had been employed to prepare houses, clear land, and plant vegetables, so that the emigrants on their arrival found good quarters and an abundance of cassada, rice, and potatoes.

6. Their town, Greenville, is on the Sinoe River, five miles from the mouth, and about two miles in a direct line from the sea. This settlement is deemed as healthy as any part of the State of Mississippi, and the land as rich. The territory purchased by the Mississippi Society is narrow on the ocean, widening as it runs back, and contains over 100 square miles. Of the thirty-seven emigrants by the brig Mail, twenty-six had been set free by Mr. Anketell, who had taken much pains to prepare them for freedom and usefulness.

7. An event occurred in the autumn of this year which cast a gloom over the infant but prosperous settlement of Greenville, and, in some measure, disturbed the peaceful relations existing between the colonists and natives. About the 10th of September the Governor left Greenville for Monrovia on business as well as for his health. On his way he attempted to visit Bassa Cove. Landing about two miles below the settlement, he was robbed and murdered by the natives. The Governor seems to have placed too much confidence in a native whom he had with him,

---

* If errors are found in the brief notices given of the Sinoe and Bassa Cove settlements, it is because the desired information in relation to them could not be obtained.

and to whom he had exposed the fact of his having a large sum of money about him. The faithlessness of this fellow in disclosing the circumstance of the money no doubt occasioned the murder.

8. This outrage led to a war between the natives and the settlers of Bassa Cove, who had one or two of their people killed, several wounded, and some of their horses destroyed. Previous to the news of this outbreak the most cheering intelligence had been received from the Bassa Cove settlement, of their health, their temporal and spiritual prosperity. Accounts from all the colonies were generally encouraging, though the Monrovia settlements were in want of adequate funds to carry forward their contemplated improvements, having for some time received but little pecuniary aid from the Society.

9. An official communication from Lieutenant-Governor Williams, dated July 31st, contained the following: "The interest manifested on the subject of agriculture is daily increasing, and the prospect brightening. All here feel the necessity of raising such articles of food as are required for our own wants, and in such quantities as to supply those wants. The greatest and only difficulty is to believe that, with the most abundant supply of African produce, the articles to which we were accustomed in America are not indispensable to our existence.

10. "The country is comparatively quiet; how long it will remain so can not be conjectured. The elements of war and discord are always existent in African society. Your suggestions in regard to the propriety of altering and amending the constitution I have thought best to submit to the consideration of the people at large. For this purpose I called a meeting in each settlement, in order to ascertain the public sentiment. The suggestion was immediately acted upon, and a committee of ten persons was appointed, who now have the subject under consideration. These persons are authorized to suggest such alterations and amendments, to any extent, as they may think adapt-

ed to our present state, and submit them to the Board. We are again destitute of stationery, and are very much in want of animals for draught work on farms."

11. It is much to be regretted that suitable working animals, with wagons, carts, plows, and drags, had not been early introduced into the Colony. With these, agriculture would have advanced rapidly, and buildings would have been erected with comparative ease. To substitute the hoe for the plow, in agriculture, and manual labor for teams, in conveying building timber from the forest, and stone from the quarry, was tedious, expensive, and discouraging. That so much has been accomplished under such privations and disadvantages, excites our wonder.

CHAPTER L.
A LYCEUM—PAPER CURRENCY.

1. Had the colonists been enabled, in 1825, to use the plow and drag in cultivation, they could, for the last ten years, have furnished provisions for all the emigrants as they arrived. Dr. Taylor wrote from Millsburg in August: "With regard to the last emigration, it must be said they have done wonderfully well. They are all at work with very few exceptions. I hope and pray that the Society may soon raise her head; that her coffers may be filled to overflowing. I think that if the bitter opponents of the colonization scheme would only come to Millsburg and look at the prospect, and see that all that is wanting to make this a splendid place, and the people independent in means, they could but say, I will give my support to this enterprise; though I advocate the elevation of the man of color in America, I am now convinced that this is the place where he can enjoy real freedom."

2. The Rev. B. R. Wilson, who was engaged in the manual labor school at Millsburg, and at the same time was pastor of a church in that place, consisting at first of but nine members, wrote as follows: "We have now a well-organized church of about seventy members, and a fine school of native boys and girls, some of whom begin to read, and several profess to have religion, and have joined the church. I am more and more pleased with Africa."

3. A colonist wrote, from Edina, to his former master: "You wish to know my situation, and how I like this part of the world. I am doing well, I have two good houses and three lots, also forty acres of land, ten of which are in culture — coffee, cotton, cassada, plantains, banana, beans, rice, yams, papaws, and melons, these grow all the year here. One acre of land is worth two in the United States. In a word, sir, no man can starve that will work one third of his time. It is a beautiful country indeed. I would not return to the States again, to live, on any consideration whatever, even if slavery were removed. But, sir, we are freemen here, and enjoy the rights of men. What shall I say about want? Why, sometimes we want sugar and tea, also butter and meat. But time will remove all this. I have plenty of milk, and make butter, but there are a great many who have not cows and goats in abundance.

4. "You would do well to send out some brandy to preserve such things as snakes, scorpions, and other things, as spirits are prohibited here, and hardly used among us, and can not be bought for money. I have the satisfaction to inform you that this is a flourishing settlement indeed. The people thrive. All my children are well, and my wife has good health. The children are good English scholars, and James is studying medicine with Dr. Johnson." A lyceum was formed in Monrovia for the diffusion of knowledge throughout the Colony. A committee was appointed to collect specimens of natural and artificial curiosities.

Two of each kind were to be forwarded to some scientific body in America or elsewhere, one retained, the other described, labeled, and returned at the expense of the lyceum. The president and corresponding secretary were to communicate with similar associations in the United States and elsewhere, and invite their aid and coöperation in advice, book, specimens, and whatever else might contribute to the object of their association.

5. It was stated in the *Liberia Herald* of the next month, that since the formation of the lyceum, some few collections of shells, rocks, minerals, and plants had been made, that arrangements were on foot for a commodious room, in which the specimens could be kept and displayed to advantage. The question for the next debate was, " Whether it was good policy to admit indiscriminately persons of all nations and color to become citizens of Liberia ?"

6. Since the foundation of the Maryland Colony, it has been the object of the Board to send regularly a spring and fall expedition. The spring expedition brought out thirty-six emigrants by the Columbia, of Baltimore, and the fall expedition, fifty-three emigrants by the Oberon, with Dr. McDowell and Dr. S. F. McGill. Dr. McDowell had practiced medicine several years in Liberia. Dr. McGill, who is a colored man, had resided there from his childhood, with the exception of the last three years, spent in acquiring a medical education at Dartmouth College, New Hampshire, where he received his diploma. He brought with him an excellent medical library, and it was expected that by practicing with Dr. McDowell, he would become qualified to succeed that gentleman as colonial physician, at the expiration of the year for which the Board had engaged his services.

7. Dr. McGill was instructed to select one or more young men of suitable capacity, and commence instructing them in medicine, with a view of having them sent to the United States to attend the necessary lectures. In this way it was hoped that permanent medical skill could be

secured in the Colony. It was evident that nothing was wanting but care during the first few months of their residence, to make this as healthy to the colored people as any place from which they emigrate.

8. The paper currency was found to answer fully the purpose intended, and it was with none more popular than with the natives themselves. While the system of barter was in vogue, a native scarcely ever sold an article to a colonist, and received merchandise in exchange, without being obliged to divide a portion of it among such friends as happened to be present when the bargain was struck; but when he was paid a piece of paper, this partnership of profits could not take place. This was perfectly understood by the natives, and hence the popularity with them of the paper currency.

9. Governor Russwurm wrote to the Board: "The direct tendency of the currency is to draw all business to the Society's store, and to induce the colonists to put by a part, instead of taking up, as formerly, every cent of their earnings. I think our next step will be a savings bank, or a benefit society for mutual relief in cases of sickness."

10. Of the new code of laws which had been prepared with great care, the Governor wrote: "We are all much pleased with the new code of laws. The powers of the judges are well defined, and will save, among an ignorant community, much contention. I have not heard even a murmur against the code, though it strikes at the root of many preconceived opinions." He added: "The people are civil and orderly. No properly established law of the Colony has ever met with open opposition; no violence has ever been threatened to the lawful authorities. No instance of riot or general uncontrollable excitement has occurred, and no instance of open quarreling or fisticuffs has come to my knowledge, directly or indirectly, since the first establishment of the Colony."

CHAPTER LI.
MONROVIA.

1. Monrovia, which contains about 300 houses and 2,000 inhabitants, is built on a depression of the ridge which sweeps inland from the cape. About midway the length of the principal street the land swells up like an earth-wave, and sinks immediately down the street, crossing the summit and following the declivity. On the summit is Fort Hill, where, in December, 1822, in the infancy of the settlement, the heroic Ashmun, rising from his bed of sickness, with thirty-four brave colonists repulsed an assault made by 800 savages.

2. The houses are detached, being built on lots of a quarter of an acre each. They are of good size, some two stories, but most of them one and a half, consisting of a single story of frame resting on a basement of stone, with a portico front and rear. Many of them were neatly, and two or three handsomely, furnished. There were twelve houses under construction, mostly of stone; and there were, besides, a few which looked in good preservation; but most of the frame dwellings presented an old and dilapidated appearance, owing to the humid climate during half the year, the scarcity of whitewash and paint, and the ravages of the beeg—a bug—a destructive species of *termite*. For the last reason, all the new houses not built in the native fashion—of wattles, mud, and grass—are constructed of stone, while the old frame ones are abandoned to decay.

3. In almost every yard there were fruit-trees—mostly the lime, the lemon, the banana, the pawpaw, and the coffee-tree; sometimes the orange, and now and then the sour-sop and the tamarind. The oranges were good, but scarce, and the lemons large and fine. The cocoa grows

abundantly, and the pomegranate, the fig, the vine, and a tree bearing the cashew-nut are to be seen, but not in abundance.

4. The soil is thin and not productive, resting upon a ferruginous rock which occasionally crops out. The gardens are inclosed by wooden palings, generally in a state of decay, or by stone walls without mortar. In them were only a few collards and some cassada, sweet potatoes, and arrow-root. But it is not the proper season for vegetables, and a few months hence these gardens may, and doubtless will, present a more gratifying appearance. The suburbs, the river, and the inner harbor are commanded by Fort Hill, as the outer anchorage is by that of Fort Norris at the cape.

5. The view from Fort Hill is a very fine one. To the west and southwest it overlooks the houses and trees and far out upon the sea; on the north and east Stockton Creek and the two branches of the Mesurado flow gently through an alluvial plain; and to the southeast the eye follows the direction of the ridge which stretches far into the interior. On Broadway, south of Fort Hill, is the government-house —a large stone building, with arched windows and a balcony in front. The lower floor is used as a court-room and printing-office, and the upper as the hall of legislative council; behind it is the jail; directly opposite is the President's mansion—a double two-story brick house, with a front portico, its roof sustained by lofty columns. It is the most imposing building in the place.

6. There are five churches, all well attended. Indeed, I never saw a more thorough-going church community, or heard a greater rustling of silk on the dispersal of a congregation, than here; all were at least sufficiently attired, and the dresses of the children were in better taste than those of their mothers. One of the most gratifying things I noticed was the great number of well-dressed and well-behaved children in the schools and about the streets.

7. The schools are also numerous and well attended. I

did not see sufficient to justify the expression of an opinion, except that, while I noticed the attendance was full in almost every one, it seemed to me that, in some instances, the acquirements of the teachers were surpassed by the capacities of their scholars; but for all the purposes of rudimental education the materials are ample. I feel a delicacy in alluding to this subject, and only say what has escaped me from a solicitude that the generation now coming forward may sustain the institutions of the republic.

8. The colonists were all decently clothed; and of the natives moving about the streets, with very few exceptions, the most indifferently clad wore a long loose shirt, but their heads and legs were bare. One of the latter I saw reading apparently a book, which he held before him as he walked.

CHAPTER LII.

NEW VIRGINIA AND MILLSBURG.

1. OPPOSITE to Caldwell is the settlement of New Virginia, where, in 1847, the Government of the United States built a receptacle for liberated Africans. Higher up are Kentucky, Heddington, and Millsburg. Heddington was fiercely attacked by the natives in 1841, and gallantly defended by a missionary and one of the colonists; the leader of the assailants was killed and his party dispersed. These four are little more than a close contiguity of small farms; but Millsburg, at the head of navigation, and the farthest inland settlement in Liberia, is a flourishing village and missionary-school station; and on the opposite side of the river is the mission of "White Plains."

2. From its situation, Millsburg must be comparatively healthy, and is certainly beautiful. The river, separated by an island into two channels, there forces itself over a

rocky ledge with the rushing sweep and hoarse sound of a rapid. The ledge is, however, a narrow one, and a channel through it might be blasted with gunpowder, or it could be flanked by a canal. Above the ledge the stream is unobstructed for about ten miles, and the country through which it flows is yet more rolling and beautiful than it is below the rapids. The soil is a rich mold, formed by the vegetable decay of centuries, resting on a substratum of clay, and covered with a luxuriant forest.

3. At the rapids are a number of islands, clothed with luxuriant vegetation; and, as was remarked by the lamented Dr. Randall, the islands differ from each other in their verdure, and from that of the mainland. Each one seems to have caught, in the autumnal inundations, the seeds and roots of particular plants and shrubs brought down from the interior; for, while differing from those on the main, no two resemble each other in their peculiar foliage.

4. Above the islands the country is represented as most beautiful, bearing trees of immense size, clear of undergrowth, and having their branches interwoven with vines, and decorated with gaudy parasitic plants, forming a shade impervious to the sun, and imparting a coolness to the atmosphere which is truly delightful. The stream, irregular in its width, sometimes forces its way through fissures in the rocks, and at others forms deep pools, where the water is so transparent that the bottom is distinctly visible.

5. It seems as if the foot of man had never trodden these lovely solitudes, where the silence is only interrupted by the murmuring sound of water, the scream of the fishhawk, and the chattering of monkeys pursuing their gambols among the trees. This must, however, be taken *cum grano salis;* for in the rainy season the river overflows its banks and inundates the country.

6. The River St. Paul's has its source in the same range of hills from which the Karamanka issues; and, by barometrical measurement, these hills are 1,400 feet in height, which is about the elevation of the head waters of the Mis-

sissippi. The scenery of the upper St. Paul's will, therefore, compare with that of the Karamanka, although more than two degrees intervene between their outlets.

7. The late Major Laing thus describes the country bordering on the latter river: "The valleys are picturesque and fertile, and are watered by numerous rivulets, which, running from north to south, collect behind the lofty hill of Botato, and contribute in swelling the river Karamanka. I was frequently induced to stop to contemplate the lovely scene around me, consisting of extensive meadows clothed with verdure; fields, from which the springing rice was sending forth its vivid shoots, not inferior in beauty and health to the corn-fields of England in March, interspersed here and there with a patch of ground studded with palm-trees; while the neighboring hills—some clothed with rich foliage, some exhibiting a bald and weather-beaten appearance—formed a noble theater around me.

8. "We left the town of Nijiniah, on the Karamanka, and having walked an hour and three quarters, gained the summit of one of the hills; and in one direction, on the opposite side, a scene quite panoramic broke upon the view: an extensive valley, partly cultivated and partly covered with a long, natural grass, about five feet high, with lines of stately palm-trees, as regular as if laid out by art, and here and there a cluster of camwood trees, their deep shade affording a relief to the lighter hue of the smaller herbage.

9. "These, with a murmuring rivulet, meandering through the center, exhibited the appearance of a well-cultivated and tastefully arranged garden, rather than a tract amid the wilds of Africa; while in the distance, mountain towered above mountain in all the grandeur and magnificence of nature."

10. On both shores of Stockton Creek, as well as on the Mesurado, are many alligators' nests. They are about four feet high, and five in diameter at the base, made of mud

and grass, very much resembling haycocks. The female first deposits a layer of eggs on a floor of a kind of mortar, and she and her mate having covered this with mud and herbage, she lays another set of eggs, and so on to the top, there being sometimes as many as 200 eggs in a nest. All is plastered over with mud by the tail, and the grass around the nest is beat down with the same member, to prevent an unseen approach of enemies. The female then watches the nest until the young are hatched by heat of the sun; when she takes them under her care.

CHAPTER LIII.
THE JALOFF AND MANDINGO RACES.

1. THE Jaloff is the tallest race of men I have ever seen, and forcibly reminded me of the fabulous accounts of the Patagonians. They inhabit the vast district extending along the coast from the Gambia to the Senegal. Their frames are rather slight than muscular; they are coal-black in their complexions, and have the short, crisped hair peculiar to the negro race; but have not the thick lips, flat nose, and low, receding forehead which, in our ideas, are associated with the features of the African. On the contrary, with the Caucasian, they have prominent noses, and their foreheads are high but narrowing at the temples.

2. Each one carries himself as stately as if he were a monarch, the women as much so as the men, and with the same proportion as elsewhere, in the respective size of the sexes. I am not alone in the opinion that the females are, on an average, as tall as men are with us. It is a very interesting race. The Europeans here represent them as easily managed by gentle means, but exceedingly danger-

ous when provoked, and as being very expert in the use of fire-arms. In point of stature they correspond with the Berri, a tall race of men toward the other side of the continent. The Jaloffs are high-toned and courteous, and, in contradistinction to the other tribes, are called by foreigners the "gentlemen of Africa."

3. The Mandingoes are from the banks of the Gambia, from Manding down to the coast. It is a numerous and powerful race, with more of the characteristic features of the negro than the Jaloffs. They are represented as lively in their dispositions, prone to traffic, and with some taste for literature—a literature confined to the Koran. It is said they read no other book, and are taught no other lessons in their schools but an unmeaning repetition of its laws and precepts. I question the correctness of the assertion. The songs of the Jelli, or singing men, would bespeak a higher intellectual cultivation. Mr. Laing visited in 1822 the walled town of Kakundi, in the country of Melicouri, and was there introduced to King Yaradee, one of the chiefs of Sulima.

4. On that occasion was recited the following song, which is almost as poetic and far more genuine than the fabled poems of Ossian. It commemorates an advantage gained by Yaradee over the Foulahs, at the time when ten thousand of them, headed by Ba Dembah, laid siege to Falata: "Shake off that drowsiness, brave Yaradee, thou lion of war! Hang thy sword to thy side, and be thyself! Dost thou not behold the army of the Foulahs? Observe their lines of muskets and spears, vying in brightness with the rays of the departing sun!

5. "They are strong and powerful; yea, they are men! and they have sworn on the Al Koran that they will destroy the capital of the Sulima nation. So, shake off that drowsiness, brave Yaradee, thou lion of war! The brave Talaheer, thy sire, held the Foulahs in contempt. Fear was a stranger to his bosom! He set the firebrand to Timbo, that nest of the Islamites; and, though worsted at

Herico, he scorned to quit the field, but fell like a hero, cheering his war-men. If thou art worthy to be called the son of Talaheer, shake off that drowsiness, brave Yaradee, thou lion of war!

6. "Brave Yaradee stirred. He shook his garments of war, as the soaring eagle ruffles his pinions. Ten times he addressed his gree-grees, and swore to them that he would either return in triumph to the sound of the war-drum, or that the cries of the Jelli should bewail his fall. The war-men shouted with joy. Behold! he shakes from him that drowsiness, the lion of war! he hangs his sword by his side, and is now himself!

7. "Follow me to the field! exclaimed the heroic Yaradee! Fear nothing! for, let the spear be sharp, or the ball be swift, faith in your gree-grees will preserve you from danger. Follow me to the field! for I am roused, and have shook off that drowsiness. I am brave Yaradee, the lion of war! I have hung my sword by my side, and am myself. I have shook off that drowsiness. The war-drum sounds, and the sweet notes of the balla encourage warriors to deeds of arms. The valiant Yaradee mounts his steed! His headmen follow! The northern gate of Falaba is thrown open, and they rush from it with the swiftness of leopards. Yaradee is a host in himself! Observe how he wields his sword! They fall before him! They stagger! They reel! Foulah men! you will long remember this day! for Yaradee has shook off his drowsiness, the lion of war! He has hung his sword by his side, and is himself."

8. By way of contrast of the turn of thought and mode of expression, I give the account of a Bornou man, related by himself: "My years were eighteen. There was war. At that time my mother died; My father died. I buried them. I had done. The Foulahs caught me. They sold me. The Housa people bought us. They brought us to Tomba. We got up. We came to the Popo country. The Popoes took us. To a white man they sold us. The

white man took us. We had no shirts. We had no trowsers. We were naked. Into the midst of the water—into the midst of a ship they put us. Thirst killed somebody. Hunger killed somebody. By night we prayed. At suntime we prayed. God heard us. The English are good. God sent them. They came. They took us. Our hunger died. Our thirst died. Our chains went off from our feet. Shirts they gave us. Trowsers they gave us. Hats they gave us. Every one was glad. We all praised the English. Whoever displeases the English, into hell let him go."

9. The Mandingoes manufacture cotton cloths and dye them with indigo and other vegetable dyes in colors so fixed as to resist, it is said, the action of acids and light—a quality surpassing that of any other known dye-stuff in the world. The Mandingo indigo-plant, as it is here called, has a deep-green leaf, with a number of spear-shaped leaflets along the sides of a common leaf-stalk, opposite to each other and abruptly winged, and may therefore be classed among compound leaves. From thirty leaves of this plant nearly an ounce of pure indigo has been obtained. The Mandingoes are skilled also in the tanning of hides and the preparation of leather; and the specimens which I saw of their bridles, whips, pouches, sword and dagger sheaths, and powder-horns far surpass all I had conceived of native manufacture.

CHAPTER LIV.
LIBERIA—PAST, PRESENT, AND FUTURE.

1. For about twenty-five years the Colony of Liberia remained under the control of the American Colonization Society, which had planted, and up to that time had fos-

tered it. But the Society could not protect it against the impositions of jealous foreigners, who, finding a youthful but growing civilized and Christian community on the coast, having no official connection with any powerful government, did all they could to annoy and crush this young people. The community could not appeal to any government for protection—could not avail itself of the rights guaranteed by the law of nations, for it was not a nation.

2. The only way left to the people to secure themselves from annoyances and impositions was to assume the control of their own political affairs, declare themselves a sovereign and independent state, secure recognition, and thus be able to treat with foreign nations. The people met in convention, earnestly discussed the matter, and agreed to declare themselves an independent state. The Society interposed no objection, but quietly withdrew its supervision and left them to the government of themselves. On the 26th of July, 1847, they presented to the world a Declaration of Independence.

3. The nationality of Liberia then came into existence under peculiar circumstances. Its independence was achieved peaceably, without the accessories of battle and smoke, the noise of the warrior, and garments rolled in blood. When, therefore, we speak of the independence of Liberia, we do not speak of it in an antagonistic or aggressive sense, as *against* any other nation, but simply in a particular, individual, or distinctive sense, in contradistinction to, or separation from, any other nation.

4. But peaceably and quietly as this nationality has been brought about, it has done and is now doing immense good. The declaration of the independence of Liberia, the establishment of the first republican government on the western shores of Africa, did not, it is true, solve any intricate problem in the history of nations. It did not shed any new light upon mankind with reference to the science of government. It was not the result of the elaboration of any novel principle in politics. But it has

poured new vigor into the poor, dying existence of the African all over the world.

5. It has opened a door of hope for a race long the doomed victims of oppression. It has animated colored men everywhere to fresh endeavors to prove themselves men. It has given the example of a portion of this despised race, far away in the midst of heathenism and barbarism, under the most unfavorable circumstances, assuming the responsibilities and coming forward into the ranks of nations; and it has demonstrated that, notwithstanding the oppression of ages, the energies of the race have not been entirely emasculated, but are still sufficient to establish and to maintain a nationality.

6. Soon after the Declaration of Independence, Liberia was welcomed into the family of nations by Great Britain and France. Then followed, one after another, all the great nations of Europe, except Russia, and that great empire has recently given tokens of friendship. The emperor sent to the capital of Liberia, in January, 1865, on a complimentary visit, a first-class Russian frigate, the Dneitry Donskoy.

7. Liberia is in treaty stipulations with Great Britain, France, the Hanseatic States, the Netherlands, Belgium, Denmark, Sweden and Norway, Italy, Portugal, the United States, and Hayti. The United States, though rather tardy in according them a formal acknowledgment, has, nevertheless, always treated them as a *de facto* government. Her squadrons on the coast have always been at the service of the government of Liberia; and their gallant officers, whether Northerners or Southerners, Red Republicans, Abolitionists, or Democrats, have always cheerfully responded to the call of that government. And the highest diplomatic representative they have yet had the pleasure of receiving from abroad is the accomplished Abraham Hanson, Esq., United States Commissioner and Consul-General.

8. They are now gradually growing in all the elements

of national stability. The resources of the country are daily being developed. Their exports of sugar, coffee, arrow-root, ginger, palm-oil, camwood, ivory, etc., are increasing every year—a fact that gives assurance of the continued growth, progress, and perpetuity of their institutions. The form of the government is republican. They have copied, as closely as possible, after the United States, their legislative, judicial, military, and social arrangements being very similar to those of this country. A writer in *Fraser's Magazine*, in quoting the dictum of Sir George Cornwall Lewis, that "man is an historical animal," says that it is "confirmed by the remarkable definiteness with which new nations repeat in embryonic development the stages through which their ancestral nations have passed." Liberia is another illustration.

9. In organizing a government for themselves on that far-off coast, there seemed to be an historic necessity that the people should adopt the republican form—and adopt it with nearly all the defects of the Republic whence they had emigrated, and for which they entertained a traditional reverence. But they are learning by experience. The people are now occupied with the discussion of fundamental changes; and it is very likely that the ideas of the progressive portion of the Republic will soon become a part of the organic law of the land. And when once the country is freed from the frequent recurrence of seasons of political conflicts, which, among a small people, must always be injurious, there will be nothing to interfere with their progress.

CHAPTER LV.
THE ST. PAUL'S RIVER IN 1866.

1. It was in the spring of 1840, on our first return voyage to the United States, that we stopped at Monrovia for a week or two, and were the guests of that truly great and good man, the late Governor Thomas Buchanan. He was evidently not an agriculturist in his tastes or habits of life. He had a distinct mission, and apprehended it. That mission was to train a young community to self-reliance and self-respect, politically and socially. The former object he had to some good extent accomplished by drilling Liberians in military tactics (for which he had an evident fondness), and leading them to victory against their most boastful and formidable foe, Gatoombah, who at a distance of forty miles interior, from a strongly fortified town, had invaded an outpost of the settlement at Heddington, and threatened further aggressions.

2. Governor Buchanan, with the aid of the future President Roberts and General Lewis, assaulted the defiant warrior in his stronghold, took it, and forced him to sue for peace. Amid much obloquy he was laboring to advance also the social character of the Liberians, at the time of our visit. But, though chiefly occupied with these objects, and with establishing honorable relations between his own and foreign countries, he of course looked forward to the time when Liberia should develop her vast agricultural resources.

3. And with a view of giving us some idea of these, he proposed a row in his barge up the river. But certainly this was not very inspiring. For he only proceeded about seven miles by Stockton Creek, connecting the Mesurado with the St. Paul's River, through the dismal swamp of mangroves lining this stream of water to its

happy exit into the St. Paul's. Here one gets the life-giving sea-breeze coming fresh through the mouth of the St. Paul's, three or four miles distant. But the Governor did not even reach that point. Through an opening in the mangroves, he conducted me to what, by courtesy I suppose, was called "the Government Farm." Certainly, even to one not accustomed as he had been to the splendid farms of Pennsylvania, this was a forlorn object.

4. The wreck of an old sugar-mill, that had never made any sugar, a few cotton plants indicating an abortive effort to cultivate this valuable article, was all that indicated that we might be standing on a farm. It was said that some parties among them, the late Mr. Blackledge, had essayed something like a sugar farm higher up on the St. Paul's, but evidently, though he afterward became a very successful planter, at this time his efforts and those of others similarly occupied were held in low repute by the merchants and shopkeepers of Monrovia.

5. Now let us contrast this with what we saw and heard on Friday, April 20th, when at the kind invitation of Mr. W. Spencer Anderson, we rowed up the St. Paul's twenty miles, to dine at his residence on Gandilla Farm. Emerging from Stockton Creek, of which the less said the better, except to warn foreigners to beware of passing through its foul atmosphere early in the morning or late in the evening, we meet the pleasant sea-breeze coming up from the mouth of the St. Paul's. And at once we feel we are in a civilized country. On the right, in Lower Caldwell, near the spot where Rev. Mr. Cesar, first Episcopal missionary, drowned himself in a fit of insanity, is the modest but neat establishment of Mr. Powers, with store and hotel.

6. Here, too, is a modest frame building with quite as modest a congregation, called St. Peter's Episcopal Church. Proceeding up the river, we saw two Baptist and Methodist churches, each of brick, on either side of the river. Just opposite to Mr. Powers', on the Virginia side of the

river, is the neat, home-like residence of Rev. J. W. Roberts, Bishop of the Liberia Methodist Conference. The settlement of Virginia here extends back three or four miles from the river. Above Mr. Roberts', we soon see the fine brick houses of Mr. William Blackledge and Rev. A. F. Russell. Presently we come to Clay Ashland, where besides Grace (Episcopal) Church are three others, representing what is called the University of Virginia, the "Quadrangular Orthodoxy."

7. Here are many fine brick houses, the township of Clay Ashland extending back four or five miles, and now we never lose sight again of cultivated fields and comfortable brick houses. Best among these are those of the Messrs. Cooper, DeCoursey, Anderson, Howland, and Washington, sugar planters. By the time we reach the Gandilla Farm, we have passed four steam mills, all hard at work. We find Mr. Anderson just grinding off his last cane. There are many wooden mills besides those propelled by steam.

8. An intelligent friend has given us the following, as an approximate estimate of the sugar crop on the St. Paul's in 1866: Sharp, 120,000 lbs.; Cooper, 30,000; Anderson, 35,000; Howland, 40,000; Roe, 30,000; sundry smaller farmers, 150,000; total 575,000 lbs. The coffee crop also is considerable, though we are not able to state how much.

CHAPTER LVI.

EXTRACT FROM MESSAGE OF PRES. WARNER, 1865.

1. IT affords me inexpressible pleasure to refer to the cessation of the unhappy contest in the United States; and especially as it has terminated in the permanent extinction, I trust, of human bondage throughout that great country.

2. An unbounded prosperity, doubtless, lies before that nation, rid, as it is, of the incubus which, from its foundation, has preyed upon its vitals. But in the month of July, in the midst of our rejoicings at the triumphs of the banner of freedom, a feeling of unutterable horror and indignation was sent throughout this land, pervading every household, and saddening every heart, by the intelligence that the President of the United States, the illustrious Abraham Lincoln, had fallen by the hand of an assassin.

3. Liberia, perhaps more than any other independent community, and for peculiar reasons, felt the shock of the melancholy death, and bewailed the loss of Abraham Lincoln. How prophetical was the remark which, nearly two years since, he is said to have uttered, that "When this war is done, I shall be done too."

4. On the 10th of May last we had an accession of 346 immigrants by the brig Cora from the island of Barbadoes. They were sent out under the auspices of the American Colonization Society; but owing to the people being from a country not included in the constitutional provisions of the Society, but more particularly on account of the high prices of provisions, the usual six months' supplies could not be furnished them.

5. This threw them, after being two months in the country, upon the support of the government, until such time as they should be able to support themselves. For this emergency the government treasury was both unprovided and unprepared, and it became therefore a subject of serious consideration and much embarrassment. To relieve the people, however, everything was done that the state of the finances would permit.

6. Just here I take great pleasure in stating, in justice to the citizens generally, and to the Ladies' Benevolent and Union Sisters of Charity Societies in particular, that from these respective sources the newly arrived and necessitous immigrants received very considerable assistance and unremitting attention during their illness. Much gratitude

is also due, and I most cheerfully record the expression of the same, to the American Colonization Society, for its very liberal donation of $10,000 expended in transporting the West Indians to these shores, and supporting them here two months. If any benefit is to be derived from the enterprise it will be exclusively ours.

7. Those of the immigrants who removed from Monrovia are located, some at Carysburg, and others on the road leading thither. Some of them have not done so well. Some have died, mostly from disappointment after the first emotions of joy. These appear to have been carried away by romantic notions of the country to which they were coming. They entirely overlooked, or did not sufficiently appreciate the costs and sacrifices of leaving scenes and associations with which from their birth they had been connected.

8. They did not take into account the ocean to be crossed, the difficulties of a new country, an acclimation more or less severe to be passed through. They saw nothing but "the land of promise," and the gift of twenty-five acres of land; when unexpected trials came upon them, therefore, they sank under their weight. I am happy to say, however, that the great majority of the immigrants are doing well, and promise to be a valuable acquisition to our little commonwealth.

9. On the subject of immigration we can not but feel a deep interest. Our population is still exceedingly scanty. Our need of population is immediate and urgent. Our immense resources can not be developed, the fruits of the earth, spontaneously produced, can not be gathered, the fat of the land can not be made available, simply for the want of minds and hands to engage in the necessary operations. Surely with the vast latent capabilities of this country, we have the ability to become a power, by no means to be despised, in the agricultural and commercial world.

10. We have again and again invited our brethren in the United States to come over and help us fill up the vast

solitudes which for centuries have remained uninhabited; while they in exile in the Western Hemisphere are jostled and elbowed and trampled upon by an oppressive race. But my hopes are as strong as ever, and my confidence remains unshaken in the destiny of Liberia. She is yet to be the asylum for the oppressed American negro, and a beacon for the guidance of the benighted tribes of this continent. I may not be able to predict the methods by which Africa's exiled sons are to be restored to her bosom, but I feel certain that such an occurrence will in some way or other take place.

11. It is the most likely solution of the vexed negro question in the United States, and the only one that has yet suggested itself to the most distinguished statesmen and philanthropists of that country. And it is gratifying to notice that this view of probable events is beginning to be entertained by some of the leading black men also.* Things are evidently tending to that condition when the most indifferent of our oppressed brethren in the United States will be compelled to give the question of emigration a serious, studious, and systematic consideration—a question upon which their physical and political well-being greatly depends.

12. Africa is to be opened. The eyes of the enterprising in Europe are intent upon the discovery of the secrets of science and of wealth hidden in the unexplored regions of this continent. The necessities of commerce and the desire of mankind will compel this land to contribute to the comfort and luxury of other quarters of the globe. We in Liberia have been permitted to make a very promising opening; and applications are being made to us by capitalists in foreign lands, or their agents, to be allowed to take part with us in the work of subjugating this continent.

CHAPTER LVII.
VIEWS OF AN INTELLIGENT EMIGRANT.*

1. I HAVE the honor to state that, as undoubtedly many of you are well aware, my family and myself left the city of New York, in the barque "Thomas Pope," on the 3d of June, 1865, for the Republic of Liberia. After a very pleasant voyage of thirty-five days we arrived at Monrovia, July 9th, about four o'clock in the afternoon. Monday, at noon, we landed safely on the soil of Africa, without any serious accident. Our reception at the time, and treatment since, have been all that we could desire.

2. I found Monrovia beautifully located on Cape Mesurado, handsomely laid out, and in time, when she has had the benefits of population, capital, industry, and enterprise, will be a great and magnificent city! Nature has fully contributed her share toward the accomplishment of this grand result. True, there are some obstacles to be removed, but these seem to have been placed here only to serve as a *stimulus to the industry and enterprise of the colored emigrants* from America. With some improvements the harbor of Monrovia could afford a safe shelter for all the navies of the world! All the sea-captains with whom I have conversed here say that there are but few harbors in the world superior to Mesurado Bay.

3. So far, I have found the climate very delightful. It is never cold, nor extremely hot. Up to this time, the

---

* The author of the above communication, H. W. Johnson, Jr., was for many years a (colored) resident of Canandaigua, N. Y., where he rose, by his own exertions, from the humble position of a barber, to the honored rank of a legal practitioner at the bar of the Supreme Court of the State of New York. He went to Liberia because he thought he could be more useful and happy there than in America.

lowest I have seen the mercury is 66°, and the highest 86°. The grass is always green, and the flowers always in bloom. Fruits and vegetables indigenous to this climate, and those that have been transplanted here from other countries, grow and ripen during the whole year. In regard to the face of the country, in a word, it is picturesque and *grand beyond all conception.* The view of Monrovia and the adjacent country from College Hill, the fort, and lighthouse, is perfectly magnificent!

4. Although we have had the fever in our family during the last six months, and have suffered severely in body, mind, and in purse, yet I have seen no cause to regret that I came to Liberia. On the contrary, I return thanks to God, that through the influence of some friends of colonization, the aid rendered by the Society, and the favorable representations of the Rev. Mr. Crummell (Professor in Liberia College), that my mind ever conceived the thought and encouraged the idea to come to this country. All that has transpired since I left America, and all I have witnessed since my arrival here, have only confirmed me in the belief that *Africa is the best home for the oppressed black men of America!*

5. While in America, I was weighed down with the thought that I was constantly in the presence of those who considered me inferior to them for no other reason *than because I wear the dark skin given me by my Creator!* The wisdom of a Solomon, the virtues of a saint, nor the wealth of the Indies can lift this burden from the soul of a sensitive colored man who *values liberty, self-respect, independence, and manhood!* But from the time I landed on the soil of Africa, down to the present, I have felt like a new man—I have felt as free as the air we breathe, and the *ponderous weight of human bondage has rolled off from my soul.* My citizenship is acknowledged; my rights respected; my wrongs redressed; and my manhood fully recognized! This is what Liberia will do for every black man who seeks an asylum on the soil of Africa.

6. With regard to the means of obtaining a living here, they are ample, cheap, and abundant, and *sure, if the emigrant will rely upon the cultivation of the soil.* You must not infer from this that there are no other means of obtaining a living and amassing a fortune in Liberia. By no means. On the contrary, here is a broad field for the citizen, the merchant, the mechanic—for those who have qualified themselves for the learned professions, etc. The country being new, and its resources almost inexhaustible, no country in the world can hold out greater inducements for colored men of intelligence, industry, and enterprise than Liberia.

7. In view of this fact, how lamentable it is that so many thousands of intelligent colored men in America, possessing fine talents and ample means, will continue to "hug their chains," "kiss the rod that smites them," finally die in despair, and entail upon their children the same wrongs which they (themselves) have endured for ages past and gone, when they can obtain all they desire within the limits of the *Republic of Liberia!* Merciful God! what stupidity and blindness!

8. I mean to state the facts as they really are. I will not deceive any one. A person coming to Liberia must not forget he is coming to a new country—that but little over forty years ago the place upon which Monrovia now stands was a dense, unbroken wilderness and bush—infested with beasts and serpents; inhabited by ignorant, degraded, superstitious, wild, and hostile tribes of natives; that the slave trade then existed with all its bloody horrors and inhuman atrocities!

9. What a change has taken place on this spot since that eventful period! Churches of the true and living God, temples of justice, halls of learning, neat and comfortable dwellings, well-regulated towns and villages, cultivated fields, and a growing commerce now fill their places! In fine, the seeds of a Christian civilization have been planted, deeply rooted, and have sprung up on the soil of Africa,

and given birth to a new Republic, which, in our day, will afford an asylum to the down-trodden and oppressed colored man in every quarter of the globe; and spread religion and law, light and civilization throughout every portion of this broad and beautiful land.

CHAPTER LVIII.
ADDRESS OF THE HON. ABRAHAM HANSON,
CONSUL-GENERAL FROM THE UNITED STATES.

1. In May, 1862, I accepted the humble, but honorable office of Commercial Agent of the United States in Monrovia. In December, 1863, the position of Commissioner and Consul-General of the United States to the Republic of Liberia was intrusted to my hands, the duties of which I still continue to discharge. I have resided in Liberia about three years. During this time I have interested myself in whatever promised to extend and strengthen the commercial and friendly relations between the two countries. I have made several visits along the coast and up the rivers, going from farm to farm, and from house to house, and thus, from verbal statements and personal observation, have acquired a knowledge of the industrious habits and domestic comforts of the citizens.

2. In every direction new plantations are being commenced, and old ones materially enlarged and improved, so that I can testify that the progress in this department promises well for the future, and full development of the rich resources of the prolific soil.

3. Coffee bids fair to become the basis of many an independent fortune. It is cultivated with ease, and with comparatively small expense. Its maturity and fruitfulness

are not retarded, but rather advanced, by the use of the intervening space for the growth of smaller plants. The entire lack of suitable machinery for hulling has, heretofore, deterred many from engaging in this branch of agriculture, but this want, I am happy to state, is soon to be supplied, and you may expect in a few years a regular shipment of large quantities of coffee, as palatable and nutritious as any that is produced in any other part of the world.

4. Sugar-cane has, I think, received a much larger share of attention than coffee, owing chiefly to the fact that it yields an earlier return. There are four steam sugar mills along the banks of the St. Paul's River, besides several wooden mills. Had I been a commercial man, I could have brought home orders for a dozen mills from parties who are generally responsible, and who offer a reasonable guarantee to secure the payment. Specimens of cane have been brought to my office more than sixteen feet in length, and from seven to eight inches in circumference at the base, of one season's growth. More than one third of the juice of such cane is lost to those who have only wooden mills to express it.

5. The article of cotton is not yet extensively cultivated, though I believe it is attracting more attention than formerly, and that which has been exported has commanded a high price and much praise for its superior staple. But it would be presumptuous in me to enter into a minute detail of the various productions of the soil of Liberia before such an audience as I conceive this to be. I may say for the satisfaction of the officers and members, as well as the patrons of this Society, that I know from observation, that the glowing reports which now come to you, from month to month, and which appear in your various periodicals and magazines, are, in the main, founded upon tangible facts.

6. There is not, there need not be on all this globe, a richer soil, a soil which yields more prompt and ample re-

turns to the labor of the industrious husbandman, than that of Liberia. She has land enough to *give* a free home to millions who may go hence to aid in her future progress; a home where numerous, various, and substantial products may be obtained with less than half the labor required in many other countries. .And, moreover, it is obvious to those who know the habits of the aborigines, their aptitude to trade, especially, that as Christian civilization and commerce advance, the door of the almost illimitable interior will be thrown open, not by force of arms, by deeds of blood, or exterminating influences, but by the firm and steady progress of the arts and sciences.

7. The present condition of the people of this Republic is encouraging. On every hand, I have seen the proofs of useful industry. All along the rivers, as well as in the settlements on the coast, the bamboo hut, the log cabin, and sometimes the frame house, begin to give way for the commodious and substantial stone or brick edifice. They are furnished as good taste would dictate, not with what is usually termed elegance, but with modern conveniences to an extent beyond what many would expect to find in that far-off land. In accepting of the generous hospitalities of Liberian merchants and planters, I have always found their tables supplied with the substantial elements of food.

8. Perhaps it is expected that I should say something in reference to the climate of Liberia. From its location on the globe you will naturally infer that it is uniformly warm. My residence in Monrovia is in 6° 9′ north latitude, but though so near the equator, the air is tempered daily by breezes from the sea. The seasons of the year are two, the rainy and the dry; the former commences with May, and the latter with November. The thermometer averages about 75° Fahr., and seldom rises above 90° in the shade. Yet, with all these elements of comfort, *it is not the white man's home.* Africans who have descended from an ancestry absent from the continent for from one to two cen-

turies, can, with good habits and proper care, survive the change and enjoy health, while the white man droops and dies.

9. My observation leads me to the conclusion, that a greater amount of mortality is occasioned by unnecessary anxiety, unfounded apprehensions of danger, unreasonable and immoderate bodily exercise, want of abstinence from improper food during convalescence, the want of suitable remedies during the fiercest attacks of fever, than from the actual, and, if I may use the terms, the avoidable or curable effects of fever.

10. Hear what the eloquent and learned Hon. E. W. Blyden said to his fellow-citizens, on the 26th of July last, the anniversary of the independence of the nation which he serves as Secretary of State. Speaking of their location on the coast, he says: " Here is a land adapted to us, given to us by Providence—peculiarly ours, to the exclusion of alien races. On every hand we can look and say it is ours. Ours are the serene skies that bend above us; ours the twinkling stars and brilliant planets—Pleiades, and Venus, and Jupiter; the thunder of the clouds; the roaring of the sea; the rustling of the forest; the murmur of the brooks, and the whispers of the breeze."

11. The Liberia College stands as a noble monument of the munificence of its founders. Under the presidency of the Hon. J. J. Roberts, the benefactor of his race, and with the coöperation of the able faculty, a foundation is being laid, broad, deep, extensive, and permanent, to raise up instruments for Africa's redemption from thralldom and from darkness.

12. As the immigrant plants his feet upon the soil of his ancestors, and directs his wandering gaze from point to point, he beholds Christian temples rearing their humble but inviting fronts. He listens to the " church-going bell." He hears voices, joining in hallelajahs to God, which rend the still air, and ascend as incense to the skies; while countenances irradiated with ineffable, heaven-born

brightness assure him that here Jehovah is known and worshiped; that Christ is honored and adored; and that the Holy Ghost diffuses his convincing, quickening, regenerating, sanctifying, saving power. Among all classes in Liberia, from the President down to the humblest walks of life, you can find those upon whom the badge of Christian discipleship is placed with honorable prominence.

13. And now I must close by asking, Who can take a careful glance at what the people of Liberia were; at the circumstances which have surrounded them; at what they have accomplished, and at what they are doing to-day, and not pause, and wonder, and give God thanks, and take courage? Liberia lives, yonder, a striking monument, not less remarkable to me than the bush burning with fire, yet unconsumed! And what is more, my humble faith in the immutable promises of God assures me that she shall continue to live and grow, for she is emphatically a foster-child of Providence. In spite of the supineness of some of her professed friends, and the sneers and open opposition of her cruel foes, she is stronger to-day in moral power and political wisdom than ever she has been before.

14. Were I a member of that race, with my knowledge of the tremendous weight that still oppresses them, and of the illimitable field which invites them to Liberia, with its innumerable facilities for comfort, independence, and usefulness, I should gather my family around me and embark on board the first vessel bound for that distant shore, even if I had to avail myself of the generous aid which the Colonization Society offers.

CHAPTER LIX.
AFRICA AT THE PRESENT DAY.
BY EDWARD EVERETT.

1. AFRICA at the present day is not in that state of utter barbarism which popular opinion ascribes to it. Here, we do not sufficiently discriminate. We judge in the gross. Certainly there are tribes wholly broken down by internal wars and the detestable foreign slave trade; but this is not the character of the entire population. They are not savages. Most of them live by agriculture. There is some traffic between the coast and the interior. Many of the tribes have a respectable architecture, though of a rude kind, but still implying some progress of the arts. Gold dust is collected; iron is smelted and wrought; weapons and utensils of husbandry and household use are fabricated; cloth is woven and dyed; palm-oil is expressed; there are schools; and among the Mohammedan tribes the Koran is read.

2. You, Mr. President, well remember that twenty-one years ago you and I saw, in one of the committee-rooms of yonder Capitol, a native African who had been forty years a field slave in the West Indies and in this country, and wrote at the age of seventy the Arabic character with the fluency and the elegance of a scribe. Why, sir, to give the last test of civilization, Mungo Park tells us in his journal that in the interior of Africa lawsuits are argued with as much ability, as much fluency, and at as much length as in Edinburgh.

3. Sir, I do not wish to run into paradox on this subject. I am aware that the condition of the most advanced tribes of Central Africa is wretched, mainly in consequence of the slave trade. The only wonder is that with this cancer eating into their vitals from age to age, any degree of

civilization whatever can exist. But degraded as the ninety millions of Africans are, I presume you might find in the aggregate, on the continent of Europe, another ninety millions as degraded, to which each country in that quarter of the globe would contribute its quota. The difference is, and it is certainly an all-important difference, that in Europe, intermingled with these ninety millions, are fifteen or twenty millions possessed of all degrees of culture up to the very highest, while in Africa there is not an individual who, according to our standard, has attained a high degree of intellectual culture; but if obvious causes for this can be shown, it is unphilosophical to infer from it an essential incapacity.

4. But the question seems to me to be put at rest by what we all must have witnessed of what has been achieved by the colored race in this country and on the coast of Africa. Unfavorable as their position has been for any intellectual progress, we still all of us know that they are competent to the common arts and business of life, to the ingenious and mechanical arts, to keeping accounts, to the common branches of academical and professional culture.

5. Paul Cuffee's name is familiar to everybody in my part of the country, and I am sure you have heard of him. He was a man of uncommon energy and force of character. He navigated to Liverpool his own vessel, manned by a colored crew. His father was a native African slave; his mother was a member of one of the broken-down Indian tribes, some fragments of which still linger in the corners of Massachusetts. I must also allude to the extraordinary attainments of that native African prince, Abdul Rahhahman. If there was ever a native-born gentleman on earth he was one. He had the port and air of a prince, and the literary culture of a scholar.

6. The learned blacksmith of Alabama, now in Liberia, has attained a celebrity scarcely inferior to his white brother who is known by the same designation. When I lived in Cambridge a few years ago, I used to attend, as one of

the Board of Visitors, the examinations of a classical school in which there was a colored boy, the son of a slave in Mississippi, I think. He appeared to me to be of pure African blood. There were at the same time two youths from Georgia, and one of my own sons, attending the same school. I must say that this poor negro boy, Beverly Williams, was one of the best scholars at the school, and in the Latin language he was the best scholar in his class. These are instances that have fallen under my own observation. There are others I am told which show still more conclusively the aptitude of the colored race for every kind of intellectual culture.

7. Now look at what they have done on the coast of Africa. It is only twenty-five or thirty years since that little Colony was founded under the auspices of the American Colonization Society. In that time what have they done; or rather, what have they not done? They have established a well-organized constitution of republican government, which is administered with ability and energy in peace, and by the unfortunate necessity of circumstances, also in war. They have courts of justice, modeled after our own; schools, churches, and lyceums. Commerce is carried on, the soil is tilled, communication is open to the interior. The native tribes are civilized; diplomatic relations are creditably sustained with foreign powers; and the two leading powers of Europe, England and France, have acknowledged their sovereignty and independence. Would the same number of persons taken principally from the laboring classes of any portion of England or Anglo-America have done better than this?

8. Ah! sir, there is an influence at work through the agency of this Society, and other societies, and through the agency of the Colony of Liberia, and others which I hope will be established, sufficient to produce these and still greater effects. I mean the influence of pure, unselfish Christian love. This, after all, is the only influence that never can fail. Military power will at times be resisted

and overcome. Commercial enterprise, however well planned, may be blasted. State policy, however deep, may be outwitted; but pure, unselfish, manly, rather let me say heavenly, love never did, and in the long run never will, fail. It is a truth which this Society ought to write upon its banners, that it is not political nor military power, but the moral sentiment, principally under the guidance and influence of religious zeal, that has in all ages civilized the world. Arms, craft, and mammon lie in wait and watch their chance, but they can not poison its vitality.

9. Whatever becomes of the question of intellectual superiority, I should insult this audience if I attempted to argue that in the moral sentiments the colored race stand upon an equality with us. I read a year or two ago in a newspaper an anecdote which illustrates this in so beautiful and striking a manner that, with your permission, I will repeat it.

10. When the news of the discovery of gold reached us from California, a citizen of the upper part of Louisiana, from the parish of Rapides, for the sake of improving his not prosperous fortunes, started with his servant to get a share, if he could, of the golden harvest. They repaired to the gold regions. They labored together for a while with success. At length the strength of the master failed and he fell dangerously sick. What then was the conduct of the slave in those far-off hills? In a State whose constitution did not recognize slavery, in that newly gathered and not very thoroughly organized state of society, what was his conduct? As his master lay sick with the typhus fever, Priest and Levite came, and looked upon him, and passed by on the other side. The poor slave stood by him, tended him, protected him, by night and by day his sole companion, nurse, and friend. At length the master died.

11. What then was the conduct of the slave in those distant wastes, as he stood by him whom living he had served, but who was now laid low at his feet by the great Emancipator? He dug his decent grave in the golden

sands. He brought together the earnings of their joint labor; these he deposited in a place of safety as a sacred trust for his master's family. He then went to work under a Californian sun to earn the wherewithal to pay his passage home. That done, he went back to the banks of the Red River, in Louisiana, and laid down the little store at the feet of his master's widow.

12. Sir, I do not know whether the story is true, I read it in a public journal. The Italians have a proverbial saying of a tale like this, that if it is not true it is well invented. This, sir, is too good to be invented. It is, it must be true. That master and that slave ought to live in marble and in brass, and if it was not presumptuous in a person like me, so soon to pass away and to be forgotten, I would say their memory shall never perish.

"Fortunati ambo! si quid mea carmina possint,
Nulla dies unquam memori vos eximet ævo."

13. There is a moral treasure in that incident. It proves the capacity of the colored race to civilize Africa. There is a moral worth in it beyond all the riches of California. If all her gold—all that she has yet yielded to the indomitable industry of the adventurer, and all that she locks from the cupidity of man in the virgin chambers of her snow-clad sierras—were all molten into one vast ingot, it would not, in the sight of Heaven, buy the moral worth of that one incident.

CHAPTER LX.
NATIVE AFRICANS IN LIBERIA.

1. LIKE the aborigines of our own country, those of Africa are divided into numerous tribes, each tribe having a dialect differing to a greater or less extent from those

of the contiguous tribes, and each being characterized by some national peculiarities; the difference, however, in appearance, customs, and superstitions not being very great among the different tribes within the territory of Liberia.

2. The principal tribes in Liberia and its immediate vicinity are the Dey, Vey, Bassa, Queah, Golah, Pessah, Kroo, Fish, and Grebo; the last-named being that tribe in the immediate vicinity of Cape Palmas.

3. The government among the different tribes may be regarded as a kind of compound of the patriarchal, the oligarchal, and the monarchical. In every tribe there is one man who is recognized as the head king, to whom all the other kings and chiefs of the tribe are nominally subordinate. African kings, however, are very numerous. Indeed, in almost every community there is one man who is regarded as a king; his jurisdiction extending over a single hamlet, or a small tract of country, including within its limits several small hamlets.

4. As in European monarchical governments, so among the native tribes of Africa, royalty and governmental authority are usually hereditary. The legal successor of a departed king, however, can not assume his royal station and authority without the concurrence of all the other kings of the tribe; and not unfrequently some other individual, not of the royal family, is appointed by the other kings, with the concurrence of the people over whom he is to preside, in consequence of the minority of the rightful successor—though he may be a man of thirty years of age, or more—or of some other difficulty either imaginary or real. The kingly succession is not so scrupulously observed in Africa as in Europe. And not unfrequently, like Bonaparte and Cromwell, some daring adventurer, sometimes of another and distant tribe, will usurp the power and authority rightly belonging to another, and set up a dominion or kingdom for himself, *vi et armis*, as in the case of the celebrated Boatswain, who rendered valuable assistance to the early settlers of Liberia.

5. In most cases the title is the only thing of which African kings can boast. None of them are ever burdened with wealth. Indeed, most of them are miserably poor. I have seen half a dozen kings, and as many chiefs and headmen, at one time, sitting on the ground as humble mendicants, in submissive patience, awaiting to receive a "dash" (present) of a few pounds of tobacco, from a gentleman in Liberia, at whose place of residence they had assembled.

6. In addition to those persons who are dignified with the honorable appellation of king, there are others of subordinate authority who are generally called headmen. In each hamlet, however small, there is a headman, who has more or less control over all the other residents of the place, and who is responsible for their conduct. The principal mark of distinction between the kings, or the headmen, and the rest of the people, usually consists in the size of the garments which they respectively wear; those of the former generally being rather more extensive than those of the latter. Their style of living does not differ materially from that of any of their subjects, and their palaces can not generally be distinguished from the residences of their untitled subordinates.

7. The natives about Liberia invariably reside in towns or hamlets, few of which contain more than five hundred inhabitants, and most of them less than two hundred. The whole country, except in the immediate vicinity of these towns or hamlets, which are very numerous, presents a deep unbroken forest, the solemn silence of which is seldom disturbed, save by the footsteps and voices of travelers and the noise of wild animals. The houses or huts in which they reside are generally rudely constructed of sticks, usually lined with strong bamboo mats, with which the dirt floors are also sometimes covered. They are always covered with thatch, and sometimes they are daubed outside with mud. Some of their huts are constructed with a little regard to taste and convenience, some are

pretty substantially built, but most of them are filthy, smoky, ugly, disagreeable hovels, presenting indubitable evidence of extreme indolence and improvidence on the part of the inmates.

8. Their almost universal style of dress consists simply of a piece of cotton cloth, or a cotton handkerchief, fastened loosely about their loins; in addition to which a kind of hat is sometimes (not generally) worn, composed of the fibers of some one of the numerous indigenous vegetable substances or of a kind of grass. In addition to the ordinary "girdle about the loins" some of the natives, particularly the kings and headmen, wear a kind of robe loosely thrown across one shoulder and wrapped around the body. These robes are generally manufactured in the country, from the native cotton, which they spin by a very simple though tedious process, and weave into narrow strips, never more than six inches wide, by a process exhibiting a little ingenuity, but not less tedious than that of the spinning.

9. A great deal of their time is occupied in dancing and singing, and in a variety of nonsensical plays. These plays are frequently kept up day and night for several successive days, and sometimes for several weeks. I have frequently heard the sound of their rudely-constructed drums, and other instruments of music, at nearly all hours of both day and night. Some of their musical instruments are quite fanciful in appearance; but none that I ever saw exhibited much ingenuity in their construction. They have various systems of gambling, and many of them are very expert in some of their games. It is not uncommon to see half a dozen, or more, strong, healthy natives sitting on the ground busily engaged in gambling, the amount at stake being a pipe full of tobacco.

10. Several of the tribes have national marks by which the members of a particular tribe may be distinguished from those of any other tribe; in addition to which the bodies of some are variously and sometimes very fantas-

tically tattooed, particularly the breast, back, and arms. Their process of tattooing consists in making numerous small incisions in the skin, over which they rub a kind of paste, usually made of the ashes of a particular shrub, mixed with palm-oil, which leaves an indelible impression, somewhat darker than the contiguous surface.

11. Domestic slavery is very common among all the tribes to which I have alluded, and I presume among all the numerous tribes throughout the whole of Africa. So far as I was able to learn, the Kroomen and the Fishmen are the only tribes on that part of the western coast who do not enslave persons of their tribe; they never enslave each other, and they are seldom enslaved by others. They, however, frequently possess slaves of other tribes, and they are the most active "aiders and abettors" of the nefarious traffic on that part of the coast. They are generally employed in conducting the slaves from the marts on the coast to the slave ships; and from them principally is derived the information relative to the state of the trade.

12. In most cases the slaves owned by individuals of any tribe are of some other tribe. Those who are captured in the wars, and thus reduced to slavery, are generally sold to foreigners; while many of those who are purchased are kept for years by the individuals to whom they belong. It is not uncommon for one man to own several scores of slaves; and in some cases, among the wealthy sons of the forest, several hundreds of their fellow-beings submit in humble obedience to the authority of their princely master. It is not improbable, indeed, that at least five sixths of the whole population of Africa are slaves. In visiting an African hamlet, however, a stranger would be at a loss to distinguish slaves from free men, or even from their masters. But, though they are of similar complexion, and though no prominent mark or badge of distinction can be seen by strangers, yet slaves are easily recognized by other members of the same community, and by members of other

communities of the same tribes, and even by individuals of contiguous tribes.

13. In many cases, however, they live as well as their masters do; and in some cases the state of bondage is apparently only nominal. But, like slaves in other countries, they are always deprived of certain civil and political immunities, which deprivation of course tends to degrade them in the estimation of their more highly favored neighbors. On some parts of the coast, however, as in the vicinity of the Gaboon River, and perhaps in many other parts of Africa, slaves are generally treated with the utmost severity, and are regarded by the free people with the utmost detestation. I have been informed that among some tribes they are held in so little estimation, that the master may take their lives (which is not unfrequently done) for the most trifling offense, with perfect impunity, no legal process ever being instituted to punish the inhuman master in any way; and the only punishment which any other free man would have to endure for a similar offense, would be the payment of the valuation of the slave to his master.

14. In many communities the number of slaves is much greater than that of the free persons; and it might be supposed that insurrections would be common. This, however, is not the case. It might also be supposed that slaves would frequently run away, inasmuch as no recognized marks of distinction between masters and slaves exist in Africa. But they seldom resort to this expedient to obtain their freedom, knowing as they do that such a course (to use a familiar simile) would be a jump from the frying-pan into the fire, inasmuch as they would be doomed to slavery by the people among whom they had fled; and very probably their situation would be worse than before.

15. The ordinary valuation of an able-bodied slave is about thirty dollars in goods, being from fifteen to twenty dollars in money. Young females generally sell for a

few dollars more than males. Very often the wives, or some of them, of African "gentlemen" are their purchased slaves. And sometimes when they get tired of their "better halves" they do not hesitate to sell them to the highest bidder. The custom of fathers selling their children, which is not, I think, so common as it is usually represented in written accounts of the horrors of the African slave trade, arises from the circumstance of the mothers of those children being slaves, and their offspring being so regarded, notwithstanding, as in some instances in other countries, father and master are terms of synonymous applicability.

16. In regard to the various superstitious notions of the ignorant and degraded aborigines of Africa, it would be difficult to measure their extent in any community, or to fathom the depth of degradation and misery thus handed down from one generation to another.

CHAPTER LXI.

THE SUPERSTITIOUS CUSTOMS OF THE NATIVES.

1. AMONG the numerous absurd opinions of a superstitious character which prevail in Western Africa, and which lead to the most foolish practices, the universal belief in *witchcraft* occupies the most prominent position. And associated with this belief, and arising from it, are many of the most nonsensical practices of which the mind can conceive. So grossly absurd, indeed, are the incoherent views of the uneducated native African, in reference to the magical influences of witchcraft, that it is next to impossible to witness their foolish practices, resulting from this belief, even after making every allowance for their want of facilities of intellectual culture, without arriving at the conclu-

sion that there is a natural obliquity of the African mind, unparalleled in all other countries.

2. This prevailing and settled belief in the influences of witchcraft often leads to murderous practices, by which thousands of these poor, degraded beings are hurried into eternity. A most absurd superstition, common among them, is that no person (except very old and worn-out people) dies unless by the agency of some other person, who according to their notions "made witch" for the deceased individual, no matter what may be the circumstances attending his death, whether by protracted disease or by accident. Suspicion generally rests on one individual or more, who was known to have been at enmity with the deceased; or the family of the dead person are consulted, and they seldom fail to accuse some one of having "made witch" for their dead relative. It sometimes happens, however, that no particular person is accused; in which case it is incumbent on the "*gree-gree man*," or doctor (a very important and influential personage in every community), to point out the culprit.

3. The accused person is obliged to undergo the infallible ordeal of "drinking sassa-wood," especially if the deceased had been a person of consequence. This drinking of sassa-wood, which is a universal test of witchcraft, consists in swallowing large quantities of an infusion of the bark of the sassa-wood tree, gulping it down until the distended stomach will not receive any more. If the person rejects from his stomach this poisonous infusion, and lives, his innocence is established; but if he retains it, and consequently dies, his cruel tormentors are satisfied of his guilt.

4. Any person is liable to be accused of witchcraft, or of having caused the death of a deceased person; but generally some old person is fixed on—one whom they wish to get out of the way; or some person with whom the relatives of the deceased are at variance, and on whom they wish to take revenge for some imaginary or real injury.

This is a very common way of being revenged. Sometimes the individual who dies points out before death the person who is accused, and in some cases it is for some injury done many years before, by the accused person himself, or by one of the same family who may already have died. The natives of Africa generally are very revengeful. They harbor such feelings for a long time; nor are they very particular as to the individual on whom they take revenge—if he or she belongs to the same family it is enough.

5. Although the drinking of sassa-wood is professedly regarded as a test of witchcraft, yet perhaps, in most cases, the death of the unfortunate individual who falls a victim to this murderous practice is previously concerted; and in those cases in which the death of the accused person is not desired by the principal operators in this tragical ordeal, the infusion is made so weak as not to produce death. But sometimes the victim is unceremoniously beat to death after having swallowed the liquid; so that, in some cases, the result of this operation of drinking sassa-wood is premeditated. And though a considerable number recover after having submitted to this absurd ordeal, yet thousands, perhaps millions, have been immolated on this altar of African superstition.

6. Most of the natives carry something about them which they call "*gree-gree*," the object of which is to protect them from the various ills to which "flesh is heir." Each of these gree-grees is carried for some specific purpose—to protect them from some particular danger. They are generally suspended around their necks, and are made of various substances, in all imaginable shapes. They are all consecrated by the gree-gree man or doctor. Some are made of the end of a ram's horn, filled with a mysterious charm by the gree-gree man; others are more complex in their workmanship, and of course more various in their potency. Some persons are literally loaded with these foolish amulets. They have gun gree-grees, water, fire,

poison, war, and I know not how many other kinds, to protect them from different kinds of danger. And it is very difficult to induce any of them to sell any of these foolish appendages.

7. The prevailing form of worship among the aborigines in the vicinity of Liberia (if, indeed, it can be said that they really worship anything) is what may be emphatically called *devil worship*—a kind of superstitious reverence and dread of his Satanic majesty—which consists, not in public acts of solemn worship, but in undefined conceptions of the power and agency of the devil in all their affairs, and in various nonsensical methods to court his favor or to avoid his displeasure.

8. In the vicinity of many of the towns a small place is set apart in the dense forest which is called the "devil-bush." At a certain age, or some time during boyhood or adolescence, the male youths are admitted formally into the privileges and duties of manhood, by being brought into the vicinity of the devil-bush and receiving certain mysterious instructions from the "devil-man," who remains concealed from view. Previous to this important period in the life of the young neophyte, he is not permitted to take any part in the affairs of state, or even to know anything of the judicial proceedings—a proscription which extends not only to the young, but to all who have not been initiated into the wonderful mysteries of this chartered university. The mysterious, mighty devil-man is none other than one of their own people, who, at certain periods, emerges from his temporary concealment, dressed in the most fantastical manner, and presenting a most frightful appearance. While he is entering the town, in order to engage in the "devil-plays," he blows a huge horn; at the sound of which the women and children are obliged to fly for their lives.

9. The principal object of the ceremonies of the "devil-bush" seems to be to keep the *women* under subjection. In Africa, as well as in every other uncivilized country,

women are made "hewers of wood and drawers of water;" they are compelled to perform a great part of the labor necessary to the subsistence of their lordly spouses—they sow the rice, plant the cassada, and attend to the principal duties of husbandry, and in all things they are obliged to yield submissively to the will of the men. They are not permitted to be present, or even to be within sight or hearing, under penalty of death, during the ceremonies of the "devil-play;" nor are they allowed, at any time, under any circumstances, to enter or to come near the place of residence of the vicegerent of the arch-deceiver. They are kept profoundly ignorant of all these proceedings, and of everything else which would tend to place them on an equality with their tyrannical rulers—the men.

10. A place similar to the devil-bush is set apart in the vicinity of most of the towns as a seminary for young females. This is called the "gree-gree bush." A small spot of ground is cleared in the midst of a dense piece of forest, a few huts are erected on this cleared spot, and in this sacred retreat, consecrated to female chastity, the young and innocent damsels are placed and kept under the direction and instructions of an old woman, whose business is to instruct them in all the duties pertaining to their condition as maidens, and to the connubial state. Those girls who are placed in this female seminary are generally, perhaps always, betrothed, or rather sold, by their parents before their entrance—sometimes, indeed, from their infancy. And here they are generally kept until the time of celebration of the nuptials with their previously affianced lords. Males are never permitted to enter the abode of these innocent creatures, under any circumstances whatever—not even their fathers or brothers. Nor are the girls allowed to leave their allotted place, except when accompanied by their aged preceptress. And even on occasions when they are brought out of their place of confinement they are not permitted to say anything to any individual of the other sex.

11. The natives in the vicinity of Liberia universally believe in the existence of a Supreme Being, but they never offer any kind of religious worship to him, and their conceptions of his character are exceedingly groveling and undefined. They also believe in the existence of a principle within the body which must survive its dissolution, but they have no definite ideas respecting the future state of existence. Indeed, in all that relates to the nature of the human soul, and to its future destiny, their views are exceedingly indefinite, and they abound in contradictions and absurdities. To reduce the discordant elements of the native African's creed to anything like the unity and consistency of a system would require a heavy draught on the imagination of the compiler.

12. In reference to the moral and intellectual condition of the native tribes in the vicinity of Liberia, and I may add throughout the greater part of Western and Southern Africa, a picture sad and gloomy meets the eye of the observer, and causes the Christian philanthropist to mourn over the moral desolation of these degraded beings. For centuries they have been utterly destitute of the restraints of morality, as well as of the benign influences of Christianity; and from one depth of degradation to a deeper still, they have been sinking until, among many of the tribes, the last vestiges of humanity almost seem to be merging into an allied proximity with the wild beasts of the forest.

13. In energy and activity of mind they are inferior to most other portions or classes of the human race. In the language of one who well understands the African character: "A few local associations; a limited number of acquaintances among their own people (all equally ignorant); some knowledge of raising the bare necessaries of life; a few traditionary stories, handed down from father to son, and rehearsed in their social groups as pastime; and a superficial knowledge of the superstitions of their forefathers, comprise about the sum total of their stores of

knowledge. They saunter through life conscious that they shall exist hereafter, but strangely indifferent as to the nature or conditions of that existence." And in reference to the mental imbecility and the indifference to intellectual improvement among these degraded sons and daughters of Ham, I may add, in the language of the same careful and experienced observer (Rev. J. L. Wilson) : " In whatever point of light we contemplate the African mind, it presents little else than an inextricable maze of ignorance, credulity, and superstition, from which it can never be disengaged except by the life-giving and light-imparting influences of Christianity."

CHAPTER LXII.

EMIGRATION IN 1851-2.

1. On the 1st of November, 1851, the barque Morgan Dix sailed from Baltimore for Liberia with a company of 149 emigrants, sent out under the auspices of the American Colonization Society. They were all landed at Buchanan, in Grand Bassa County, about the 10th of the following month (December). Several of this company were men of considerable intelligence, prudence, and enterprise; and we were happy to learn that they lived, and did well in their adopted home. A large number of these emigrants were, however, such persons as we would not select as emigrants to Liberia, if we could always exercise the privilege of selection. And, as was feared, the mortality among this company was considerable—much greater than the usual mortality among emigrants in passing through the process of acclimation—the whole number of deaths for the year following having been thirty-seven.

2. Several of these were very aged persons, and several young infants. These people were under the medical care of Dr. J. S. Smith, who was as well qualified to conduct emigrants safely through the acclimating process as any other physician that has ever practiced in Liberia, and whose practice was generally attended with great success. Dr. Smith attributes the death of most of those who died of this company to other causes, than sickness produced by the ordinary agents of disease, operating in Liberia.

3. He says: "The Morgan Dix company were generally intractable, and were influenced more by animal appetites than by reason. Those who were not given to inordinate indulgence of the appetite, and had stout hearts, have done well. Besides, many of them were infirm and of feeble constitutions—some having been the subjects of typhoid fever, and not a few were subjects of confirmed dyspepsia." Again, he says: "There were several who were given to strong drink; and some of them were exceedingly imprudent in the excessive use of fruits.

4. Under date of July 29th, S. A. Benson, Esq., our agent at Buchanan, writes as follows: "The immigrants by the Zeno, Liberia Packet, and Ralph Cross have not had much mortality among them; but the mortality of the Morgan Dix's company has been considerable, owing to their imprudence—they would not heed advice, would eat fruit such as old settlers do not indulge in; as instance, one got out of his bed at night while sick, went under an orange-tree in my garden, and ate two dozen oranges at midnight, and boasted of it next day. Such a set of hard-headed people, as a general thing (though there are some worthy exceptions), I never saw before. The most of those who were prudent have not lost one of their family."

5. In November, 1852, three fine new barques sailed for Liberia: the Joseph Maxwell, from Wilmington, N. C., November 22, with 150 emigrants; the Linda Stewart, from Norfolk, Va., November 27, with 171 emigrants, 129

of whom were from Virginia, 39 from North Carolina, 2 from New York city, and 1 from New Jersey; and the Shirley, from Baltimore, November 27, with 2 emigrants sent out by this Society, and 34 by the Maryland State Colonization Society.

6. The whole number in the three vessels was 321 (exclusive of Marshall Hooper and wife, who are returning to their home in Liberia), of whom 289 were born free, 22 were emancipated in view of emigrating, and 10 purchased their own freedom or were purchased by their friends. Of the whole number, 144 were from North Carolina, 7 from Georgia, 2 from the District of Columbia, 1 from Pennsylvania, 1 from New Jersey, and 1 from Indiana. Some of these emigrants are men of considerable intelligence and enterprise; and we have reason to hope that many of them will become valuable citizens of the new Republic.

7. Five white missionaries of the Baptist Church sailed for Liberia in the Linda Stewart: the Rev. Mr. Sherman and wife, of Philadelphia; the Rev. Mr. Goodman and wife, of Ohio, and Mrs. Crocker, widow of the late Rev. W. G. Crocker, who, after six years' labor in Liberia, died at Monrovia in 1844. Mrs. C., after an absence of a few years from Liberia, is now returning to her former field of labor and usefulness.

8. The following-named missionaries sailed in the barque Shirley: the Rev. Levi Scott, Bishop of the Methodist Episcopal Church, who goes to meet the Liberia Annual Conference; the Rev. J. W. Horne, who expects to take charge of the Methodist Episcopal Seminary at Monrovia, and Miss Reynolds of the same Church; also the Rev. Mr. Scott and wife, and Miss Freeman of the Protestant Episcopal Church. The three latter are destined for the mission of that Church at Cape Palmas.

9. On the 23d of December, 1851, Mr. Abraham Cauldwell was appointed by the New York and Liberia Agricultural Association their traveling agent to Africa. He

returned to New York on the 12th of November, 1852, and gave the following account of Africa, and of the benefits to be obtained by emigration to that country, which was published in the New York *Tribune* of December 1:

10. "I will endeavor," he writes, "to give you as true a statement as my humble ability will permit. In truth and soberness, it would be needless for me to tell you that Africa flows with milk and honey, or that corn grows without planting. Liberia truly is a garden spot; her lands are beautiful, her soil is most fertile, her prairies and her forests are blooming and gay, her rivers and streams abound with fish, and her forests with game. She has a republican constitution; a most excellent code of laws are strictly observed. There are several churches and schools in Monrovia, and they are well filled with scholars. The Monrovians are the most strictly moral, if not the most strictly religious, people I ever saw.

11. "I shall now speak of emigration, of which I have some knowledge. In 1823 I emigrated to Hayti, and in 1839 I emigrated to the Island of Trinidad, West Indies, and lastly to Africa, where I find a peaceful home, where storms of prejudice never come on account of my complexion.

12. "I have been noticing, for several years, the movements of the Abolition Society, and once thought they were right, and still believe they are sincere, and really desirous to elevate the colored man. Some of them have shown it too plainly for me to be mistaken. For instance, Mr. Gerrit Smith, who gave away part of his fortune. Many others have also sacrificed their good names and their money. But, alas! how many good men have been deceived. I, for one, have been blind to my best interest. I hesitate not to say that colonization is the only thing to elevate the colored man. It is vain for many of us to talk of settling on Mr. Smith's land, or of emigrating to Canada and settling on land without money, which, comparatively speaking, few have.

13. "Africa holds forth inducements whereby the colored man may be elevated without money and without price. When I arrived in Liberia, the government granted me sixty lots, of ten acres each; thirty lots lie upon the St. Paul's River, that being all the land unoccupied on the bank of the river that I could obtain; and thirty more immediately in the rear, but not more than a quarter of a mile back. The land is beautifully situated on the river. The soil is very fertile and well timbered. It is within two miles of the town of Millsburg.

14. "The government grants ten acres to each family, and if they want more they can get it from the government for about fifty cents per acre. I have also built nine houses for you on the land, one large house, and eight others of lesser size for families. I have also cleared and planted down, in cassada, coffee, and other products, about nine or ten acres. I also bought three acres of cassada, grown and fit for use, which is ready for the emigrants who have to settle part of that land. Though I have contracted but for six hundred acres, thousands of acres can be obtained in the rear, if required. There are also many beautiful mill-streams on the tract, and the best of water.

15. "There is no danger of not having success in emigrating to Liberia; for I assure you, if you settle on those lands, having a house already built and a garden planted, and if you will but work two hours in each day, you can not fail to do better than by working the whole day in America. You can raise sweet potatoes, yams, cassada, cotton, coffee, and all other vegetables. You can also raise two crops a year. Besides, you can raise geese, turkeys, ducks, chickens, pigs, horses, cows, sheep, goats, and everything to make you happy, with far less expense than you can in America.

16. "There is a wide field open for farmers. If a man plants ten acres of coffee, in four or five years he will realize a handsome income. Coffee requires very little

labor, and is of more value than anything America can produce from your labor in twenty years. Everything grows abundantly. It is a fine country for cotton, corn, and rice, though cotton is not much planted as yet. There is a market for your produce in Monrovia. Beef sells at 10 cents per pound; turkeys from $4 to $5 a pair; chickens 25 cents a pair; eggs from 15 to 37 cents a dozen; rice from $1 to $2 a bushel; sweet potatoes 75 cents a bushel.

17. "You can also salt down beef, pork, and fish. I would in particular recommend farmers to emigrate to that country. If you go there to labor by the day, month, or year, you will not make much, for laborer's wages are very low. I would advise emigrants to take as much house-furniture as they need, for everything they want here they want there, besides a little money, if they can. Mechanics may find work, though wages are low. Men of capital, as mechanics, can do well, and are much wanted."

CHAPTER LXIII.

THE CHESAPEAKE AND LIBERIA TRADING COMPANY.

1. THE Liberia Packet was built in 1846, and sailed on her first voyage in December of that year. She was sent out by the Chesapeake and Liberia Trading Company, which went into operation under a charter from the State of Maryland. The building of this vessel was an era of no little magnitude in colonization operations. It was with great difficulty that funds could be raised for the purpose, and at her completion only $16,000 of the $20,000 necessary were subscribed. To show the condition of affairs at that time, we copy a programme of operations contained in the October number of our Journal—1846.

2. "This charter was obtained in the hope and belief, that an amount of stock, sufficient to put one vessel in operation, would be subscribed for by colored people of the United States and Liberia; as such a measure would tend much to disabuse the minds of the colored people here of the false impressions, which they have heretofore entertained, with regard to Liberia, and bring them and their transatlantic brethren nearer together. This hope, however, has not been fully realized. Many among the colored people, who were most anxious to have the thing established, have declined making good their subscriptions; and the result has been, a subscription for a majority of the stock necessary for building the Packet, by several white gentlemen favorable to the scheme. All such subscriptions, however, are made on the condition of a transfer of the same at its fair market value when it shall be desired by any colored person, either in the United States or in Liberia.

3. "The whole amount of funds originally obtained on subscription to the 'Cape Palmas Packet,' has been invested in the stock of this Company, in the name of the Maryland State Colonization Society, as it was believed the present plan would prove equally advantageous to the Society in its general results, and more economical. A very liberal subscription has been made in advance by several prominent citizens of Liberia, which we doubt not will be increased, on the first voyage of the Packet, to the amount desired : viz., one half her value. It is intended to keep the vessel running regularly between the ports of Baltimore and Norfolk, and the several Liberia colonies, making two, or three, or even four voyages a year, these depending in a great measure upon the amount of freight or emigrants, offered by the Colonization Societies.

4. "It is not intended to take freight for other parties, unless the Missionary Societies having stations in the colonies, should see fit to guarantee a certain amount of freight annually, as the Colonization Societies have done; in

which case, the same facilities for regular shipments would be granted them. Cabin passengers, to the extent of the accommodations, will be taken at the usual rates, and every attention paid to their convenience and comfort. The under officers and crew of the vessel will be colored men, and it is intended to put her in charge of a colored man as master, as soon as one competent can be found. Letters and packages will always receive attention, and be delivered as directed, if practicable.

5. "In many respects we fell sadly short of the mark. We soon found it idle to think of over three voyages per year, and from occasional detention on the coast of Liberia, waiting freight, and, in the United States, awaiting emigrants, we found it very difficult to fix any particular time for sailing; consequently, great disappointment was the too frequent result. We failed also to increase the subscription of colored people to the stock, and were often obliged to take the stock of original subscriptions at par; so that, up to this time, only $3,325 of the $25,000 worth of stock is held by colored people, and of this amount only $375 in this country, although it has paid a cash dividend of ten per cent. per annum, since the Company went into operation.

6. "Again, we failed in getting a colored master and colored officers and crew. For a time we succeeded in getting good colored officers; but, after trying in all the Northern ports, could not find a man suitable to take the place of Haley, first officer, should he be promoted to the command. So the project was for that time abandoned. Nor have we any hope that a suitable colored man to command a foreign trading vessel, could now be found in this country; the soil is unfavorable to the production of the man. He must come from Liberia.

7. "But notwithstanding our failure to do all that we anticipated, we can confidently say, the six years running the Packet between this port and Liberia has done much good. Her quick passages have brought Liberia nearer

to this country, she having several times made passages in but a few days over the month, and twice within the month. Her superior accommodations rendered the passage of emigrants far more agreeable than ordinary trading vessels heretofore chartered. Her regular return to this port enabled many of the Liberians to visit the United States, thereby increasing business relations between us; and enabled hundreds of others, whose circumstances would not permit their again crossing the Atlantic, to send letters and packages to their friends.

8. "The visits of the Liberians to this country, which have no doubt been quadrupled in consequence of the establishing of the Liberia Packet, have done more to excite an interest in Liberia among the free colored people of this country, than all the speeches and writings of the friends of colonization since the Society commenced operations. One important advantage to colonization has resulted from the operations of the Chesapeake and Liberia Trading Company, not promised or estimated in the outset: viz., the cheaper transportation of emigrants. In the contract between the Company and the Colonization Societies, the Company bound itself to carry all emigrants offered at certain rates, and these rates were rather below the average rate at which emigrants had been hitherto sent in transient vessels.

9. "This was all the Company asked; and, had the Society been bound to furnish a quota at certain times, the expenses of transportation might be supposed to be about the same as they had previously been. But the case was far otherwise. The Societies could not *guarantee* any fixed number. The Company has often prepared for a larger number, say 150, and when the time of sailing arrived, perhaps fifty would not be ready to embark, thereby rendering it necessary for the Company to procure freight from other sources, or sail an empty vessel. Again, few emigrants would be offered, and not enough freight solicited, or merchandise purchased, to fill the Packet;

but when the day of sailing approached, the number of emigrants would often be doubled, and the Company obliged to put their own cargo in store for another voyage.

10. "The Colonization Societies, therefore, have been gainers by employing the Company as agents for carrying on their operations. Without the Company's aid, they would often have chartered larger vessels, and been obliged to send them out half filled, or embark in a commerce not legitimately within the scope of their operations. The Company has also not only chartered, but bought and even exchanged vessels, when emigrants were offered out of the Packet's time, and transported them at the established rates. We claim, therefore, that the operations of the Chesapeake and Liberia Trading Company for the past six years have been productive of incalculable advantages to colonization, and in no respect detrimental to it.

11. "The Company is not now (January, 1853) the owner of any vessel. The first three years of the operations of the Company proved conclusively, that the Liberia Packet was entirely too small for the purpose intended. The increase in the number of emigrants, the increased quantity of their effects consequent upon the movement of a better class, the increase of freight offered by different parties to their Liberian correspondents, required a vessel of near, or quite, 500 barrels capacity, and it was determined to sell the Liberia Packet when opportunity offered.

12. "In the autumn of 1851, the American Colonization Society had a choice lot of emigrants, from the valley of Virginia, and a steam saw-mill, to send out. A vessel of suitable size could not be readily found in this port to charter, and the Company purchased the barque Morgan Dix, a vessel of 276 tons, for the purpose. She made one successful voyage, and prepared for another. When nearly ready for sea, the number of emigrants increased so much that she was judged too small, and she was exchanged for the barque Ralph Cross, of near 4,000 barrels capacity. This vessel was put in first-rate order

for the accommodation of emigrants, and sailed for the coast with a full cargo in May, 1853. The Liberia Packet arrived in July, and was disposed of. A large expedition was planned for the Ralph Cross, November 1st, and we waited her arrival without hearing of her loss until the 10th."

CHAPTER LXIV.

THE PESSAY TRIBE.

BY REV. GEORGE L. SEYMOUR.

1. As to the country, I would remark that I have seen and heard of no better. In this region the face of the country is undulating, presenting a most healthful aspect; heavily timbered, good for house and mill purposes, and everything, in short, where timber is called into requisition; soil mostly of a sandy loam, productive of all tropical vegetation, as also varieties common in the temperate zones; water, as good as the best in the Union, except your mineral; *their* equal, doubtless, may, by discovery, be found in this land of mystery. The rock or stone consists principally of three kinds: 1st, the blue granite, like that at Monrovia; 2d, the gray or sand mixed formation; 3d, the iron ore; the first two good for building; in fact, the latter may be employed in that way if persons have a fancy for that kind of material.

2. I add, in answer to another question, that the following productions thrive well, viz.: Indian corn, rice, millet (a kind of breadstuff having a stem like the corn-stalk, with an ear on the top like puss-tail flag), and another kind much like the broom-corn; sweet potatoes, yams, tania, egg-plant, cucumbers, arbor beans, tomatoes, radishes, mustard, pineapple, plantain, banana, guava,

papaw, granadilla, orange, lime, lemon, cotton plant, indigo, all common to this part of the country. The cola tree (which acquires an enormous bulk, and produces abundantly a bitter nut, much in request as an article of commerce), peanuts, black-eyed peas, coffee, cocoa for chocolate, and a variety of pepper, may be found on the mission premises; and yet these are not all the country affords by many sorts. I shall strive to procure them all. Shalots, or onions, are found in the country, better than I have seen raised on the sea-coast, some of which we have in our garden; there are many little herbs for salad, etc. I have no names by which to term them, not being a botanist.

3. I wish to say that the people are a kind and peaceable race, industrious and ingenious, hospitable to strangers, but, like all savages, revengeful to their enemies; yet for all that, the head men are very considerate about entering into important measures, easily governed, and quite affectionate to each other; while, at the same time, they are disposed to tricks of dishonesty to each other, and will take advantage of strangers if they have an opportunity. In body they are robust, and much better proportioned than the Bassas; of about the same stature, wearing very little cloth as a common thing. I should not forget that their color is more generally inclined to a light brown than that of the Bassas; and those interior of us are still lighter, as they are from a more northern district. Their food consists of rice principally; of course they make use of palm-oil, the palm-tree being found throughout the country, so far as I have traveled.

4. As regards their knowledge of God, of course it is very indefinite; yet they all have some confused idea of a great First Cause. But one thing, very favorable to the spread of the Gospel is, I have observed, that this tribe is not given up to the use of the gregree or fetish, like the Bassas. I have been in many a Pessay town and have yet to see a gregree house; while, at the same time, one hardly sees a Bassa town without one; the people wear

horns and trinkets. A favorable omen, indeed! Some of them tell me of the Mohammedan worship among the tribes more to the north and east.

5. The Pessay is the only tribe that manufacture iron, so far as I have seen, though it is said that some other tribes also work it. They spin the cotton and weave it into cloth, many samples of which you have doubtless seen on the coast while visiting us. They make their clay owls and pots, also pipes; all of which answer very well the purpose intended. Their habitations consist of mud-walled huts, very low, not allowing you to stand erect in them, with thatched roofs, some square and others round, having projections, giving the appearance of a huge mushroom. They are agriculturists in their general occupation; and they engage in the slave trade to a limited extent, as the chance of shipment is too uncertain for those on the coast to make a large demand; and in that one particular, the Republic of Liberia has worked a revolution that is felt a great distance interior of us.

6. Polygamy is practiced by this tribe, but they do not treat their women as uncharitably as the Bassas, but do more for them in the way of farming, for they cut the brushwood, and after burning, char it up for planting in all cases, which is not done by the Bassas, except when the farm burns badly; they also cut the same farm over the next season, and sow rice and plant cassada—a thing not done by the Bassas, except those near the Pessay tribe. In the circumstance of a person dying, they do not burn up the house of a dead person like the Bassas, nor do they remove away, but reside for many years in one locality, and for that purpose they build more substantial dwellings. Their implements of husbandry are the bill-hook, ax, and hoe, and with these simple articles they do a great amount of labor.

7. I have seen here farms of many acres cut and planted in rice, corn, cassada, etc.; and the largest farm I think would measure about forty acres, belonging to one or two

persons of a town. The people about us trade in rice, camwood, and colas; fowls, sheep and goats, bullocks, peanuts; they make palm-oil for their own use, but not for sale, except the little for us, which is much less than we want for table purposes; and the people interior of us trade in bullocks, cloth, sheep, goats, iron, etc., and take in exchange guns, powder, tobacco, crockeryware, beads, cutlasses, foreign cloths. The European goods are best liked by both Bassas and Pessays, not on account of texture so much as their width, dye, and figure or print, and in fact (strange as it may appear) they do not fancy the American goods as well as those above mentioned; and one reason they give is that the American goods are too heavy and strong; but the American musket, powder, and tobacco, and many other articles of trade, are eagerly sought after by the tribes interior of the Republic.

8. The habit of the African in general to wash frequently is proverbial; there is but little sickness among them, and they are quite expert in herb medicines; have their doctors, who appear to be persons of considerable note, yet not to that degree as to assume the aspect of superstitious assurance. As I have intimated before, they have no form of religious worship, of course no priest. As instruments of hunting and war they use the musket, arrow, spear, and knife or cutlass. For both hunting and war, the arrow point is dipped in a deadly poison, the slightest scratch of which I am informed causes death; and they shoot with such precision and at such a distance that the victim is sure of a mortal wound, and this fact is too well known by the Bassas on the borders of the Pessay country to encourage them to provoke a war.

9. I should have mentioned before that this tribe cultivate a good quality of tobacco, the leaves of which I have measured, and found them nine inches wide by eighteen long.

Thus upon the whole I consider this people an interesting tribe—for their aptness to learn is much in advance of the Bassas; and their dialect is peculiarly adapted to the articulation of English, and they speak it with a clearness that would deceive many an ear, not having that roll and grumble about it which belongs to the Bassa dialect; they pride themselves in making efforts to speak the English, and are attentive at religious worship. The children acquire the knowledge of letters very fast.

CHAPTER LXV.

LETTER FROM G. W. HALL, ESQ.

BRIG "HANNAH," OFF CAPE SIERRA LEONE.
December 16, 1857.

1. I HAD anticipated the pleasure of writing to you from Cape Mount, but early yesterday morning our ship met this brig bound for Sierra Leone and a market. Her consignee came on board and desired me to accompany him. Accordingly, in less than two hours, I bade adieu to my agreeable companions and comfortable quarters, for the sake of business, and once more seeing the settlement of Sierra Leone. I hope this course will not prevent, but merely delay for a few weeks, my visit to Liberia. Although the wind did not blow like fury, as a friend of ours hoped it would, the M. C. Stevens had a very fair passage, she being only thirty-one days out when I left her, and then within one hundred miles of Cape Mount, her first point of destination.

2. There, most of her emigrants are, for the first time, to press the soil of their freedom; there to feel, if ever, that heart-throbbing which the first full freedom of manhood so uniformly inspires. Most of them, you are aware, were born slaves, and are now made free by will of their kind owners. Many bring with them funds sufficient to build

their simple frame dwellings, fence in their lots, and to secure them from suffering during their first year's experience in Africa; others have nothing with which to commence a new life in a new world but stout hearts and sturdy frames; and very few of them, or their children, are educated men; but many, and by far the greater number of Liberian youth, possess a "common school" education, and make honest and industrious citizens. We may well hope that this, the third company of the M. C. Stevens, will not fall far short of the best which has preceded it.

3. Most of the men are farmers; that class numbering forty-eight, all young or middle-aged, and healthy; blacksmiths, 3; tobacco-workers, 5; carpenters, 2; painters, 1; waiters, 2; steam engineer, 1 (a free man from Charlotte County, Va.); one brickmaker and rock-mason, who is a liberated slave from Kentucky, and one solitary barber. Many friends of colonization in America think that this simple material is too rude for Africa, and they would choose in its stead the more polished freeman of Northern cities, quite forgetting that in a new country the sturdy laborer is equally as indispensable as the man of education and refinement. It is certainly a matter for regret, that free colored men of the North do not more often turn their attention to Liberia, and resolve to aid with their might to build up and firmly establish this new Republic, the only present home of the colored man. Instead of doing this, they say to colonizationists, Make us a home in that strange land, which shall, before we enter it, vie with your own boasted home.

4. Make in Africa internal improvements, make roads, build bridges, that, when we reach it, there shall remain nothing more for us to do but to enjoy your generous bounty. They can not, will not, emigrate to such a country, with clodhopping slaves, clad in linsey-woolsey, and just redeemed from massa's plantation. Liberia does not this day contain two hundred citizens who are Northern

born. Nearly all that she has been, is, and perhaps all that she ever will be, is owing to white philanthropy, and to the energy and intelligence of colored men born south of Mason and Dixon's line, men whose fathers were slaves, or who were in some instances themselves born slaves.

5. The Rev. Elijah Johnson, whose name shines brightly, if not brightest, in Liberian history, was born a slave in Maryland, and emigrated from New Jersey in 1820. David Moore, long the treasurer of the colony, and afterward of the Republic, one of the most honest and valuable citizens Liberia ever had, was once a Mississippi slave, by trade a tanner, and a man of very limited education.

6. The father of President Benson, who is undeniably an educated gentleman, was a plain farm-hand from Frederick County, Md., but he was a man of natural abilities, and a fit counselor for the white agent of his day. Liberia needs men of intelligence, wealth, and energy; but she needs the laborer too, that which constitutes the bone and sinew of every country. In our own land even, but a small proportion belong exclusively to the educated and refined classes, and we have the best of precedents that in the settlement of a new country, but a small proportion should belong to it. Some writers say not more than one in every ten.

7. The population from which a few friends of colonization would select emigrants for Liberia is unhappily composed of barbers, waiters, boot-blacks, and the petty shop-keepers of our cities, some of whom have acquired a business education well adapted to their present position, and when possessed of capital, would be very desirable acquisitions for the Liberian towns; but they can not endure the hard labors and rough usage of country life, where new lands are to be cleared and a virgin soil cultivated; they must continue to be, to a certain extent, the trading class of any country.

8. Moreover, as there are so few avenues open to them

for professional advancement, our country contains a very limited number of educated colored men; and the late Governor Russwurm, of Cape Palmas was, and Rev. Alexander Crummell now is, the best representative of that few in Liberia; they were college-bred, and in every sense of the word literary men. But Liberia can not now support many such in the positions that they would naturally desire to occupy. Mr. Crummell having resigned his position in the Episcopal Mission for private reasons, has retired upon his farm; but an amateur farmer without capital everywhere fails to glean more than a scanty subsistence, and Liberia is no exception to this rule.

Mr. Crummell, however, is not likely to continue his farming operations. The Episcopalians at Monrovia, heretofore dependent upon the American Mission Board, now propose to raise the means for erecting a church edifice, and to secure Mr. Crummell as its pastor. Should this plan be carried out, it will show that men of talent and education (if such proof be needed) are appreciated in Liberia, and that men bred to professional pursuits will be supported there in due time.

9. The ship M. C. Stevens brought out this voyage a young man from Baltimore, who is a regular graduate of Dartmouth College, and is fully qualified, color excepted, to practice at the Baltimore bar. His success is almost certain, as there is not another lawyer in Liberia who was bred to the profession; a second one might be equally successful, and thus this business would gradually pass out of the hands of quacks, who now hold it without depending upon their practice for support. But a score of lawyers would inundate the country as surely as would the same number more than supply the requisitions of some of our Western towns. The conclusion of the matter is, that with an attachment to freedom, and with a determination to do with their fullest energy whatever good thing they may find to do, it will require but little trimming to make all classes fit most admirably together; each will subserve the

other's interest, and all will be united in efforts to elevate their race. Then will foreign philanthropy or foreign speculation aid them as our country has ever been aided, in building roads, and making every kind of internal improvement that the mind can conceive or the heart desire. Then will Liberia become an envied nation, and a long-suffering people be redeemed.

CHAPTER LXVI.

LETTER FROM MONROVIA.

The following is from a letter dated Monrovia, February 2d, 1858:

1. With the exception of a slight financial embarrassment, the affairs of government are moving on prosperously. Our President, S. A. Benson, possesses in an eminent degree the ability and qualifications to administer public affairs; and by his urbanity and courtesy has rendered himself emphatically the people's President. He encourages, by every advisable means, the development of the country's resources; and by precept and example—being himself a practical farmer—he excites the people to generous rivalry in agricultural pursuits, so that this branch of industry has received an impetus greater than has ever been experienced previously.

The St. Paul's River exhibits the appearance of unusual activity; several large farms of sugar-cane are being cut, keeping one small steam, and three ox, mills in constant operation. About one half the cane cut from the farm of the late Mr. Richardson has been ground, yielding 2,000 pounds of sugar and about the same number of gallons of syrup.

2. A cotton farm has just been started on the Junk

River, by Hon. D. B. Warner; should it be successful, there will be a large yield, which will doubtless induce others to make similar experiments.

The corner-stone of Liberia College was laid January 25th, with the assistance of the Masonic Grand Lodge of Liberia, and its subordinates. I have not seen a plan of the building, but judging from the extent of the foundation, and such casual description as I could obtain from the builders, the edifice will be the most imposing in Liberia. There was great delay in selecting a suitable site, caused chiefly by local interest and prejudice, but the final decision has located it in Monrovia, the policy of which has been doubted by many. The chief objection is, that such an institution should not be situated near a large town.

3. The Legislature adjourned January 23d, after a session of six weeks. One of the most important bills passed during the session, related to the French plan of procuring emigrants from this coast. I am unable to give you a synopsis of the bill, as it has not been printed as yet; but the restrictions which it imposes will have the tendency to abolish the system from that part of the coast over which this government maintains jurisdiction. The course we have pursued in regard to this system has so affected the French Government toward us, that she has retracted the gift of a sloop-of-war made some time since, although we had sent an agent to France to receive it, according to agreement. But it is preferable to lose the vessel, though it is much needed, than to be remiss in frowning down a system which has proved to possess but a very few more of the attributes of humanity than the slave trade.

4. The Methodist denomination of Liberia, heretofore under the jurisdiction of the American Bishop, has increased in prosperity and importance to such an extent, that it was deemed expedient to have a bishop especially for this country, one who was a citizen of the Republic and identified with the interests of the people. Accordingly, the Conference which has just adjourned, elected to

that position the Rev. Francis Burns. It is a judicious election, as Mr. Burns has been Superintendent of the Methodist Mission in Liberia for a long time, and no one is better acquainted than he with the condition and wants of this people. He expects to visit the United States during the ensuing summer for the purpose of being ordained.

President Benson writes, under date of Monrovia, January 30, 1858:

5. Your very fine ship, the M. C. Stevens, is in port, homeward bound, and I embrace the opportunity of re-acknowledging your interesting favors by her, all of which have been perused and their contents duly noted. I perceive by yours, as well as other journals, that Liberia and the great Colonization cause, have been malignantly, and somewhat ingeniously, attacked, by that unreasonable portion of the press of your country which invariably expects a demonstration of greater perfection in intelligence, morality, and industry, in Liberia, by Liberians, than they ever expect to witness in countries (including their own and themselves) which have had twenty times the advantages of Liberia. A single delinquency of emphatic occurrence in Liberia, creates more pretended surprise and disrespectful animadversion among and by a class in the United States, than do the tens of thousands of similar daily occurrences among themselves, with all the advantages under which they have been raised.

6. I am happy to say that our public affairs are moving on as usual; some particulars in regard to them you will have no doubt gathered from my Message to the Legislature, of the 10th ult. (copies of which I sent you *via* England, per December mail). The report of the Adjudicating Committee of the National Fair, held in this city on the 14th to the 21st ult., is now in course of printing. It has produced an almost magical effect upon the industrial skill and energy of our citizens, so that the Legislature have made a standing arrangement to hold them successively in the different counties every year.

7. I consider that we are now approximating nearer to substantial prosperity than ever. It is true, times are hard for money, and we sensibly feel the falling off of the oil trade during the last year; yet, after all, the people raise enough to eat, and the failure of the oil season, together with other things, have caused them not only to see the propriety of raising something for exportation, but actually to prepare and commence doing so; and if no untoward circumstance arises, I think you and other friends of this Republic will become increasingly gratified and encouraged by authentic annual reports of manly progress in all those industrial pursuits that are so essential to individual and national prosperity.

8. And if nothing but a temporary failure in the oil trade will induce some of our principal men to see the folly of basing our commerce upon what should be regarded as an auxiliary, instead of principal, commodity; if nothing else can bring them to see that the Americo-Liberians must be their own producers, and are not to depend upon the native Africans otherwise than as auxiliaries, then I hope that a blight may rest upon the palm-tree, until they begin to practically demonstrate that this lesson is effectually learned. The more intelligent citizens are particularly encouraged; and notwithstanding the tightness of the monetary market, and the great responsibility resting upon me (attended with a proportionate degree of cares and perplexity), yet never was I more encouraged in my life than during the last eight months; for during the most gloomy times last year, I plainly recognized the hand of Providence; I knew it would all be for our good, individually and nationally.

CHAPTER LXVII.

NEW SETTLEMENT.

(FROM REV. G. L. SEYMOUR.)

BUCHANAN, *February* 1, 1858.

1. I RECEIVED your kind letter of December 16th, 1857, which found me in this place, preparing to return to my station in Pessay, after an absence of a few weeks, for the purpose of obtaining aid from the Government and individuals to assist in defraying the expenses of an exploration interior of Liberia.

2. And I have to say that I have been blessed in my exertions to the amount of about three hundred dollars; and as I received aid from Government (of course in service of the same) in the important enterprise, about which all appear interested, I feel compensated for the letter I sent in answer, if but one good idea is advanced in behalf of Africa, and do trust that it will awaken the sympathy of our colored brethren in the United States for their fatherland; for be assured, sir, that it is Africa's own children who are to do the work, under God.

3. I do not know that it would be well to undertake the purchase of any part of the camwood country alone, with a view to secure the wealth thereof; for the natives think it common property; and, of course, many would disregard the contract and impose upon the owners.

4. The three head men referred to, are constant in their solicitations for Americans to reside with them; each of them will be pleased to hear from you on the important subject of interior settlements at or near their dominions; and I believe they will perform all they promise. I shall deem it a pleasure to inform them that I have an answer to the communication in their behalf; if it is but a few lines in my letter, it will please them, for they have an

idea that the Society can accomplish much toward settling Americans in their midst. I am compelled to regard this as one of the indications of the harvest, ripening fast.

5. The extension of settlements interiorward is not so dangerous an experiment as may be supposed, if the right kind of persons can be employed; and the Government will have but little to do in affording protection, if a friendly intercourse is maintained by those that go, in the first instance. Our Government is at this time cramped for want of means. Therefore they can do but little toward defraying the expenses of a wagon-road now, but will take hold of the thing in due time if the necessary means can be secured.

6. I need not remind you, that the means to perpetuate the work on a broad plan is at the disposal of any and all, who take hold of it in a masterly way; and the Government will no doubt undertake it in a few months. You are correct in the supposition, that the wood country and our station are beyond the jurisdiction of the Republic—they are about seventy-five or eighty miles beyond.

7. There would be difficulty in transporting a company of emigrants with luggage to our place, yet it can be done for about twenty-five or thirty dollars apiece, and perhaps less on an average. I have thought it best to begin a settlement with old citizens, and heartily adopt your sentiments as to their moral and religious character.

CHAPTER LXVIII.

THE FUTURE OF AFRICA.

1. THE friends of African colonization have every reason for substantial encouragement in the great work in which they are engaged. Erroneous impressions of the capabilities of the African race are entertained by many in this

country, arising from the fact of so many of them having long been in slavery within the bounds of this republic. The impression is strengthened by the other fact, that so great a number of the free sink into a state of degradation. It were easy to account for so deplorable a result on natural and well-known principles, without contravening the theory of African capability.

2. The wonder is, that so many promising cases have been found, in which genius and energy have developed themselves in a striking degree. We know a jet-black negro, who, by the courtesy of the professors and students of one of our medical institutions, was permitted to attend the course of lectures, and passed his examinations with an ability equal to most of his fellow-students, and superior to many. Indeed, everything about him seemed *white*, except his color. None could be more quiet and respectful in his manners, none graduated under the seal of a deeper approbation from the professors, who are *colonizationists*. He is now practicing with success in Liberia.

3. The effect of the principles of colonization on well-disposed minds among our native colored people is seen in various forms. Take, for example, the commercial firms in Liberia, who have studied the mercantile theory, and have applied the knowledge they acquired to the production of wealth. Some of them have succeeded to admiration. As few have failed there as in this favored country, perhaps fewer in proportion to the number engaged in business.

4. A poor colored boy, who was a common newspaper carrier in one of our cities, was smitten with an ambition to "be something," and he went to Liberia. There he became quite a scholar for a Liberian, a noted lawyer, and an orator. We have read his letters with surprise, and a printed oration of his on the life of a deceased officer of the Republic excited our admiration. The flowers of an African imagination were freely distributed through his composition; but this was natural to him. He might not

have studied Blair or Whately, but the effusion is very creditable, and lifted him high among his peers.

5. A more sober style of thought and expression appears in the messages of the colored Presidents to their Legislature, as befits the dignity of their station. Many of our governors have not surpassed them. Good, sound sense has ever characterized these documents. Their policy is simple, their wants few, and their ambition is chastened by the necessities of their position. The power and influence which the official leaders have exercised over hostile or restless adjacent tribes are truly remarkable.

6. The peculiar condition of the people keeps them near the protecting providence of a superior Power, and they are not slow to inculcate this idea in their official documents. Armies and navies they have none. They rely for peace on the comity and good-will of enlightened foreign nations. And this has been extended to them freely and honorably. Of the interior of Africa, heretofore almost a blank on the map of the world, modern scientific travelers and religious missionaries are continually bringing new information. It is impossible that the labors and discoveries of such men as Moffatt, Livingstone, Barth, Bowen, and Wilson should be in vain. From them we learn of stalwart races, noble chiefs, in lands of singular fertility and abundant resources.

7. We hear of languages copious, mellifluous, and even systematic in their details, which, when reduced to a regular grammar, exhibit moods, tenses, and terminations almost as perfect as the Greek, Latin, or English. What is not the printing-press yet to achieve for Africa? How are the triumphs of Christianity yet to adorn that land?

8. An officer in the service of one of their kings had been degraded for some crime. He was saved from death by the intercession of the missionary. The sable warrior disdained the boon of life, if he was to be deprived of the rank and privileges, the badges and honors of his position,

and rejected the commutation of his sentence, which, to the astonishment of the other nobles, the missionary had obtained for him. Clasping his hands on his bosom, he exclaimed: "Oh, king, afflict not my heart. I have merited thy displeasure. Let me be slain like the warrior. I can not live with the poor." Raising his hand to the ring he wore on his brow, he continued: "How can I live among the dogs of the king, and disgrace these badges of honor which I won among the spears and shields of the mighty? No, I can not live! Let me die, oh, Pezoolu!" And he was precipitated over the Tarpeian precipice into the yawning waters below, to be devoured by crocodiles. Such is African pride on one hand, and African despotism on the other. Christianity will humble the one, and destroy the other. There are Africans who have never been made slaves, even in regions where the slave trade has been triumphant. Such are the Kroomen, the watermen of the coast.

CHAPTER LXIX.

RESOURCES OF AFRICA.

BY DR. LIVINGSTONE.

1. DR. LIVINGSTONE, the celebrated African traveler, recently made an address before the Chamber of Commerce in Manchester, England, in which he spoke at length of the resources of Africa.

He said that the African ought to be encouraged to cultivate the raw materials of English manufactures; and he was so fully convinced of the elevating tendency of lawful commerce, together with the probable influence which the course specified promised to have on the slave trade and slavery, that he proposed to devote the next few years of his life to special efforts in that direction. A peculiar and rather annoying combination of circumstances had placed the great Anglo-American race, on which undoubtedly the hopes of the world for liberty and progress rested, in a very trying position.

2. Our demands for sugar and cotton were daily increasing; those demands were at present met in a great measure by slave labor; but the great body of Anglo-Americans would unquestionably prefer to have their wants supplied by free men, and he ventured to hope that the discovery of a new region, well adapted for raising those articles, might be a providential opening for enabling us to escape from our anomalous position.

3. Before attempting to give some idea of this new field for commercial enterprise, it might be mentioned that, while he proposed to try to make the Zambese River a permanent path to the inland healthy region, with a view to the wide diffusion of civilization and Christianity, and endeavoring to link the interests of the African with our own, he had felt that it would not be right in him to do this at the expense of those who contributed their money for purely religious purposes; but the gentlemen he now addressed, in common with others, had contributed handsomely, in the way of testimonial funds, to relieve his mind from care with respect to his family, and he begged to tender them his very grateful acknowledgments.

Mr. Cheetham, M. P., asked Dr. Livingstone what were the peculiar productions of the districts which he had visited?

4. Dr. Livingstone said, It would be observed that the country through which the Zambese flowed was abundantly watered by the numerous rivers which joined it. South of latitude twenty degrees there was a country remarkably destitute of water, where one might travel four full days without obtaining a single drop of water, there being no rivers south of that line; but the country to the north of it was totally different.

5. While in the south the vegetation was altogether thorny, there being a prodigious number of different kinds of thorns, the northern and well-watered country produced a vegetation without thorns. The majority of the trees there were evergreens; many of them had the appearance of laurels and orange-trees. In that country there were a great many different kinds of fruit, most of which he believed to be totally unknown to Europeans. He brought home about twenty-five or twenty-six different kinds of fruit, some of which were valuable as yielding oil. Nearer to the coast, eastward, the people cultivated large quantities of cucumbers; and their best salad oil was made from the seeds of the cucumbers.

6. Throughout the whole country the ground-nut was cultivated in large quantities—used as food and for oil. In Angola the natives knew of a very great many different dyes, which they were not very willing to make known to Europeans. In reference to cotton, very large quantities of it were cultivated by the natives, and one small district, between the rivers Conza and Loanda, produced 1,300 cloths annually of cotton, grown by the natives, spun by the women, and woven by the men.

The west coast was by far the best field for cotton. On the east it was cultivated a little, but it was not so good. It clung to the seed, and an iron roller had to be used to separate it. The quantity grown on the east side was very much smaller than on the west side, but the natives had never been induced to cultivate cotton; they had never been offered anything for it, and they only cultivate a little to make clothes for themselves. He believed, if they had a market, they would cultivate largely; for wherever they had the opportunity of selling anything, they immediately began to collect it.

7. There was a trade between Loando and Brazil in wax, which was necessary for the churches in Brazil. In the central country the people had no idea that sugar could be got from the sugar-cane, although the sugar-cane

abounded in their country; and when he told them of it, the chief asked him to make some. He explained that it could only be done by machine. Then, asked the chief, would he bring him a machine from his own country? He explained that he was a poor man, and it required something considerable to purchase one. The chief replied: "Why, the whole of the ivory of the country is yours, and if you leave any of it, it is your own fault." Angola produced beautiful wheat, and he saw it growing on the high lands with ears the length of the hand. The high land produced it without irrigation, and it might be grown there to almost any extent.

8. The east side of the country also produced wheat. The Zambese overflowed large tracts of country annually, like the Nile. The Portuguese had been in the habit of cultivating the wheat on that side of the country; all it required was, that a slave woman with a little hoe should make a hole in the ground, drop a few seeds in, and push back the soil with her foot. In four months there was a crop of beautiful wheat. This simple operation answered all the purposes of our subsoiling, plowing, draining liming, and manuring. The higher they went up, the better the wheat was. In reply to subsequent inquiries, Dr. Livingstone said there were extensive tracts of forest land. There were nine seams of coal. He examined one near Tete, which was about sixty-eight inches in diameter; the coal having been tilted to the surface by volcanic action. Lieutenant Hoskins, who had command of one of the gunboats now gone to China, had given his opinion that the bar at the real mouth of the Zambese, was no impediment to commercial purposes, as there were twenty-two feet of water upon it; and, though the river was rather tortuous, he would not hesitate to take up a steamer of the same capacity as his gunboat. The river was at the flood during four or five months of the year.

CHAPTER LXX.
VOYAGE TO LIBERIA.

BY DR. JAMES HALL.

1. THREE days after the arrival of the ship at Monrovia, she was followed by the British steamer Hecla, which brought up the Commissioner and troops; the palaver having been set as before detailed. The entire operation, from the receipt of Governor Drayton's application for aid, to the disbanding of the troops, was conducted in a manner most creditable to all concerned, the President of the Republic, the Legislature, the Commissioner, officers and men, the Government of Maryland in Liberia, King Will and his people, and last, though not least, Capt. Alpin, of the Hecla, who with a kindness and liberality most commendable, promptly tendered the use of his vessel to Commissioner Roberts, in transporting the troops, baggage, and munitions of war to Monrovia.

2. The business of the ship having been completed, it only remained to finish ballasting with sand, no freight being offered, and leave for home. Our visit having thus far been one of labor and anxiety, relieved occasionally by the hospitality of old friends, we determined on devoting one day to pleasure, going "up the river," as they say, in Monrovia; and it is a phrase not without meaning and importance. From *up-the-river* they get their daily bread or vegetables, which often supply the place of bread—*up-the-river* live the sturdy farmers and planters of Mesurado County—*up-the-river* lie the *country seats* of many of the Monrovia merchants and leading men; in fact, *up-the-river* is felt to be the home of the Liberians, their little inland kingdom, to which they expect to retire when all the world shall again go a slave-hunting. So up-the-river we must go.

3. One of our friends kindly tendered us the use of his light six-oared gig, and favored us with the company of himself and his interesting lady. To insure a safe return ere night-fall, an early start was necessary; therefore we put off for the shore by sunrise, found our friends at the water side awaiting us, and were soon headed up the Stockton Creek. Everything promised a most charming time of it, and we will anticipate the conclusion by saying, that we have seldom experienced a more delightful day. The party was just large enough, four in number, to sit comfortably in the well-cushioned stern sheets of our beautiful shallop, a nice canvas awning screened us from the rays of the sun, and the swiftness at which we were impelled through the water by six athletic Kroomen, gave us the advantage of a perpetual breeze as we sped through the tortuous Stockton.

4. Here, again, the recollections of former times came over us, when we daily passed through this body of mangrove on our way to Caldwell to visit the receptacles of newly-arrived emigrants. But we recognized no point or landmark of old, scarcely did we know new, Georgia landing. All is one dreary sameness after leaving Mesurado and sight of the harbor. There is no change in the scene except what is caused by the time of tide. At low water you see the roots, or, more properly, the legs of the mangrove trees, tripod-like, but innumerable, supporting their twisted and irregular trunks. Underneath are channels of water and black mud, on which are plenty of snipes and other varieties of water-fowl, looking up an honest livelihood among the small deer, which always abound in such localities. You not unfrequently see the beautiful gold-streaked iguana and other smaller species of the lizard tribe, crawling around among the mangrove roots; occasionally, too, an alligator lies stretched on the mud embankment, dozing away the time, or watching for his dinner.

5. At high water all is covered up; the roots and lower

limbs of the mangrove-trees are submerged in the water, and one seems to be gliding through a floating leafy forest; no sign of animation, excepting the water-fowl screaming through the creek, looking in vain for food, and occasionally a monkey swinging on the mangrove limbs, now fearless of alligators and other foes. All is bush and water. A passage through the Stockton to the St. Paul's is at all times, and in all seasons, one of the most monotonous and disagreeable undertakings imaginable, neither conducive to pleasure, comfort, or health. 'Tis a dead pull of five or six miles through malaria that can almost be *felt*, or too certainly felt, afterward. We, however, noticed one very great difference between a passage now and twenty-five years since. Then, it was not only dreary and monotonous, but lonely, seldom meeting or passing any human being on the way, unless a provision or lumber boat of the agency, going to or returning from Caldwell. Now, the creek was alive with boats and canoes, many of the latter loaded with vegetables for the Monrovia market. Boats, canoes, and people, a curious and mixed-up lot they were. We met two or three pretty good boats, pulled by Kroomen with oars, one the doctor's, the others belonging to farmers and traders on the St. Paul's; but the majority were canoes of all varieties, from the light-curved Kroo canoe, to the heavy burthensome dug-out of the colonists; some manned by colonists, some by natives, and some not manned at all, but *womaned*.

6. In more than one instance we saw colonist women paddling the canoe and the men sitting idle; whether husband, father, or passenger, we could not say. But even here, in this humble and unfeminine occupation, the passion for finery and dress is by no means extinct; jaunty bonnets, pink and yellow ribbons, and light muslin dresses, were not uncommon; the latter, however, well tucked up around the waist, clear of the water, while using the paddle. We recollect witnessing the debarkation of *up-the-river* people at Monrovia on parade day, before going to

Cape Palmas; soldiers with their wives, daughters, and, possibly, sweethearts. The men had little to do, save haul up the canoe, dry their feet, and put on shoes and stockings. Not so the females; it took them no little time to get in fix to go up-town. We noticed a number go behind one of the warehouses and carefully arrange their dresses, add a cape or collar from a box, adjust ribbons and bonnets, holding in one hand a little sixpenny German looking-glass, and then walk off with an air of gentility and pride, not without grace. It spoke well for the tidiness and good charater of this most humble part of the population of Liberia.

7. But to return to our voyage up the river. We said we recognized no old landmark on our way up the Stockton, but we did expect to find our old boat-landing at Caldwell, the junction of the Creek with the St. Paul; but not a vestige of it was to be seen, not even of the old Government House or any of the old receptacles—all gone —the landing overgrown with thick, heavy grass, and the houses, probably, resolved into their original elements. Africa is no place for monuments. The tooth of Time is said to destroy all works of man; but softened by the heat and moisture of Africa, old Time might easily work great changes were his tooth extracted; birth and death, decay and reproduction, so constantly and rapidly succeed each other. Glad were we to emerge from the Stockton and enter upon the beautiful, broad St. Paul's; 'twas like leaving a cellar for open day, so different was the scene before us.

8. Truly, the St. Paul is a noble river, and were it not for the obstructions at Millsburg, would ere this have thousands of Americo-Africans lining its borders far interior to our present settlements. The banks on the southeast side, at Caldwell, and for some distance up, are rather low, but yet are lined with cottages, mostly old settlers; for it was settled for some mile or two up in our early Liberian life. On the opposite shore, the bank rises more

abruptly—it ranges from ten to twenty, thirty, and even fifty feet high in some places. On this side, no attempt had been made at settlement when we left Monrovia, in 1833.

From all that has been said of the St. Paul in our colonization prints, letters from colonists, by those whom we have seen there located, and the constant reference to *up-the-river* in Monrovia, we had not been led to expect great changes and improvement; but, in this case, we are gratified to say, our expectations fell far short of reality. We can not say that the indications of prosperous wealth are greater or exceed our anticipations; but the evidences of comfort and good living do. We think we have never seen a place more charming, or where we would sooner choose to live and die, than on the banks of the St. Paul.

9. There is very little to be said about it, or, rather, we are finable to convey by words an adequate idea of its charm and beauty. One must be acquainted with tropical scenery to form any just estimate. The river is from half to three fourths of a mile broad; the current free but not rapid, gliding down with a smooth, unruffled surface, stronger in the center, eddying under the slight curves and projections of the shore, although the course from Millsburg to its mouth is very direct; the water turbid, especially in the rainy season. As we left Caldwell, we began to pass the farms of emigrants on the opposite shore; in fact, both sides were lined with farms and gardens, alternating with occasional reaches of wood, from Caldwell to Millsburg. Having no time to spare, we landed but twice on our way up; and therefore can not describe the different towns, or even name them. All appeared to be one continuous settlement, and required no naming for our enjoyment or satisfaction. The farms were generally cultivated, even to the water's edge, or top of the bank—grass, or garden and field vegetables, alternately. The plantains and bananas formed a conspicuous feature in the landscape, generally lining the river bank.

Many houses were immediately on the river; others, and generally the larger ones, some distance removed, with a lawn in front. Material used, brick and wood; we do not recollect a stone building. Some of the brick houses were quite large, square buildings, and must have been expensive. Most likely, all that the individual possessed, or could get credit for, was put into the house—this is the weak side of the Liberians. But, paid for or not, owned or not by the occupants, we have never seen in any tropical country so many good and comfortable dwellings within the same distance of each other, or more indications of comfort and a full supply of the necessaries of life.

10. When approaching what is, or was, called College Hill, we landed and walked over it, and can not imagine a spot more suitable for the proposed college. From this we passed on to what is termed Clay-Ashland, where we made a flying visit to many of the emigrants who went out in our ship;—poor people! they were then undergoing their first attack of fever—heavy toll to pay for entering their fatherland. We also jumped on shore at the former home of our old friend Zion Harris, the Nimrod of Liberia and great snake-killer, killed at last in his own bed by lightning. He had a strong premonition or warning of his approaching death, which he expressed to sundry persons. It certainly can not be said, in philosophical explanation of this, that he brought down the lightning upon himself. We obtained a brief sketch of his death from his devoted wife, and on parting, exhorted her to keep intact Zion's beautiful farm. She gave assurance that she would do so, and that she had engaged a man to help her in the work. Too late, we saw, for condolence.

11. The ultimate point or intended terminus of our visit was Richardson's, the sugar planter, sixteen miles from Monrovia, which we reached about eleven o'clock, but to our regret, learned he was absent, having gone down to Monrovia very early, probably arriving there before our departure, as we did not meet him on the way. We, how-

ever, patiently awaited his return, knowing that as soon as he learned we were on a visit to his place, he would instantly set out for home. In an hour or so we had the pleasure of seeing him pulling rapidly up in a canoe. Another hour was spent in dinner, etc., when we sallied out to look at his establishment. The house is situated about one hundred yards from the river, at some forty feet elevation above it, and is far from being of the first class of dwellings; the lower part being used for a store or trade room; but Richardson's ambition reached beyond having a big house. Near the landing was a large kiln of good brick, one half of which had already been laid in the foundation and first story of a capacious sugar-house. Into the latter he intended to put a large steam-power and sugar-mill, already ordered from the United States. He had planned a wooden railway from the mill to the water's edge, by which he could load and unload boats with steam power, intending also to use it for sawing and other purposes when not engaged in cane grinding.

12. Everything appeared to have been judiciously arranged for practical operations on a large scale. On proceeding back from the house, we passed a large garden, well laid out and fenced, with a great variety of fruit and vegetables under way. Farther on, we came to his pasture ground, also well fenced; and feeding in it, were some twenty head of fine large cattle, mostly of a cream-colored, long-horned kind, from the interior. Going through this, we came upon his field of sugar-cane, estimated by him to contain an area of sixty-five or seventy acres. We passed entirely through the lot to a farm-house on an elevation at the farther side, in which lived his head farmer or manager—if Mr. R. could be said to have any manager besides himself. Here, then, was before us, under our own eyes and no mistake, the ground-work of a large and extensive sugar plantation, of large mechanical operations, and also of a great commercial establishment (for Mr. R. carried on a profitable trade with the natives from the

interior). And by whom, and by what means, was all this brought about? Simply by the energy, ability, industry, and frugality of one man, and that, too, in three years, and little or no capital to start upon! Let these facts speak trumpet-tongued to the confusion of all opponents of Liberia and Colonization, be they Northern or Southern fanatics, or the discontented, whining, begging, home-sick emigrants, who write home begging letters, willing to return to bondage, for the flesh-pots.

13. It is well known that this man, who had done so much for himself, for Liberia, and for his race, was drowned in the St. Paul River but a few months after we parted from him, and we repeat what we then wrote to a mutual friend, that we never so deeply regretted the death of any man. As we spoke of Zion Harris' premonition or anticipation of his decease, we will state a fact in connection with the death of Richardson, even at the risk of being considered superstitious. A week or two after our return from Liberia, a young lady, who came passenger with us, a teacher in one of the mission schools, was detained at our house over-night by a heavy rain. In the morning, at breakfast, she remarked, "It is said that the dream of a person on sleeping in a house the first night, will prove true, but I hope mine will not, for I dreamed that Mr. Richardson was drowned in the St. Paul River." Two months after came the news of the fact, happening, as nearly as we could calculate, about the time of the dream. Would it were all a dream, and Richardson were now managing his affairs on the St. Paul!

14. Before we finished examining and admiring the extensive and varied improvements of our host, we noticed a heavy tornado rising in the east, and barely reached the house in double-quick time as the deluge came down. It did not end with a shower, but seemed to set in for a heavy rain, continuing for near two hours without intermission. Here was a pretty fix to be in—two horns of a dilemma: to turn out in this deluge, even if the Kroomen

could be bribed to do it, or to stay and run the risk, to myself and companion, of the African fever. We had about decided to saturate the system with quinine and brandy for one night, and run the risk; when, to our great joy, about four o'clock it held up, and a space opened for the sky to peep through. No time was spent in adieus or stirrup cups; we literally slid down the wet, clayey bank into the boat, yet but half bailed out, and bid our six *athletes* do their best for a guerdon. Truly they did so, for never before did we glide so rapidly through water, impelled by human force, for the distance. Sixteen long miles to the cape, and then to pass the bar, the ravenous bar, or land and cross the beach. 'Twas long after dark before we spied the cape; only distinguishable by the twinkle of lights from the dwellings and the feeble luminous spot called the light-house.

As our ship's boat was inside, we decided upon a trial of the bar, determined to return and cross the beach if it appeared at all angry, but happily all was quiet; and guided by the light from the ship till near enough to distinguish her high black hull, we soon got alongside, and were sipping our much needed tea at nine o'clock, having vastly enjoyed our trip *up-the-river.*

CHAPTER LXXI.

HOPE FOR AFRICA.

1. A VARIETY of circumstances have recently transpired which excite the liveliest hopes in regard to Africa. Public attention is turned toward that country in a manner not before known. From many quarters, and in many ways, without concert on the part of those taking the lead in the movements to which we refer, helping hands are

stretched out toward the long-neglected and long-oppressed tribes of that unhappy country.

2. The discoveries of Dr. Livingstone, and his visit to his native land, have brought matters as it were to a crisis. The attempts which have been made in former times to introduce commerce and civilization into the interior have not wholly failed. Though expedition after expedition seemed to have been baffled, yet they left traces on the banks of the great rivers, of the efforts of philanthropic people in this country; and private enterprise, starting from these points, has carried light and knowledge far into the interior.

3. Out of all these arose the contract for a monthly mail to the west coast; and, lately, a second company have started a line of steamers to trade regularly with that region, and with every prospect of success. English influence has penetrated far inland; hence when a large number of the Matabele, near Tete, who mistook him for a Portuguese, were closely scrutinizing Dr. Livingstone, they were at last satisfied, and expressed their satisfaction in language too honorable to us, and too touching in itself, to be soon forgotten—"You belong to the tribe that loves the black man!"

4. While this illustrious traveler was pursuing his way among regions hitherto unknown to Europeans, and among peoples of whose existence we had no knowledge, a new effort to carry intercourse up the Niger as far as its confluence with the Tchadda, was in contemplation. It has now been settled, with the concurrent aid of the Government. Mr. Macgregor Laird, already one of the foremost in the endeavor to civilize Africa, has engaged to have a steamer passing regularly from Fernando Po to the confluence of the great rivers, and he also runs one on his own account besides.

5. About four years ago, Mr. Moffat sent home a long and deeply-interesting account of his visit to Moselakatze, chief over one of the largest tribes, occupying a fine coun

try lying north of the Kurraman, on whose banks he was stationed. One object of the visit was to convey various communications and supplies for Dr. Livingstone to some point on his proposed journey to the east coast. Moselakatze appointed twenty of his men, with an officer, to carry on foot seventeen boxes and other packages, to the south bank of the Zambese. When the party arrived there with their treasure, they hailed the Makololo on the opposite shore, informed them of the purpose of their visit, and invited them to take charge of what they had brought for "the Doctor." Suspecting treachery, the Makololo at first declined. In consequence, the Matabele left the supplies on the bank of the river, and devolved upon their suspicious neighbors the responsibility of keeping them safely. The Makololo subsequently crossed the Zambese, conveyed the packages to an island, protected them from the weather, and in that state Dr. Livingstone found them, more than a year afterward, in perfect safety. Not an article was pillaged; and when Dr. Livingstone arrived, his heart was cheered with the books, letters, and, to him, other valuable supplies, which had so long waited his arrival.

6. Most of the missionaries stationed on the African coast have cherished a deep and anxious desire to carry their labors inland; and no one can examine any maps of these districts, and compare them with those of former days, without being struck with the obvious tendency of such agencies to penetrate into the country behind them. The few who have gone somewhat into the interior have found a comparatively healthy country, open and prairie-like, a people far superior in habits and knowledge to those who are on the coast, where the degrading influence of the slave traffic has been most felt, and practicing many of those curious customs, and maintaining those peculiar social laws which Dr. Livingstone found in existence among the tribes whom he saw.

7. Should God graciously vouchsafe his blessing, mis-

sions in Africa will assume a new character, and those already in operation there will receive a fresh impetus. These missions will soon be second to none in importance. The old civilization of Africa will be brought back, but happily this time not associated with heathenism and idolatry, but intimately blended with the Christian morals and faith. We bid these enterprises God-speed. The great purpose for which so many have toiled in hope, and which has surmounted every opposing obstacle, will be no longer regarded as vain and fruitless, but one rich in the promise of a grand success. Surely light begins to dawn on Africa.

CHAPTER LXXII.

THE NEW NATIONALITY.

1. Congress admitted at its late session a new member into the family of nations with which this Government has diplomatic relations. It is *Liberia*—land of the free—situated on the west coast of Africa, between ten degrees on each side of the equator; extending about six hundred miles along the shore, and from fifty to one hundred miles into the interior, comprising about thirty thousand square miles of territory, with more than three hundred thousand inhabitants, of which some fifteen thousand are emigrants, and their descendants, from the United States.

2. It is wholly a country of colored people. No person can be a citizen who does not admit that African blood runs in his veins. Its present chief magistrate, Stephen Allen Benson, is a man of pure negro extraction—a native of Maryland in this country, carried by his parents, when a child of six years, in 1822, to that colony, which was then forming the nucleus of Liberia. Its government

resembles our own. It has a "Declaration of Independence," a "Constitution," a Legislature, composed of a Senate and House of Representatives elected by the people, a Supreme and other courts of justice, a small navy, and a well-trained militia. The President and Vice-President must be thirty-five years of age, and have property to the amount of $600; and their term of office is two years. The members of the House are elected for two years, and of the Senate for four years. Universal freedom prevails under its jurisdiction.

3. The English is the national language. The tastes, and customs, and sympathies of the people are eminently American.

It has able men in the professions, industrious men in the field, skillful men in the shop, shrewd men in the market. It has good citizens, with more than fifty Christian churches, and three thousand communicants, and as many Sabbath-school children. It has schools and seminaries, and a college with competent instructors. The press, also, is there, with its regular issues of the newspaper and other publications.

4. Monrovia, the capital of Liberia, so named after President Monroe of this country, a distinguished friend of the settlement, is beautifully situated on Cape Mesurado, about seventy-five feet above the level of the sea, in $6°$ $19'$ north latitude and $11°$ west longitude. Its population is about three thousand five hundred. Its position is peculiarly favorable for commerce with the interior, by means of the St. Paul, the Junk, and other navigable rivers.

The college edifice lately erected there has a commanding site, on a twenty-acre field for play-grounds—granted by the Government. It was built by the beneficence of good people in Boston, Massachusetts, and vicinity. Four thousand acres of land are donated to this institution by the Liberian Legislature. Ex-President Roberts (a Methodist) is President; Rev. Alexander Crummell (an Episcopalian) and Rev. E. H. Blyden (a Presbyterian) are Professors.

It is already supplied with a respectable library and geological cabinet, and will in a very short time receive pupils.

The entire faculty are just now on a visit to this country. The buildings, streets, manners, and customs of the people of Monrovia are very much like those of places similarly situated in this country. The inhabitants are as industrious, moral, religious, and happy as those of any like place in the world.

5. The Monrovians are great Sabbatarians. Says Gerard Ralston, of London: "They go constantly to church; and so closely do they respect the Sabbath, that when the Prince de Joinville, the captain of the French frigate Belle Poule, came into their port on Sunday, and offered to salute their flag, it was declined because of their unwillingness to have the Sabbath desecrated. So, also, when Captain Eden, of one of Her Majesty's ships, was ordered to call at Monrovia to salute the flag, provided it would be returned, when he was informed that it could not be done on that day, being Sunday, but it would be done on the following day (Monday). Captain Eden, being pressed for time, saluted on Sunday, with the understanding that the salute would be returned to the first British cruiser that came into port."

6. The climate of Liberia is warm, but equable, and tempered by frequent rains and daily sea-breezes. The year has two seasons—the wet, beginning about the middle of May, and the dry, commencing at the middle of November. The average temperature of the former being about seventy-five degrees, and of the latter about eighty degrees, so that the heat is never so great there as it is at times in this country. This is a salubrious clime to the man of color, but noxious to the whites. "Many attempts," says Gerard Ralston, "have been made by different nations—Portuguese, Dutch, English, French, Danes, and Swedes—to establish settlements of white colonies on various intertropical portions of the African coast, and all

have failed from the same cause—the deadly nature of the climate.

7. The average length of the life of the white man there is said to be less than four years, while the colored immigrant will live as long as others of his race in America. All immigrants, however, have to pass through a brief acclimating fever, in which death now rarely occurs. It is remarkable that foreigners must spend the night on board ship, while they may be on land from eight o'clock A.M. to eight o'clock P.M., with safety from the miasma.

The two largest rivers within the present limits of Liberia are the Cavally, in the southeast, navigable to vessels of fifteen feet draft for eighty miles, and the St. Paul, in the northwest, navigable for sixteen miles to ships of twelve feet draft, and extending into the country three hundred miles, through a fertile and beautiful region.

8. Numerous small streams, some of which are half a mile wide fifty miles from the ocean, are navigable for small boats various distances. Excellent fish abound in all these streams. The soil yields a rapid and abundant reward, being exceedingly fertile and prolific for almost every kind of tropical fruit. Half a million of coffee-trees are under cultivation, and considerable quantities of this article are exported to Europe and this country. A single individual raised last year sixty thousand pounds of sugar. Cotton, being also indigenous to the soil, is beginning to be extensively cultivated, and a large trade in this staple, it is expected, will soon be opened with the nations in the interior. They raise and *manufacture* into cloths annually, as estimated by Mr. Crummell, not less than one million of pounds.

9. Palm oil and the palm nut are prominent articles of export, the annual traffic of which, on the west African coast, is valued at more than *ten millions of dollars*.

Forty vessels are owned and manned by the Liberians, and their commerce with this and other countries is already greater than that of New York for the first half century of its existence.

From recent official tables, it appears that of sixty countries with which the United States have established commercial relations, Liberia stands number eighteen in the scale of importance, the value of our annual trade with her being—exports $2,062,723, imports $1,755,916.

10. The facilities of Liberia for expansion into the interior are abundant. Explorations have been made eastward from Monrovia to the distance of some three hundred miles, which bring to light the most tempting inducements to the formation of new settlements and the introduction of the arts of civilized life. The native tribes are favorably disposed toward the Republic—and in their physical, mental, moral, and social condition they promise much more of good than many of the coast tribes. Vast resources of wealth, agricultural, mineral, and industrial, have been found in these "regions beyond," and their capabilities are such that all the colored population of the globe could not exhaust them for ages. A wide and most inviting field is here open for all the people of color in this country, and for the most enterprising commercial, philanthropic, and Christian labors. It is fit that the Republic which has opened the door to this interior region should be recognized by our Government. We rejoice that this act of justice and policy is at last done. All honor to the noble men, dead and living, *of every part of our country*, who have labored for this auspicious result.

CHAPTER LXXIII.
NEW GEORGIA.

1. Rev. Alexander M. Cowan writes thus in regard to New Georgia: "New Georgia has two principal streets, on which most of the inhabitants reside. Some few cross-streets have dwellings on them. One hundred and fifty-nine town lots, of one fourth of an acre, have been drawn, but not more than twenty-one of them are now occupied by the original settlers, because they are too far off from their farm lands. The soil is a white sand with very little loam in it. The streets are remarkably clean. The houses are mostly of one story, and are framed buildings; some, however, are built of poles, daubed with clay. All the houses are raised from two to three feet from the ground, and are placed on pillars of wood or brick, to give a free circulation of air, especially in the wet season. This practice prevails in Liberia.

2. "They have no stone in this settlement. The improved lots are planted with cassada, sweet potatoes, eddoes, yams, beans, melons, cucumbers, etc., with a suitable proportion of the pawpaw, pine-apple, tamarind, cocoa-nut, orange, lime, guava, plantain, and banana. * * *

3. "The orange is, in size and branches, like an apple-tree, and bears twice a year, having the oranges scattered in its branches. They can be found on some of the trees every month in the year, though the principal ripening of them is in May and June, and in November and December. There can be seen at the same time on the trees, the bud, the blossom, the full formed fruit, and the ripe fruit. They have two kinds, the sweet and the sour. The sweet are better than the Havana and the New Orleans oranges.

4. "The lime is much like the orange-tree in its growth and yield, but differs in size, the lime being the smallest in growth. The guava-tree abounds here. It is like our

peach-tree. The guava is not fit to eat from the tree, but makes a very rich preserve. Its size is that of a common peach.

"The Georgians spoke the English language with a foreign accent. Their children had not that accent in their speech. They were ready to give me information in regard to their means of support, their productions, their schools, and their religious privileges.

5. "They raised cotton, spun it, and, in some measure, wove it into cloth. Their dress, the cultivation of their land, their social intercourse, and their religious improvement bespoke much for their comfort, their industry, and morals. Order seemed to prevail throughout their town. In their yards, and at their doors, I could see the female members of the households in their every-day dress, brought out of their houses from curiosity to see me, a white person, walking up and down their streets, *gazing* at what I saw in their town. I was very much gratified at the cleanliness and good manners I witnessed among them as a body—for there was a difference in the comforts and style of the people. In every place there will be, and must be, for good order, males and females who have proper ideas of what constitutes a good, orderly, and moral society, and who will give a particular personal exhibition of its several parts in their daily life. They have two churches, Methodist and Baptist, two day-schools, and two Sabbath-schools. Many of the children read and spelt for me, showing that they had an 'aptness to learn.' * * *

6. "Great contentment prevailed among them. I need not say they were citizens of the Republic, and that the officers of their town were elected out of their own class of persons. I did not see a mulatto among them. I went into a house and stated I would be glad to have dinner, but with no special preparation for it, as I wished to see what could be furnished me, on such a call, to eat. I was soon seated at a table, having before me cold mutton, cas-

sada, rice, and sweet potatoes. The mutton was not as fat as Kentucky mutton, but it was sweet, tender, and juicy. I was pleased with my dinner. They gave me to drink the juice of the granadilla. It grows on a vine. * * *

7. "I bade this people farewell, with the full conviction that the Gospel of Christ, with its attendant means, as education, civilization, and a proper sense of duty that man owes to his fellow-man, in a social and civil state of life, can, and will, elevate all religion, in knowledge, and manners of life. Here has been this evidence before my eyes. And their children coming on the stage of life, with these advantages (which their fathers possessed not in their youth), will act with higher views from their citizenship, and with more enlarged ideas arising from the spiritual, social, and political benefits furnished them by living in Liberia, than they could possibly have had if they had been born, and lived, and died in the United States."

8. Also, W. S. Hall, speaking of this people, says: "They were located on Stockton Creek, and their town, called New Georgia, now boasts two Christian churches, in which Sabbath-schools are regularly held, in addition to two day-schools. A few of those sent from here have learned to read, and very many of them are respectable members of a church. They long since took the oath of allegiance to the Republic of Liberia, and most of them possess the requisite property qualification entitling them to a vote. One of their number has been a member of the State Legislature. A few have married colonist females.

"They are not traders, but simple cultivators of the soil, and market gardeners for the town of Monrovia, four miles distant.

9. "They are an honest and industrious people, and highly respected as such by the Americo-Liberians, with whom they associate on the most brotherly terms of equality. The adults will speak in broken English, and can not be considered wholly civilized men; but their children have

had the benefit of a common-school education, and would not be recognized as differing in any respect from those whose parents were born in this country."

CHAPTER LXXIV.

FOREIGN RELATIONS IN 1862.

1. THE Foreign Relations of Liberia have been extended and multiplied during the year, and with one or two exceptions, have remained undisturbed. The purpose of demolishing the barricades among the chiefs near Cape Mount has been accomplished without any hostile demonstration, and the effect to commerce and order proved beneficial. Some of the interior chiefs appear dissatisfied, and difficulties among tribes of Fishmen near Cape Palmas, which were thought to be settled, have sprung up again. Several cruel acts of the superstitious trial by poison having been perpetrated, President Benson proceeded against them with one hundred men, in the Seth Grosvenor, joined by others, and compelled them to keep the peace and pay the cost of the war. It is justly remarked by President Benson, touching the murderous practices to some extent prevailing among tribes under the protection of the Republic:

2. "The time has come when such homicidal practices by natives living at least within the vicinity of our settlements should be promptly checked. If the Government has the right and power to stop them (which I presume no one will deny), then it becomes a moral duty, and the neglect of such a duty involves moral delinquency and national guilt."

3. The honorable vindication of the character of Liberia by her government in the affair of the French vessel, the Regina Cœli, induces the expectation that she will be able

to show the world how unjustifiable was the recent attack of a Spanish man-of-war steamer upon the single man-of-war schooner in the harbor of Monrovia. This was not more an assault against Liberia than an affront to the majesty of England (since it was in retaliation upon the English man-of-war for destroying the Spanish slaver in the Gallinas), and we may look to the power of Great Britain to maintain her own policy against the slave trade, and her sense of the solemn treaty obligations of Spain. We can not think that the magnanimity of Spain will permit her to attempt to coerce the young and feeble Republic of Liberia (acknowledged as a free state by at least ten of the civilized powers of the world) to cast aside her responsibility to God, to herself, and humanity.

4. In his last message, President Benson observes that it is impossible for Liberian merchants to succeed in honest competition in ports of the United States under the great pressure of existing discriminating duties; and it has been deemed right and proper to impose on the vessels and cargoes of the United States in her ports, similar discriminating duties. This is mutually disadvantageous, but of far greater injury to our citizens than to hers. The acknowledgment of the independence of Liberia, recommended by the President to Congress, would naturally be followed by other measures that would place the commerce, mutually, of that Republic and the United States upon a just basis.

5. Benevolence, like business, must submit its plans to the unbending laws of nature, and learn from physical science how to direct its operations; but pure benevolence turns naturally toward the light, and, by a divine ingenuity, is apt to conform its labors to these physical laws.

6. The mixed motives which suggested the Liberian Colony merged on the fact that a great physical law had been violated in transferring the natives of tropical Africa to our wintry climate, and that the error was to be corrected by sending them back. At an early day they be-

gan to be removed southward on this continent, but benevolence and social justice required their return to the land of their fathers.

7. Working under this law, Benevolence adapted to this colonization the favoring incidents which have conspired to remove doubts, answer objections, and silence the clamors of those violators of nature who sought to absorb this tropical race by intermarriage with our own; the colonization of these people somewhere in tropical regions has become a national policy, while the most thoughtful and experienced find reasons of the highest order, reaching to the permanent welfare of all races of men, in favor of the Colony of Liberia.

8. While navigators crept along the shores of Europe, each nation found the supply of its wants and the means of its increase only within its neighborhood; but when the ships of Portugal returned from India, and the ships of Spain from the Mexican Gulf, loaded with the rich products of the tropics, the nations of Europe began a new career of civilization, and looked to the interchange of conveniences and luxuries over the whole face of the earth. This career was restrained by their limited means of navigation, and still more by the indolence of the people of the tropics, and their unwillingness to prepare large supplies of the products of their soils and mines for the European market; but ships were rapidly multiplied, and large bodies of laborers and mechanics were carried to equatorial regions. But these colonists were subdued by the climate, and demoralized and swept away by the habits of the barbarians; and the adventurers came to the natural and fixed conclusion that tropical products must be obtained by the labor of the equatorial races.

9. Following this conclusion, the adventurers tried various motives to induce regular and effective industry among the natives, and, failing in this, they resorted to enforcement. The slender race of Asiatics, which had entered America on the western side sunk and perished

under the toil exacted by their masters; and the hopes of Europe concerning the wealth of the New World were checked a second time.

10. Observation has shown that men from the equator become hardy by removing a few degrees farther to the north. Acting on this idea, the people of Guinea were brought to the borders of the Gulf of Mexico. They were found equal to the labor, and more effective on the northern than on the southern border. Now, the abundance of the tropics is poured into Europe; what had been the delicacies of the few—the sugar and its products, the coffee and the rice, the tobacco and the cotton—became common to the whole people. The English colonies rose rapidly in the vicinity of this new labor. The Africans continued to be moved northward, and to enrich their masters; and in the newness of the country they were pushed so far into our winter climate that their labor soon became unprofitable.

11. The opening of the tropics and the mines, followed by the consequent inventions, has made the civilized world what it is in population and wealth. England employs on one tropical plant more people than she contained in the days of Elizabeth. The natives of the tropics do all the work of their own climate; they will continue to do it. Can they do it of choice? Can they do it cheerfully and hopefully? Can they make an even bargain for the fruits of their labor? Can they civilize?

12. The presence of the Caucasian, among the equatorial races, has not profited either; but has degraded the one without elevating the other. Can tropical products be had in abundance without the controlling presence of our race? This is the great question for solution; and in view of this question I have framed the resolution, "that the colonization of tropical Africa, by Africans previously civilized in this country, opens a new and cheering prospect for the general welfare of the different races of men."

13. The prospect is new; it is new in several of its

features. It is a new fact that a body of tropical **Africans**, enjoying letters and arts, have established and administered a civil government, and maintained it by the fair and effectual administration of written laws and courts of record, during a course of years, unaided by men of our race.

14. During thirty years past they have been steadily gaining civil strength and increasing in numbers, and during all that time they have required less and less of the directing care and control of this Society. They have made steady and hopeful progress in producing for the markets of the world such articles as we expect from tropical regions. They have scared away from six hundred miles of coast the malignant little gods who have always been the scourge of equatorial Africa. They have snatched from these gods many thousands of the natives, and brought them to the knowledge of the God of the universe, and led them to Christian worship. They have conquered a pestilent climate by clearing and draining their lands. They have built goodly houses and dwelt in them. They offer a home and protection to the converts brought by white missionaries from the pagan tribes behind them. Their schools produce engineers competent to project internal improvements, and mechanics able to execute them. Their merchants are respected in the civilized world. In all these matters they are steadily advancing, while the interference of our race in their affairs is not felt.

15. Is not this a new state of things in equatorial Africa? It is so, because these people were previously civilized in this country, and prepared to do what they are continuing without the presence of our race. They are colonists, with the means and motives for sending to the markets of the world hereafter an unlimited quantity of tropical products. Will they do it?

16. There is a cheering prospect that they will accomplish a general welfare for their race and ours. The

greatness of an undertaking is measured by its duration and capacity for expansion.

17. So far as we can now see, Liberia may endure. It has the elements of constancy. It stands acknowledged by many great nations as a nationality. England is pledged by Jamaica and by Sierra Leone to protect it. France is bound by the memories of St. Domingo to protect it. Our nation will defend if she does not acknowledge Liberia.

18. If Liberia shall endure, it is capable of indefinite expansion. Every step in its organization and construction can be repeated, and repeated more easily than it was begun. A voice from large portions of this country announces voluntary emancipation; a voice in this hall announces compensation to masters, and a voice from the free African people of these States will announce a voluntary exodus to the land which nature adapted them to occupy at their return from captivity in our frosty climate.

19. Each new traveler penetrating from the coast to the eastward reports hills and valleys and streams of water where the maps had laid down a desert. The colonist will follow the traveler. A highway shall be there. The people shall press onward to the sources of the Nile; and Egypt shall at last acknowledge a civilization from the West.

20. Let the stable nationality of Liberia be assured, and the problem of tropical civilization by tropical races will be solved, and tropical products will follow; for civilization generates the wants and wishes which impel the poor to labor and the rich to enterprise. A second colony can rise by the light of the first—can profit by our mistakes, and sooner rise to independence.

21. What has been accomplished in the tropics of Africa can be ultimately extended over the same belt around the globe. Ancient colonies were formed by those who escaped from the sacking of their cities, leaving their effects to the flames, and bearing off the aged on their shoulders,

and leading the young by the hand. Their obscurity and remoteness from other nations was their safety. But our colonies will go forth with full supplies, secure in the chivalrous protection of strong nations, and ready to enter the market of the world with the first-fruits of their industry.

22. Much of the tropical race has nearly served out its time under the direction of the Caucasian race. They have earned their outfit. Send them back to the land of the sun. The wilderness and the solitary place shall be glad for them, and the desert shall rejoice and blossom as the rose. They shall go out with joy and be sent forth with peace. For God hath made of one blood all the nations of men to dwell on all the face of the earth, and hath appointed the bounds of their habitation, that by co-operative labor they should work out that good for the sons of men which they should seek after all the days of their life.

CHAPTER LXXV.

THE COLONY IN DANGER.

LETTER FROM REV. JOHN SEYS.

Monrovia, *November* 27, 1861.

1. The brig Ann, of New York, sails to-morrow, will touch at Cape Palmas, and thence proceed immediately to the United States. Although I can not now write to you as fully as I would wish, yet I trust a few lines will not be unacceptable, especially as it is not long since I had the pleasure of writing more at length.

I am happy to be able to say that a kind and watchful Providence still continues to guard the interests of this young and comparatively feeble nation.

2. The dreadful attack from the hostile Spaniards is yet

in the future, and, not unlikely, may be indefinitely postponed. Independently of the very tangible and rather destructive evidence which the Government of Liberia gave the Spanish steamer, on the 11th September, of their readiness and ability to repel any such attack upon them as was then made, it is not at all improbable that they may have heard of the very active part which Great Britain has taken in the affair. So soon as it was known at Sierra Leone, His Excellency the Governor of that colony dispatched Her B. M. steamer, the Torch, to come at once to the aid of the Liberians, and, on her return, the Falcon took her place, and has been lying for nearly a fortnight in our roads.

3. The utmost vigilance is kept up on the part of the military and naval forces of the country, and there is cause to believe that should another attack be made, the invader, to use the language of one of the officers of the Falcon to me, may find himself "blown to pieces."

Hostilities of a very serious character have been prevailing among the interior tribes for some time. Towns have been burned, murders committed, and many captives taken.

4. The Liberian Government immediately interposed, and one man, quite an intelligent native, reared in the family of one of the early settlers, and supposed to be a staunch ally and friend of the Republic, has been arrested and is now in jail, after an examination which it is believed will bring him before the grand jury, and may end seriously. Of his complicity with the head men and ringleaders of these wars on innocent allies of Liberia, there seems to be strong evidence.

5. My fears entertained and expressed some time since of a great scarcity of food, have proved as yet groundless. Notwithstanding the failure of your Mary C. Stevens at the time we all expected her, and the fact, in addition, that the visits of American vessels, with full cargoes, are becoming more and more rare, yet there has been no

want. Foreign provisions have been higher, but our native breadstuffs have been plentiful, and so far as I can judge, the crisis has passed, and there will be no want of any of the real necessaries of life in Liberia. To God be all the praise in the first place, and next a meed of praise must be awarded to our farmers, who so industriously keep us supplied with potatoes, and cassavas, and eddoes, and beans, plantains, and bananas, and scores of other good things which this wonderfully prolific soil so luxuriantly produces.

6. The liberated Africans are doing well. The Liberian Government are carrying out, in good faith, their contract with your Society, and I take pleasure in giving the required certificates to that effect. These people improve fast, and I am every day more and more convinced that to efficiently benefit the recaptured African he must be sent to Liberia. Here is found every possible inducement to him to improve, and here, if anywhere in Christendom, he can become A MAN.

CHAPTER LXXVI.

INAUGURAL ADDRESS OF PRESIDENT BENSON, 1860.

FRIENDS AND FELLOW-CITIZENS:

1. Two years ago, when addressing you on a similar occasion, it was perhaps equally as foreign to your purpose, as it was to my expectation and desire, that I should this day stand before you again, as your candidate elect, to be inaugurated for the occupancy of the presidential chair of this Republic for another term of two years. Yet, in the course of events, it has been your pleasure, in the exercise of your enlightened and sacred suffrage since that period, to designate me to serve you another term. And

it is in obedience to your sovereign will, as expressed so generally at the ballot-box last May, that I appear before you this day to take upon me the solemn oath enjoined by the fundamental law of this Republic.

2. I feel, fellow-citizens, that I would be no less highly chargeable with a dereliction of duty than I would be outraging my own feelings, were I to permit the present occasion to escape, without attempting, however imperfectly it may be done, an expression of the profound gratitude I feel toward you for the successive unmistakable evidences of confidence reposed in me, by electing me three times to the highest office in your gift. I beg now to assure you that the confidence thus reposed, will produce no effect on me, contrary to that of affording incentives to increased efforts on my part to serve the best interest of our common country.

3. To serve the best interest of Liberia, was by far the leading, if not the only motive that influenced me four years ago to take upon me, by your request, such responsible duties as are involved in the office of the chief magistracy of this Republic. And however tremulously at the time I may have approached the presidential chair, it was a source of much relief to my mind, when I remembered that my public life would be subject to your scrutiny, subject to the verdict of a political tribunal, synonymous with the power that had exalted me to the presidency. In the mandates of that tribunal, as may be expressed at the ballot-box, I hope to always cordially acquiesce, whether they be *pro* or *con.*

4. After a public life of four years spent in your midst, it would be a needless tax on your time to attempt now a recapitulation of my administrative policy. This may be proper enough when one is for the first time entering upon his administrative term. But should he continue his incumbency for successive terms, he should expect and desire his constituents to judge him by his works, instead of by his words. This course has been, as a general thing,

the uniform practice of political adjudication in republican governments. I had many unmistakable evidences of your approval of the enunciation of principles and policy, which I made upon the occasion of my first induction four years ago. The following year, in my renomination and re-election, you were pleased to give further evidence of your satisfaction and conviction, that I had striven hard to cause my administrative policy to harmonize with the theory I had enunciated. And during the early part of the year that has just closed, you were pleased again to evidence your confirmation in this belief, by elevating me this third time to the highest office in your gift.

5. These repeated evidences of satisfaction and confidence convince me that you have very rightly adjudged that, whatever is the uniform practice of one, is the only reliable exponent of his principles. In entering four years ago upon the public career into which I am being inaugurated again to-day, my duty was plain before me. I sought by every justifiable means to encourage political peace and concord among ourselves, and to give countenance only to so much agitation as might be necessary to prevent an unhealthy political stagnation, and its ruinous consequences. I also intently strove to direct the minds and action of my countrymen to those principles of political economy, without the observance and practice of which the wealthiest nation must retrograde, and the young nation must expire in its infancy; but from the observance of which, individual and national prosperity in every possible conceivable respect would result; in a word, to induce the bulk of our citizens to draw their minds away from foreign lands, and turn their attention home, to the development of our country's resources; to the cultivation of the soil, and the manufacture of the products of our country, which pursuits are the only reliable basis of a healthy and profitable commerce; internal improvements, so as to facilitate transportation, that Liberia might become more loved and appreciated at home

as well as admired and respected abroad, rendered increasingly so by the continued equitable administration of her laws to all, and her certain, though gradual, advancement in every other essential element of national greatness.

6. If Liberia is ever to be *really* independent; if ever her finances or pecuniary interest is to find a reliable basis; if she is to establish and maintain a literature here; if the area of her territory is to expand commensurately with her national age; if civilization and Christianity are to be coextensive with her territorial jurisdiction; if ever she is made in the future to disgorge her last mineral and vegetable treasures; if ever we safely escape the danger of foreign influence in our politics; if ever we attain to perfect and respectable national manhood, these great and ennobling ends are to be secured by the general diffusion of religion and letters throughout this Republic.

7. I employ the term *religion* here as a comprehensive or generic term, comprehending in the galaxy of its constituent traits and concomitants *industry* and *economy*, and that industry, too, that is of the most productive and available nature. For inspiration plainly intimates (if not expressly teaches) that "diligence in business, fervor of spirit, and the service of the Lord," if not synonymous terms, are at least tri-sisters and inseparably joined. And if there is one national industrial pursuit to be preferred to another, taking precedence because of its paramount importance, it is that which Divine Wisdom assigned man in his primitive state of innocence—the cultivation of the soil; an occupation more congenial than any other to that state of purity in which he was created, and which was calculated more than any other secular employment to preserve from contamination those sanctified affections with which he held constant communion with his Creator.

8. If at this time there be any one thing in Liberia more than another that rejoices and encourages my heart,

it is the rapid progress that my fellow-citizens have made in agricultural and other industrial pursuits. Their progress in that respect is more than sufficient to compensate me for whatever ordeal I may have had to pass through during the last four years of my public life. I am fully aware that various have been, and perhaps are, opinions in foreign lands, as to our capability for the perpetuity of our government and civil institutions. Our success is still regarded by many as a problem, yet to be solved. The opinion was based, a few years ago, mainly on what was supposed to be a natural deficiency of intellect in the race, as well as delinquency in voluntary enterprise and industry. But the rapid discoveries and lucid testimony of numerous recent travelers upon this continent have pretty well convinced the civilized world that Africa and Africans, when not contaminated by such civilized influences as are vicious, are a very different people in condition and character from those of hopeless, indolent, and brutal degradation, which opinion had so generally obtained for centuries in the civilized world.

9. Barth, Livingstone, Bowen, and Seymour, have each, to a degree, drawn the curtain aside, and presented to the astonished view of the civilized world populous kingdoms and cities. They have not only traversed extensive regions of fertile and well-watered countries, abounding in natural wealth, because their vast mineral and vegetable treasures remain yet untouched, but they also bear testimony to the annual existence of large and well-cultivated fields where plenty abounds. And some portions of this land are occupied by negroes who consider it a disgrace to be indolent; negroes dwelling in the heart of Africa, who, for centuries of seclusion from the civilized world, have maintained a somewhat respectable state of civilization; vast regions peopled by negroes, whose virtues, especially of chastity, honesty, hospitality, and industry, rival the degree to which those qualities generally obtain in the civilized world; a people admirably subject to rule and order,

and possessing to an astonishing degree those elements which, by a proper development, and if accompanied with a knowledge and practice of Bible truth, can not fail in the future to elevate them to a state of national dignity and grandeur, second to no existing race now upon the earth.

10. Fellow-citizens, in proportion as years increase upon me do I discover the vastness of the field, and the responsibility of the work marked out by Divine Providence for Liberia upon this continent. Who is it that can look through the vista of the future without being satisfied that there must, in the very nature of things, be an extensive expansion of territory; coextensive with which, we trust, will be the diffusion of religion, letters, and law, and a rapid assimilation to us of the teeming tribes of this vast continent, their confederation or consolidation with us—tribes, many of whom, in their seclusion in central Africa, now possess all the essential elements and susceptibilities of a great and noble people; and surely one can not refrain from indulging in an anticipation, almost amounting to a certainty, of a glorious future for Liberia, a future whose glory will exceed the present in brilliancy, far more than the clear noonday does the beclouded morning sun.

11. Let our friends in foreign lands, who have for many years anxiously watched our progress; whose prayers and means have for so long a time been kindly and magnanimously tendered in our behalf; whose solicitude for our well-being and success is no less than our own; let them know, let them from this moment receive this declaration most respectfully made unto them, as an assurance emanating from the heart of each individual citizen of Liberia separately, and then again as emanating in the aggregate from every heart united in one, that "Liberia will not, can not, and shall not, be disgraced by civil wars!" Let the declaration of truth go forth to them this day, that their fears of civil war among us during the last year were un-

founded; such a thought, apprehension, or intention could find no place to exist in any Liberian's head or heart.

12. Our citizens, when they become surcharged with real or imaginary political provocations, will seek and avail themselves of the medium of the press, if accessible, for relief. This is natural to them, in common with the citizens of all other republican governments, where the liberty of the press is tolerated. And though the abuse of their privilege by going to excess, as was evidenced in all the Liberian papers published the last year, is much to be regretted, and should not be encouraged, yet it should be regarded more in the light of a safety valve, relieving them, through this medium, of that which might otherwise find a less harmless escape.

13. And now, fellow-citizens, since the year which ends my second administrative term has just closed, and we are just entering upon a new year and a new term, let the political follies and inconsistencies of the last year pass away with it. Let the wise and good in foreign lands be thoroughly convinced at last of the important fact, respecting which they seem most tenaciously incredulous, that Liberians can politically dispute and contend, can wage a most intense political warfare of words, and can most independently say a great many hard things about each other in the heat of their excitement—perhaps truly and untruly—and at the same time contemplate not the least corporeal or other injury to each other; and at no time permitting the excitement and adverse political feelings to become so intensive, as to prevent them at any time from uniting on a common platform of patriotism in defense and support of the fundamental interests of our common country.

14. Let Liberians demonstrate to the world that they can, at the proper time (as is now the case), lay down their weapons of political warfare after having inflicted no further damage than words can do, only to resume their use in moderation when circumstances shall really make it necessary. Let us in future look up and forward more in-

tently than ever before to higher and nobler ends. Let Church and State keep their respective missions before them, and moving on in their respective legitimate spheres, strive to excel in being instrumental in contributing to the spiritual and temporal welfare of this land and country; in the faithful prosecution of which, in this very extensive and responsible field spread out by Divine Providence before each one individually, as well as before all in the aggregate, each and all will find enough to do, to call into requisition their every energy, their every power, their every faculty.

CHAPTER LXXVII.

TREATY BETWEEN THE UNITED STATES AND LIBERIA.

By the President of the United States of America.

A PROCLAMATION.

WHEREAS a Treaty between the United States of America and the Republic of Liberia was concluded and signed by their respective Plenipotentiaries, at London, on the 21st day of October, 1862, which treaty is, word for word, as follows:

The United States of America and the Republic of Liberia, desiring to fix, in a permanent and equitable manner, the rules to be observed in the intercourse and commerce they desire to establish between their respective countries, have agreed, for this purpose, to conclude a treaty of commerce and navigation, and have judged that the said end can not be better obtained than by taking the most perfect equality and reciprocity for the basis of their agreement; and to effect this they have named, as their respective

Plenipotentiaries, that is to say: the President of the United States of America, Charles Francis Adams, Envoy Extraordinary and Minister Plenipotentiary of the United States of America at the court of St. James; and the Republic of Liberia, his excellency Stephen Allen Benson, President thereof, who, after having communicated to each other their respective full powers, found in good and due form, have agreed upon the following articles:

ARTICLE I.—There shall be perpetual peace and friendship between the United States of America and the Republic of Liberia, and also between the citizens of both countries.

ARTICLE II.—There shall be reciprocal freedom of commerce between the United States of America and the Republic of Liberia. The citizens of the United States of America may reside in, and trade to, any part of the territories of the Republic of Liberia to which any other foreigners are or shall be admitted. They shall enjoy full protection for their persons and properties; they shall be allowed to buy from and to sell to whom they like, without being restrained or prejudiced by any monopoly, contract, or exclusive privilege of sale or purchase whatever; and they shall, moreover, enjoy all other rights and privileges which are or may be granted to any other foreigners, subjects, or citizens of the most favored nation. The citizens of the Republic of Liberia shall, in return, enjoy similar protection and privileges in the United States of America and in their territories.

ARTICLE III.—No tonnage, import, or other duties or charges shall be levied in the Republic of Liberia on United States vessels, or on goods imported or exported in United States vessels, beyond what are or may be levied on national vessels, or on the like goods imported or exported in national vessels; and in like manner no tonnage, import, or other duties or charges shall be levied in the United States of America and their territories on the vessels of the Republic of Liberia, or on goods imported or exported in those vessels, beyond what are or may be levied on national vessels, or on the like goods imported or exported in national vessels.

ARTICLE IV.—Merchandise or goods coming from the United States of America in any vessels, or imported in United States vessels from any country, shall not be prohibited by the Republic of Liberia, nor be subject to higher duties than are levied on the same kinds of merchandise or goods coming from any other foreign country or imported in any other foreign vessels. All articles the produce of the Republic of Liberia may be exported therefrom by citizens of the United States and United States vessels on as favorable terms as by the citizens and vessels of any other foreign country.

In like manner all merchandise or goods coming from the Republic of Liberia in any vessels, or imported in Liberian vessels from any country, shall not be prohibited by the United States of America, nor be subject to higher duties than are levied on the same kinds of merchandise or goods coming from any other foreign country or imported in any other foreign vessels. All articles the produce of the United States, or of their territories, may be imported therefrom by Liberian citizens and Liberian vessels on as favorable terms as by the citizens and vessels of any other foreign country.

ARTICLE V.—When any vessel of either of the contracting parties shall be wrecked, foundered, or otherwise damaged on the coasts or within the territories of the other, the respective citizens shall receive the greatest possible aid, as well for themselves as for their vessels and effects. All possible aid shall be given to protect their property from being plundered and their persons from ill-treatment. Should a dispute arise as to the salvage, it shall be settled by arbitration, to be chosen by the parties, respectively.

ARTICLE VI.—It being the intention of the two contracting parties to bind themselves by the present treaty to treat each other on the footing of the most favored nation, it is hereby agreed between them that any favor, privilege, or immunity whatever in matters of commerce and navigation, which either contracting party has actually granted, or may hereafter grant, to the subjects or citizens of any other State, shall be extended to the citizens of the other contracting party gratuitously, if the concession in favor of that other State shall have been gratuitous, or in return for a compensation as nearly as possible of proportionate value and effect to be adjusted by mutual agreement, if the concession shall have been conditional.

Article VII.—Each contracting party may appoint consuls for the protection of trade, to reside in the dominions of the other; but no such consul shall enter upon the exercise of his functions until he shall have been approved and admitted in the usual form, by the government of the country to which he is sent.

Article VIII.—The United States government engages never to interfere, unless solicited by the government of Liberia, in the affairs between the aboriginal inhabitants and the government of the Republic of Liberia, in the jurisdiction and territories of the Republic. Should any United States citizen suffer loss, in person or property, from violence by the aboriginal inhabitants, and the government of the Republic of Liberia should not be able to bring the aggressor to justice, the United States government engages, a requisition having been first made therefor by the Liberian government, to lend such aid as may be required. Citizens of the United States residing in the territories of the Republic of Liberia are desired to abstain from all such intercourse with the aboriginal inhabitants as will tend to the violation of law and the disturbance of the peace of the country.

Article IX.—The present Treaty shall be ratified, and the ratifications exchanged at London, within the space of nine months from the date hereof.

In testimony whereof, the Plenipotentiaries before mentioned have hereto subscribed their names and affixed their seals.

Done at London, the twenty-first day of October, in the year one thousand eight hundred and sixty-two.

     CHARLES FRANCIS ADAMS. [L. S.]
     STEPHEN ALLEN BENSON. [L. S.]

And whereas the said Treaty has been duly ratified on both parts, and the respective ratifications of the same were exchanged at London, on the tenth ultimo, by Charles Francis Adams, esquire, Envoy Extraordinary and Minister Plenipotentiary of the United States at the court of St. James, and Gerard Ralston, esquire, Consul-General and Commissioner for and on behalf of the Republic of Liberia, on the part of their respective governments:

Now, therefore, be it known that I, ABRAHAM LINCOLN, President of the United States of America, have caused the said Treaty to be made public, to the end that the same, and every clause and article thereof, may be observed and fulfilled with good faith by the United States and the citizens thereof.

In witness whereof, I have hereunto set my hand and caused the seal of the United States to be affixed.

[L. S.] Done at the city of Washington, this eighteenth day of March, in the year of our Lord one thousand eight hundred and sixty-three, and of the Independence of the United States the eighty-seventh.

     ABRAHAM LINCOLN.

By the President:
 WILLIAM H. SEWARD,
   Secretary of State.

CHAPTER LXXVIII.

THE ORIGINAL CONSTITUTION OF THE REPUBLIC OF LIBERIA.

ARTICLE I.

DECLARATION OF RIGHTS.

THE end of the institution, maintenance and administration of government is to secure the existence of the body politic, to protect, and to furnish the individuals who compose it with the power of enjoying, in safety and tranquillity, their natural rights and the blessings of life; and whenever these great objects are not obtained, the people have a right to alter the government, and to take measures necessary for their safety, prosperity, and happiness.

Therefore we, the people of the Commonwealth of Liberia in Africa, acknowledging with devout gratitude the goodness of God in granting to us the blessings of the Christian religion, and political, religious, and civil liberty, do, in order to secure these blessings for ourselves and our posterity, and to establish justice, insure domestic peace, and promote the general welfare, hereby solemnly associate, and constitute ourselves a free, sovereign, and independent State, by the name of the Republic of Liberia, and do ordain and establish this Constitution, for the government of the same.

SEC. 1. All men are born equally free and independent, and have certain natural inherent and inalienable rights—among which are the rights of enjoying and defending life and liberty, of acquiring, possessing, and protecting property, and of pursuing and obtaining safety and happiness.

SEC. 2. All power is inherent in the people; all free governments are instituted by their authority and for their benefit, and they have a right to alter and reform the same when their safety and happiness require it.

SEC. 3. All men have a natural and inalienable right to worship God according to the dictates of their own consciences, without obstruction or molestation from others. All persons demeaning themselves peaceably, and not obstructing others in their religious worship, are entitled to the protection of law in the free exercise of their own religion, and no sect of Christians shall have exclusive privileges or preference over any other sect, but all shall be alike tolerated; and no religious test whatever shall be required as a qualification for civil office, or the exercise of any civil right.

SEC. 4. There shall be no slavery within this Republic. Nor shall any citizen of this Republic, or any person resident therein, deal in slaves, either within or without this Republic, directly or indirectly.

SEC. 5. The people have a right at all times, in an orderly and peaceable manner, to assemble and consult upon the common good, to instruct their representatives, and to petition the government or any public functionaries for the redress of grievances.

SEC. 6. Every person injured shall have remedy therefor by due course of law; justice shall be done without denial or delay; and in all cases not arising under martial law, or upon impeachment, the parties shall have a right to a trial by jury, and to be heard in person or by counsel, or both.

SEC. 7. No person shall be held to answer for a capital or infamous crime, except in cases of impeachment, cases arising in the army and navy, and petty offenses, unless upon presentment by a grand jury; and every person criminally charged shall have a right to be seasonably furnished with a copy of the charge, to be confronted with the witnesses against him, to have compulsory process for obtaining witnesses in his favor; and to have a speedy, public, and impartial trial by a jury of the vicinity. He shall not be compelled to furnish or give evidence against himself, and no person shall, for the same offense, be twice put in jeopardy of life or limb.

SEC. 8. No person shall be deprived of life, liberty, property, or privilege, but by the judgment of his peers, or the law of the land.

SEC. 9. No place shall be searched nor person seized, on a criminal charge or suspicion, unless upon warrant lawfully issued, upon probable cause, supported by oath, or solemn affirmation, specially designating the place or person, and the object of the search.

SEC. 10. Excessive bail shall not be required, nor excessive fines imposed, nor excessive punishments inflicted; nor shall the legislature make any law impairing the obligation of contracts; nor any law rendering any act punishable, in any manner in which it was not punishable when it was committed.

SEC. 11. All elections shall be by ballot, and every male citizen of twenty-one years of age, possessing real estate, shall have the right of suffrage.

SEC. 12. The people have a right to keep and to bear arms for the common defense. And as, in time of peace, armies are dangerous to liberty, they ought not to be maintained without the consent of the legislature, and the military power shall always be held in exact subordination to the civil authority, and be governed by it.

SEC. 13. Private property shall not be taken for public use without just compensation.

SEC. 14. The powers of this government shall be divided into three distinct departments, the Legislative, Executive, and Judicial, and no person belonging to one of these departments shall exercise any of the powers belonging to either of the others. This section is not to be construed to include Justices of the Peace.

SEC. 15. The liberty of the press is essential to the security of freedom in a State: it ought not, therefore to be restrained in this Republic.

The press shall be free to every person who undertakes to examine the proceedings of the legislature or any branch of government; and no law shall ever be made to restrain the rights thereof. The free communication of thoughts and opinions is one of the invaluable rights of man; and every citizen may freely speak, write, and print on any subject, being responsible for the abuse of that liberty.

In prosecutions for the publications of papers investigating the official conduct of officers, or men in a public capacity, or where the matter published is proper for public information, the truth thereof may be given in evidence. And in all indictments for libels, the jury shall have a right to determine the law and the facts, under the direction of the court, as in other cases.

Sec. 16. No subsidy, charge, impost, or duties ought to be established, fixed, laid, or levied, under any pretext whatsoever, without the consent of the people, or their representatives in the legislature.

Sec. 17. Suits may be brought against the Republic in such manner and in such cases as the legislature may by law direct.

Sec. 18. No person can, in any case, be subjected to the law martial, or to any penalties or pains, by virtue of that law (except those employed in the army or navy, and except the militia in actual service), but by the authority of the legislature.

Sec. 19. In order to prevent those who are vested with authority from becoming oppressors, the people have a right, at such periods, and in such manner as they shall establish by their frame of government, to cause their public officers to return to private life, and fill up vacant places, by certain and regular elections and appointments.

Sec. 20. That all prisoners shall be bailable by sufficient sureties, unless for capital offenses, when the proof is evident or presumption great; and the privilege and the benefit of the writ of habeas corpus shall be enjoyed in this Republic in the most free, easy, cheap, expeditious, and ample manner, and shall not be suspended by the legislature, except upon the most urgent and pressing occasions, and for a limited time, not exceeding twelve months.

ARTICLE II.
LEGISLATIVE POWERS.

Sec. 1. The legislative power shall be vested in a Legislature of Liberia, and consist of two separate branches—a House of Representatives and a Senate, to be styled the Legislature of Liberia; each of which shall have a negative on the other; and the enacting style of their acts and laws shall be: "It is enacted by the Senate and House of Representatives of the Republic of Liberia in Legislature assembled."

Sec. 2. The representatives shall be elected by and for the inhabitants of the several counties of Liberia, and shall be apportioned among the several counties of Liberia as follows: The county of Montserrado shall have four representatives, the county of Grand Bassa shall have three, and the county of Sinoe shall have one, and all counties hereafter which shall be admitted in the Republic shall have one representative, and for every ten thousand inhabitants one representative shall be added. No person shall be a representative who has not resided in the county two whole years immediately previous to his election, and who shall not, when elected, be an inhabitant of the county, and does not own real estate of not less value than one hundred and fifty dollars in the county in which he resides, and who shall not have attained the age of twenty-three years. The representatives shall be elected biennially, and shall serve two years from the time of their election.

Sec. 3. When a vacancy occurs in the representation of any county by death, resignation, or otherwise, it shall be filled by a new election.

Sec. 4. The House of Representatives shall elect their own speaker and other officers; they shall also have the sole power of impeachment.

Sec. 5. The Senate shall consist of two members from Montserrado county, two from Bassa county, two from Sinoe county, and two from each county which may be hereafter incorporated into this Republic. No person shall be a senator who shall not have resided three whole years immediately previous to his election in the Republic of Liberia, who shall not, when elected, be an inhabitant of the county which he represents, and who does not hold real estate of not less value than two hundred dollars in the county which he represents, and who shall not have attained the age of twenty-five years. The senator for each county who shall have the highest number of votes shall retain his seat for four years, and the one who shall have the next highest number of votes two years, and all who are afterwards elected to fill their seats shall remain in office four years.

Sec. 6. The Senate shall try all impeachments, the senators being first sworn, or solemnly affirmed, to try the same impartially, and according to law ; and no person shall be convicted but by the concurrence of two thirds of the senators present. Judgment in such cases shall not extend beyond removal from office, and disqualification to hold an office in the Republic, but the party may still be tried at law for the same offense.

When either the President or Vice-President is to be tried, the Chief Justice shall preside.

Sec. 7. It shall be the duty of the legislature, as soon as conveniently may be after the adoption of this Constitution, and once at least in every ten years afterward, to cause a true census to be taken of each town and county of the Republic of Liberia, and a representative shall be allowed every town having a population of ten thousand inhabitants, and for every additional ten thousand in the counties after the first census one representative shall be added to that county until the number of representatives shall amount to thirty—afterward one representative shall be added for every thirty thousand.

Sec. 8. Each branch of the legislature shall be judge of the election returns and qualifications of its own members. A majority of each shall be necessary to transact business, but a less number may adjourn from day to day, and compel the attendance of absent members. Each House may adopt its own rules of proceeding, enforce order, and, with the concurrence of two thirds, may expel a member.

Sec. 9. Neither House shall adjourn for more than two days without the consent of the other; and both Houses shall sit in the same town.

Sec. 10. Every bill or resolution which shall have passed both branches of the legislature, shall, before it becomes a law, be laid before the President for his approval. If he approves, he shall sign it; if not, he shall return it to the legislature with his objections—if the legislature shall afterward pass the bill or resolution by a vote of two thirds in each branch, it shall become a law. If the President shall neglect to return such bill or resolution to the legislature, with his objection, for five days after the same shall have been so laid before him—the legislature remaining in session during that time—such neglect shall be equivalent to his signature.

Sec. 11. The senators and representatives shall receive from the Republic a compensation for their services, to be ascertained by law; and shall be privileged from arrest, except for treason, felony, or breach of the peace, while attending at, going to, or returning from the session of the legislature.

ARTICLE III.

EXECUTIVE POWER.

Sec. 1. The supreme executive power shall be vested in a President, who shall be elected by the people, and shall hold his office for the term of two years. He shall be commander-in-chief of the army and navy. He shall, in the recess of the legislature, have power to call out the militia, or any portion thereof, into actual service, in defense of the

Republic. He shall have power to make treaties, provided the Senate concur therein by a vote of two thirds of the senators present. He shall nominate, and, with the advice and consent of the Senate, appoint and commission all ambassadors, and other public ministers and consuls, Secretaries of State, of War, of the Navy, and of the Treasury; attorney-general, all judges of courts, sheriffs, coroners, marshals, justices of the peace, clerks of courts, registers, notaries public, and all other officers of State, civil and military, whose appointment may not be otherwise provided for by the Constitution, or by standing laws. And in the recess of the Senate, he may fill any vacancy in those offices, until the next session of the Senate. He shall receive all ambassadors and other public ministers. He shall take care that the laws be faithfully executed. He shall inform the legislature, from time to time, of the condition of the Republic, and recommend any public measures for their adoption which he may think expedient. He may, after conviction, remit any public forfeitures and penalties, and grant reprieves and pardons for public offenses, except in cases of impeachment. He may require information and advice from any public officer, touching matters pertaining to his office. He may, on extraordinary occasions, convene the legislature, and may adjourn the two Houses whenever they can not agree as to the time of adjournment.

SEC. 2. There shall be a Vice-President, who shall be elected in the same manner, and for the same term as that of the President, and whose qualifications shall be the same; he shall be President of the Senate, and give the casting vote when the House is equally divided on any subject. And in case of the removal of the President from office, or his death, resignation, or inability to discharge the powers and duties of the said office, the same shall devolve on the Vice-President, and the legislature may by law provide for the case of removal, death, resignation, or inability, both of the President and Vice-President, declaring what officer shall then act as President, and such officer shall act accordingly, until the disability be removed or a President shall be elected.

Sec. 3. The Secretary of State shall keep the records of the State, and all the records and papers of the legislative body, and all other public records and documents, not belonging to any other department, and shall lay the same, when required, before the President or legislature. He shall attend upon them when required, and perform such other duties as may be enjoined by law.

Sec. 4. The Secretary of the Treasury, or other persons who may by law be charged with the custody of the public moneys, shall, before he receives such moneys, give bonds to the State, with sufficient sureties to the acceptance of the legislature, for the faithful discharge of his trust. He shall exhibit a true account of such moneys when required by the President or legislature; and no moneys shall be drawn from the Treasury but by warrant from the President, in consequence of appropriation made by law.

Sec. 5. All ambassadors and other public ministers and consuls, the Secretary of State, of War, of the Treasury, and of the Navy, the Attorney-General, and Postmaster-General, shall hold their offices during the pleasure of the President. All justices of the peace, sheriffs, marshals, clerks of courts, registers, and notaries public shall hold their office for the term of two years from the date of their respective commissions; but may be removed from office within that time by the President at his pleasure; and all other officers, whose term of office may not be otherwise limited by law, shall hold their office during the pleasure of the President.

Sec. 6. Every civil officer may be removed from office by impeachment, for official misconduct. Every such officer may also be removed by the President, upon the address of both branches of the legislature stating the particular reasons for his removal.

Sec. 7. No person shall be eligible to the office of President who has not been a citizen of this Republic for at least five years, and shall not have attained the age of thirty-five years; and who shall not be possessed of unencumbered real estate of not less value than six hundred dollars.

Sec. 8. The President shall at stated times receive for his services a compensation which shall neither be increased nor diminished during the period for which he shall have been elected. And before he enters on the execution of his office, he shall take the following oath or affirmation:

I do solemnly swear (or affirm) that I will faithfully execute the office of President of the Republic of Liberia, and will to the best of my ability preserve, protect, and defend the Constitution, and enforce the laws of the Republic of Liberia.

ARTICLE IV.

JUDICIAL DEPARTMENT.

Sec. 1. The judicial power of this Republic shall be vested in one Supreme Court, and such subordinate courts as the legislature may from time to time establish. The judges of the Supreme Court, and all other judges of courts, shall hold their office during good behavior; but may be removed by the President, on the address of two thirds of both Houses for that purpose, or by impeachment and conviction thereon. The judges shall have salaries established by law, which may be increased, but not diminished, during their continuance in office. They shall not receive any other perquisite or emoluments whatever, from parties or others, on account of any duty required of them.

Sec. 2. The Supreme Court shall have original jurisdiction in all cases affecting ambassadors or other public ministers and consuls, and those to which the Republic shall be a party. In all other cases the Supreme Court shall have appellate jurisdiction, both as to law and fact, with such exceptions and under such regulations as the legislature shall from time to time make.

ARTICLE V.

MISCELLANEOUS PROVISIONS.

SEC. 1. All laws now in force in the Commonwealth of Liberia, and not repugnant to this Constitution, shall be in force as the laws of the Republic of Liberia, until they shall be repealed by the legislature.

SEC. 2. All judges, magistrates, and other officers now concerned in the administration of justice in the Commonwealth of Liberia, and all other existing civil and military officers therein, shall continue to hold and discharge their respective offices in the name and by the authority of the Republic, until others shall be appointed and commissioned in their stead pursuant to this Constitution.

SEC. 3. All towns and municipal corporations within this Republic constituted under the laws of the Commonwealth of Liberia, shall retain their existing organizations and privileges, and the respective officers thereof shall remain in office, and act under the authority of this Republic, in the same manner and with the like powers as they now possess under the laws of said Commonwealth.

SEC. 4. The first election of President, Vice-President, Senators, and Representatives shall be held on the first Tuesday in October in the year of our Lord eighteen hundred and forty-seven, in the same manner as elections of members of the Council are chosen in the Commonwealth of Liberia, and the votes shall be certified and returned to the Colonial Secretary, and the result of the election shall be ascertained, posted, and notified by him as it is now by law provided in case of such members of Council.

SEC. 5. All other elections of President, Vice-President, Senators, and Representatives shall be held in the respective towns on the first Tuesday in May, in every two years, to be held and regulated in such manner as the legislature may by law prescribe. The returns of votes shall be made to the Secretary of State, who shall open the same, and forthwith issue notices of the election to the persons apparently so elected senators and representatives; and all such returns shall be by him laid before the legislature at its next ensuing session, together with a list of the names of the persons who appear by such returns to have been duly elected senators and representatives; and the persons appearing by such returns to be duly elected shall proceed to organize themselves accordingly as the Senate and House of Representatives. The votes for President shall be sorted, counted, and declared by the House of Representatives. And if no person shall appear to have a majority of such votes, the Senators and Representatives present shall, in convention, by joint ballot, elect from among the persons having the three highest numbers of votes, a person to act as President for the ensuing term.

Sec. 6. The legislature shall assemble once at least in every year, and such meeting shall be on the first Monday in January, unless a different day shall be appointed by law.

Sec. 7. Every legislator and other officer appointed under this Constitution shall, before he enters upon the duties of his office, take and subscribe a solemn oath or affirmation to support the Constitution of this Republic, and faithfully and impartially discharge the duties of such office. The presiding officer of the Senate shall administer such oath or affirmation to the President, in convention of both Houses; and the President shall administer the same to the Vice-President, to the Senators, and to the Representatives in like manner. If the President is unable to attend, the Chief Justice of the Supreme Court may administer the oath or affirmation to him, at any place, and also to the Vice-President, Senators, and Representatives, in convention. Other officers may take such oath or affirmation before the President, Chief Justice, or any other person who may be designated by law.

Sec. 8. All elections of public officers shall be made by a majority of the votes, except in cases otherwise regulated by the Constitution or by law.

Sec. 9. Offices created by this Constitution which the circumstances of the Republic do not require that they shall be filled, shall not be filled until the legislature shall deem it necessary.

Sec. 10. The property of which a woman may be possessed at the time of her marriage, and also that of which she may afterward become possessed, otherwise than by her husband, shall not be held responsible for his debts, whether contracted before or after marriage.

Nor shall the property thus intended to be secured to the woman be alienated otherwise than by her free and voluntary consent, and such alienation may be made by her either by sale, devise, or otherwise.

Sec. 11. In all cases in which estates are insolvent, the widow shall be entitled to one third of the real estate during her natural life, and to one third of the personal estate, which she shall hold in her own right, subject to alienation by her, by devise or otherwise.

Sec. 12. No person shall be entitled to hold real estate in this Republic unless he be a citizen of the same. Nevertheless, this article shall not be construed to apply to colonization, missionary, educational, or other benevolent institutions, so long as the property or estate is applied to its legitimate purposes.

Sec. 13. The great object of forming these colonies being to provide a home for the dispersed and oppressed children of Africa, and to regenerate and enlighten this benighted continent, none but persons of color shall be admitted to citizenship in this Republic.

Sec. 14. The purchase of any land by any citizen or citizens from the aborigines of this country, for his or their own use, or for the benefit of others, as estate or estates in fee simple, shall be considered null and void to all intents and purposes.

Sec. 15. The improvement of the native tribes, and their advancement in the arts of agriculture and husbandry being a cherished object of this government, it shall be the duty of the President to appoint in each county some discreet person, whose duty it shall be to make regular and periodical tours through the country, for the purpose of calling the attention of the natives to these wholesome branches of industry, and of instructing them in the same; and the legislature shall, as soon as can conveniently be done, make provision for these purposes by the appropriation of money.

Sec. 16. The existing regulations of the American Colonization Society, in the Commonwealth, relative to emigrants, shall remain the same in the Republic, until regulated by compact between the Society and the Republic; nevertheless, the legislature shall make no law prohibiting emigration. And it shall be among the first duties of the legislature to take measures to arrange the future relations between the American Colonization Society and this Republic.

Sec. 17. This Constitution may be altered whenever two thirds of both branches of the legislature may deem it necessary. In which case the alterations or amendments shall first be considered and approved by the legislature, by the concurrence of two thirds of the members of each branch, and afterward by them submitted to the people, and adopted by two thirds of all the electors at the next biennial meeting for the election of Senators and Representatives.

Done in convention at Monrovia, in the county of Montserrado, by the unanimous consent of the people of the Commonwealth of Liberia, this twenty-sixth day of July, in the year of our Lord one thousand and eight hundred and forty-seven, and of the Republic the first.

In witness whereof we have hereto set our names.

S. BENEDICT, *President*, J. N. LEWIS, H. TEAGE, BEVERLY R. WILSON, ELIJAH JOHNSON, J. B. GRIPON, Montserrado County. JOHN DAY, A. W. GARDNER, AMOS HERRING, EPHRAIM TITLER, Grand Bassa County. R. E. MURRAY, County of Sinoe. J. W. PROUT, *Secretary of Convention*.

www.ingramcontent.com/pod-product-compliance
Lightning Source LLC
Chambersburg PA
CBHW032049230426
43672CB00009B/1526